THE TWO WINGS OF CATHOLIC THOUGHT

THE TWO WINGS OF CATHOLIC THOUGHT

ESSAYS ON *Fides et ratio*

EDITED BY DAVID RUEL FOSTER
& JOSEPH W. KOTERSKI, S.J.

THE CATHOLIC UNIVERSITY OF AMERICA PRESS
WASHINGTON, D.C.

Copyright © 2003
The Catholic University of America Press

The paper used in this publication meets the minimum
requirements of American National Standards for Information
Science—Permanence of Paper for Printed Library Materials,
ANSI Z39.48-1984.

LIBRARY OF CONGRESS CATALOGING-IN-PUBLICATION DATA

The two wings of Catholic thought : essays on Fides et ratio / edited
by David Ruel Foster and Joseph W. Koterski.
        p. cm.
    Includes bibliographical references and index.
    ISBN 0-8132-1302-9 (pbk. : alk. paper)
        1. Catholic Church. Pope (1978–: John Paul II). Fides et ratio.
2. Faith and reason—Christianity. 3. Catholic Church—Doctrines.
I. Foster, David Ruel, 1952– . II. Koterski, Joseph W.

BT50 .T96 2003
210—dc21
2001047745

IN MEMORY OF OUR FATHERS,

Walter J. Koterski and Ruel E. Foster,

who showed us the love of Our Father

CONTENTS

INTRODUCTION

JOSEPH W. KOTERSKI, S.J., AND
DAVID RUEL FOSTER

When Pope John Paul II's thirteenth encyclical, *Fides et ratio*, appeared in 1998, the unusual amount of news coverage which it received made clear that the pope had struck a chord. The presumption inherited from the Enlightenment that faith and reason follow divergent paths runs very deep in modern culture. But John Paul's choice to yoke faith and reason together in the title of an encyclical on the twin sources of knowledge, which have long been joined in the history of Christian thought, caught the world's attention in a way that surpassed most other papal documents.

The purpose of this volume is to help deepen appreciation for the stereophonic approach to truth that the Holy Father recommends. By stressing faith and reason as "the two wings" of Catholic thought, the pope captures in the lively image of a soaring bird the same point that theologians like Hans Urs von Balthasar communicate by calling truth symphonic. The various melodies that have resounded in the ideas of widely differing philosophers and theologians can each make a contribution to knowing the truth about the things that matter most in life. It is our conviction that the beauty of this symphony, like the flight of the bird, can be even better appreciated when one has studied the component parts. Knowing the various musical strains plucked by a composer, like knowing the muscles that propel the bird, only increases our wonder when we hear the music or see the bird on wing.

The essays of this book are grouped into three sections designed to consider the main doctrinal and historical aspects covered in *Fides et ratio* and to suggest some important directions in which this encyclical may be applied. In the first section on doctrinal perspectives, Avery Cardinal Dulles, S.J., asks a question that has long haunted Christians who felt the attraction of pagan philosophy but worried about compromising the purity of their faith: Can philosophy be Christian? Cardinal Dulles's analysis of the encyclical concentrates on the theoretical gambits open to the Christian who wants to philosophize. Prudence Allen, R.S.M., and Joseph Koterski, S.J., then treat two philosophical topics that have been the most affected by centuries of contact with the Christian faith: the philosophy of the person and metaphysics. While concern with human nature dominated Greek philosophy from the time of its origins, the concept of the person, in the strict sense, only arose in the course of theological reflections on Christ and the Trinity. The essay by Sister Allen details the teachings of this encyclical on the human person in the context of the history of Christian thought on that subject. Likewise, the history of metaphysics antedates the Christian dispensation, but the perspective on that subject changes dramatically once theorists begin to reflect on being from the perspective of creation. Father Koterski's essay surveys the encyclical's stress on the validity of metaphysics and the need for philosophers to recover this approach in their work. In the final essay in this section, David Meconi, S.J., reflects on the Marian framework that is so typical of Pope John Paul II's thought and speculates on what the pope might mean when he speaks of "philosophizing in Mary."

The second section of this volume contains a pair of essays on how this encyclical might be applied to Catholic higher education and to contemporary culture. The Most Rev. Allen Vigneron considers the significance of this encyclical for Catholic intellectual life today. He also proposes some specific applications for seminary curricula. David Foster takes up the challenge of determining some of the implications of *Fides et ratio* for Catholic universities. His essay considers five implications of *Fides et ratio*, including the contention that it supplies a Catholic rational for academic freedom that is missing in *Ex corde Ecclesiae*.

The final section of this volume reviews the historical periods which Pope John Paul II highlights in *Fides et ratio*. Father Koterski reviews the encyclical's comments on the history and importance of biblical Wisdom Literature and then expands on some of the themes found therein that complement themes the pope selected for examination. Prof. Michael Sweeney examines the treatment given to medieval philosophy and theology by *Fides et ratio*, while Prof. Timothy Quinn surveys the pope's approach to modern philosophy. Finally, Cardinal Dulles considers the Church pronouncements from Vatican I to John Paul II on the relation of faith and reason and details the contrasts and continuities that result.

DOCTRINAL PERSPECTIVES

CAN PHILOSOPHY BE CHRISTIAN? THE NEW STATE OF THE QUESTION

AVERY CARDINAL DULLES, S.J.

The Problem

The possibility of a Christian philosophy was fiercely debated in the late 1920s and the early 1930s, especially in France, where several distinguished historians of philosophy, including Émile Bréhier, vigorously denied that there had been, or could be, any such thing.[1] It was, Bréhier said, as absurd as a Christian mathematics or a Christian physics.[2] Genuine philosophy, in his opinion, had been suffocated by Christian dogma in the Middle Ages, and did not reemerge until the seventeenth century, when Descartes picked up about where the Greeks had left off.

The Catholic medievalist Étienne Gilson led the counterattack. He opened his Gifford Lectures, entitled *The Spirit of Medieval Philosophy*, with two chapters devoted respectively to the problem and the no-

---

1. A good introduction to the debate may be found in Maurice Nédoncelle, *Is There a Christian Philosophy?* (New York: Hawthorn Books, 1960), esp. 85–99.
2. Émile Bréhier, "Y a-t-il une philosophie chrétienne?" *Revue de métaphysique et de morale* 38 (1931): 133–62, at 162.

tion of Christian philosophy, which he defined as "every philosophy which, although keeping the two orders formally distinct, nevertheless considers the Christian revelation as an indispensable auxiliary to reason."[3] In a series of books and articles published over the next few decades Gilson demonstrated the vibrancy of medieval philosophy. He convincingly argued that the biblical concepts of God, creation, history, and the human person had made a decisive impact on the whole history of modern philosophy.[4]

In our own time, at least here in the United States, there seems to be a rather general recognition that Christians have a distinctive approach to philosophy. We have had since 1926 an American Catholic Philosophical Association, which now has some 1200 members, but there was nothing equivalent for Protestants until 1979, when William P. Alston, Alvin Plantinga, and several of their friends established the Society of Christian Philosophers. Today, twenty years later, it counts more than a thousand members, and enrolls a rapidly growing number of younger scholars. It is thoroughly ecumenical in its constituency.[5]

These initiatives, however, are scarcely typical of the university world, which finds the concept of Christian philosophy paradoxical, even nonsensical. Some philosophers simply rule out any consideration of revelation as lying beyond the purview of their discipline. Emotivists in the tradition of Alfred Ayer still dismiss religion as noncognitive. A host of agnostics, pragmatists, relativists, and decon-

3. Étienne Gilson, *The Spirit of Medieval Philosophy* (New York: Scribner's, 1940), 37.

4. See in particular Gilson's interventions in the debate, "La notion de philosophie chrétienne," *Bulletin de la Societé française de philosophie* 31 (April–June 1931): 37–93. Gilson's final position is well indicated in his book *The Philosopher and Theology* (New York: Random House, 1962).

5. Richard John Neuhaus, "The Public Square," *First Things* 90 (February 1999): 68–80, at 79. See also *Faith and Philosophy: Journal of the Society of Christian Philosophers,* vol. 15, no. 2 (April 1998) for reflections on the twentieth anniversary of the Society.

structionists, while differing among themselves, form a common front in opposition to revelation as a font of abiding truth.

Pope John Paul II, in his 1998 encyclical *Fides et ratio,* shows himself acutely aware of the present intellectual climate. With his customary courage, he dares to challenge current trends in both philosophy and theology and in so doing raises the question of Christian philosophy in a new form. From the very beginning of the encyclical John Paul II reminds his readers that philosophy, in its etymological sense, means the love of wisdom (§3).[6] Philosophy, therefore, is a human search for truth about ultimate questions (§73); it is a journey awakened by wonder springing from contemplation of creation (§4).

In a stricter sense, philosophy is a rigorous mode of thought; it elaborates a systematic body of knowledge in which the elements are held together in organic unity by logical coherence (§4). Ideally the system should comprehend reality in all its dimensions, but the pope acknowledges that no one system achieves this ideal. Because of the limits of the human mind and the particularities of human cultures, every philosophical system is partial and incomplete. For this reason philosophical inquiry holds the primacy over philosophical systems (§4).

Philosophy, according to the pope, operates within the order of natural reason (§9), using its own methods (§49), which differ from those of theology. Although philosophers disagree among themselves about the methods of their discipline, they appear to be unanimous in holding that philosophy does not derive its proofs from the word of God, received in faith.

Theology, by contrast, is "a reflective and scientific elaboration of the understanding of God's word in the light of faith" (§64). According to John Paul II, the starting point of theology is always the word

---

6. Here and throughout the rest of this volume, section numbers given in parentheses refer to sections of *Fides et ratio.*

of God given in history and accepted in faith (§73). By "faith" he means a free, obedient, and deeply personal decision by which one entrusts oneself to God and acknowledges the truth of what God has revealed (§13). The chief purpose of theology is to provide an understanding of revelation and of the content of faith (§93). The heart of theological inquiry is the mystery of the triune God, which becomes accessible to faith through the Incarnation of the Son and the descent of the Spirit of truth upon the Church (§93).

Three Classical Positions

Christian philosophers have reached no agreement about how philosophy is related to faith. The classical positions fall into three main types.

According to the first school of thought, sometimes called Augustinian, there is a Christian philosophy, and in fact the only true and adequate philosophy is Christian. In the early centuries of the Christian era, apologists such as Justin and Clement maintained that Christianity is the true philosophy (§38), but they seem to have been using the term "philosophy" in a broad sense as equivalent to human wisdom. In the Middle Ages St. Anselm made a sharper distinction between faith and reason. Having accepted the existence of God and the fact of the Incarnation on authority in faith, he tried to demonstrate these truths by "necessary reasons" that would compel the assent of Jews and pagans who did not credit the authority of Scripture. He apparently considered that he had succeeded in this endeavor.[7] Much later, rationalist philosophers such as Hegel contended that the mysteries of the Trinity and the Incarnation, initially accepted by faith, could be demonstrated by pure reason, at which point faith would no longer be needed in order to affirm them as true.

---

7. Anselm, *Cur Deus homo?* 2:22. For similar statements see his *Proslogion* 4 and the Appendix to his *Monologion,* "On Behalf of the Fool," 8.

Hegel and his school, being rationalists, were convinced that reason is superior to faith. They integrated theology with philosophy by letting it be swallowed up by philosophy. But it is also possible to integrate the two disciplines to the advantage of theology. In the nineteenth century the traditionalists, denying the autonomy of reason, held that all true philosophy was based on divine revelation, accepted in faith. In our own century Gilson came to the conclusion that in reasoning about God and things necessary to salvation "no one can pretend to reach truth unless he relies upon revelation to safeguard him against error."[8] The remarkable advances achieved by philosophy in the Middle Ages, he contends, were due to the guidance and enrichment it received from revelation.

While this view tends to merge the objects of philosophy and theology, it preserves a difference of method since theology proceeds by way of authority whereas philosophy relies on evidence and intrinsic reasoning. Christian philosophy, as Gilson came to use the term, meant "the use the Christian makes of philosophical reason when, in either of these two disciplines [philosophy and theology], he associates religious faith and philosophical reflection."[9] According to Gerald McCool, Gilson understood Christian philosophy as the philosophical moment in Catholic theology.[10] While retaining a formal distinction between the two disciplines, he argued that the Christian should not try to develop a philosophy independent of theology.[11]

The second classical position is the direct contrary of the first. Instead of saying that philosophy must be Christian, the neo-

8. Gilson, *The Philosopher and Theology,* 188.
9. Ibid., 198.
10. Gerald A. McCool, "How Can There Be Such a Thing as Christian Philosophy?" in *Philosophical Knowledge,* ed. J. B. Brough et al., *Proceedings of the American Catholic Philosophical Association* 54 (1980), 126–34, at 132.
11. John F. Wippel, "The Possibility of a Christian Philosophy: A Thomistic Perspective," *Faith and Philosophy* 1 (1984): 272–90, at 278.

Thomists of the Louvain school, following in the footsteps of Désiré Cardinal Mercier, hold that philosophy must proceed rigorously by its own methods, without allowing itself to be influenced by faith. Fernand Van Steenberghen, representing this school, insisted that philosophy must be open on an equal basis to believers and nonbelievers. Christian philosophers, he contended, should not allow themselves to be isolated in a ghetto, as would occur if Gilson's positions prevailed.

While concurring with the rationalists that there could be no specifically Christian philosophy, the Louvain neo-Thomists rejected Bréhier's negative assessment of medieval philosophy. The faculties of philosophy in the medieval universities, they maintained, achieved significant advances in the strictly philosophical field, without allowing faith or theology to interfere with their autonomy. The same can be done by the believer today.[12]

As Christian believers, Mercier and Van Steenberghen of course accepted revelation. They also insisted that it was possible to reflect on revelation in a scientific way. But such reflection, they maintained, was by definition theology, since it was done in the light of faith.

The two classical positions thus far described stand at opposite ends of the spectrum. The first school maintains that philosophy ought to be Christian, since it requires the positive influence of faith; the second school denies the possibility of Christian philosophy on the ground that philosophy must be a self-contained product of autonomous reason.

Between these two contrasting positions there are several mediating positions, which make up my third category. Jacques Maritain, differing only slightly from Gilson, argued that human reason, although limited in range, can achieve significant insights about ulti-

12. Fernand Van Steenberghen, "Philosophie et christianisme," in his *Études philosophiques* (Quebec: Éditions du Préambule, 1985), 11–57. In this section of the book he reprints, among other pieces, his intervention at the second day of the *Journée d'études de la Société thomiste* on the notion of "Christian philosophy" (1933).

mate questions without the help of revelation. Revelation attests to many naturally knowable truths such as the existence of God, the spirituality of the rational soul, and the dependence of the whole world on God's creative action. In dealing with truths that can in principle be known both by revelation and by reason, Christian philosophers may allow faith to indicate where the truth lies, but as philosophers they are obliged to establish their conclusions by independent reasoning. Maritain concludes with a typically Scholastic distinction: philosophy can be Christian in the order of exercise, but not in the order of specification.[13] Christian philosophy is philosophy itself conducted by a thinker who profits from revelation.[14]

A second mediating position is that usually identified with the name of Maurice Blondel. He held that neo-Thomists such as Van Steenberghen and Maritain treated philosophy too much as though it were a self-contained system, in which revelation could appear as a mere intruder. The whole supernatural order could then be written off by nonbelievers as an unnecessary superstructure over and above a self-sufficient world of reason and experience. As an alternative to this extrinsicism Blondel contended that philosophy, when it operates without any reference to faith, becomes aware of its own limits. It can discover within the human person an inner dynamism toward a goal that nature cannot reach and toward a truth that reason cannot discover. Blondel rejected the idea of a philosophy that would be Christian in the sense of being based on revelation, but he held that all sound philosophy, holding fast to its own principles, would lead to the threshold of revealed truth. It could thus be Christian in spirit and in orientation.[15]

13. Jacques Maritain, *An Essay on Christian Philosophy* (New York: Philosophical Library, 1955), 11.

14. Ibid., 30.

15. Maurice Blondel, "La philosophie chrétienne existe-t-elle comme philosophie?" *Bulletin de la Société française de Philosophie* 31 (1931): 86–92. See also his *Le problème de la philosophie catholique* (Paris: Bloud & Gay, 1932), 127–77.

Henri de Lubac, developing a third mediating position, agreed with Gilson on the necessity for philosophy to be informed by Christian revelation in order for it to learn the most important truths of the natural order. Blondel, in his view, spoke too much as though the philosopher could begin in a void without regard for tradition and culture. But in agreement with Blondel, de Lubac held that philosophy is affected by the natural desire for the supernatural; it is naturally Christian and is oriented toward revelation as its own completion. The positions of Gilson and Blondel thus correct and complete each other.[16]

Philosophy prior to Faith

Building on these classical positions, John Paul II in *Fides et ratio* distinguishes three states or stances of philosophy in relation to faith. He speaks of a philosophy prior to faith, a philosophy positively influenced by faith, and a philosophy that functions within theology to achieve some understanding of faith.

In describing the first state of philosophy, John Paul II accepts the thesis of Van Steenberghen and Maritain that there can be authentic philosophy outside of faith. Arguing rigorously from rational criteria, one can attain conclusions that are true and certain (§75). In affirming this position, the pope would seem to be on solid ground. Plato and Aristotle, while lacking the guidance of Jewish and Christian revelation, rank among the greatest philosophers of all time. They ably refuted sophistic errors such as materialism, relativism, and hedonistic pragmatism. They showed the capacity of reason to discern the intelligible features of the real order. They laid a solid groundwork for the metaphysical principles of contradiction, sufficient reason, and causality.

16. Henri de Lubac, "On Christian Philosophy," *Communio* 19 (1992): 478–506.

John Paul II, however, does not settle for a closed system of rational knowledge. With Blondel and de Lubac, he is keenly aware that an autonomous philosophy cannot be self-sufficient. The journey of philosophy, he holds, cannot be completed without faith. Just as faith seeks understanding, so, conversely, understanding seeks faith (§§16–23). Philosophy, in perceiving its own limits, can serve as a preparation for the Gospel.

This basically Augustinian position has roots that long antedate Blondel. Even before the Christian era, Plato recognized pressing questions that the philosopher could not answer without the help of a divine revelation, which he himself did not claim to have received. In Plato's *Phaedo* Simmias confesses to Socrates the difficulty of attaining certitude about the fate of the soul after death. The wise man, he says, should take the best and most irrefragable of human theories and let them serve as a raft upon which to sail through life "not without risk, as I admit, if he cannot find some word of God which will more surely and safely carry him."[17]

The insufficiency of reason was expressed in another way by Immanuel Kant, who claimed that in showing reason's incompetence to attain speculative certitude about questions concerning God, freedom, and immortality, he was making room for faith. Kant may have excessively minimized the scope of theoretical reason, and his conception of faith may have fallen short of Christian orthodoxy, but we may concur with his thesis that by recognizing the limits of reason we can better appreciate the need for faith.

Schooled in post-Kantian personalist phenomenology, John Paul II is deeply sensitive to the subjective component in human knowledge. Philosophy, as he sees it, is not so much a set of conclusions as

17. Plato, *Phaedo,* 85c–d, *The Dialogues of Plato,* trans. B. Jowett (New York: Random House, 1937), vol. 1, p. 470.

a mode of inquiry (§76). As I have said, it is first of all a process of exploration and only secondarily a matter of systematization (§4).

Philosophy, in this Augustinian perspective, is not a dispassionate clinical inquiry; it has to be pursued with trust, commitment, and creative imagination. Again and again in his encyclical, John Paul II adverts to the unquenchable thirst for truth that God has implanted in the human heart (opening sentence and §29). Modern philosophy, he observes, has the great merit of focusing attention on the human spirit and its yearning to understand (§5). Human knowledge, he says, is a journey that allows no rest (§18; §33). In the footsteps of Anselm the pope asserts that "the intellect must seek what it loves: the more it loves, the more it desires to know" (§42). The philosopher should be driven by a passion for ultimate truth, a passion that faith can intensify (§56).

The philosopher, considered in the order of actual existence, is no stranger to belief. Anyone who begins to philosophize does so as a member of a community that has received a body of beliefs and values transmitted from the past. Only after such views have been unreflectively assimilated does the philosopher bring critical inquiry to bear (§31). The tools of critical reason have themselves been forged and refined in the philosophical tradition.

Even when embarking on the quest for new insights, reason is sustained by a certain primordial faith. The discoverer begins by assuming that the thirst for truth, so ineradicably rooted in the human heart, is not vain and useless. The sense that there is an answer waiting to be found sustains the confidence and perseverance needed to conduct the search (§29). At this point in his encyclical the pope speaks in terms reminiscent of the great philosopher of science Michael Polanyi.

John Paul II, as I understand him, would agree with Blondel that the human spirit has an inbuilt restlessness toward the divine, an inner exigency for a supernatural message of salvation. But he would probably add, as de Lubac and Karl Rahner do, that philosophy would not be able to articulate the concept of the supernatural without help from revelation. When practiced in a Christian culture, philosophy receives its concept of the supernatural from the believing community.[18]

The passage from autonomous philosophy to faith does not take place without a conversion. John Paul II is sensitive to the perspectives of Christian existentialism, typified by Søren Kierkegaard and Fyodor Dostoevski. The word of the Cross, he acknowledges, seems to crush and contradict the philosopher's ideal of wisdom. The wisdom of the Cross challenges every philosophy (§23).[19] But truth cannot be incompatible with truth. "At the summit of its searching reason acknowledges that it cannot do without what faith presents" (§42). In the final analysis, truth proves to be one. Christ, who calls himself the truth, brings the quest of philosophy to a surpassing fulfillment (§34).

Philosophy Aided by Faith

Our consideration of the insufficiency of autonomous reason brings us to the second state of philosophy, which arises after revelation has occurred and been accepted in faith. John Paul II agrees with those who hold that Christian revelation can make a valid contribu-

18. de Lubac, "On Christian Philosophy," 488; Karl Rahner, *Foundations of Christian Faith* (New York: Crossroad, 1982), 24–25, 126. On Rahner see further William V. Dych, "Philosophy and Philosophizing in Theology," in *Continuity and Plurality in Catholic Theology: Essays in Honor of Gerald A. McCool, S.J.,* ed. Anthony J. Cernera (Fairfield, Conn.: Sacred Heart University Press, 1998), 13–34, at 20.

19. The contrast between Christian wisdom and rationalist wisdom, brilliantly expressed by existentialist thinkers such as Kierkegaard, is recalled by Augusto Del Noce in his article "Thomism and the Critique of Rationalism: Gilson and Shestov," *Communio* 25 (1998): 732–45.

tion to philosophy, as may be seen from the examples of outstanding thinkers such as Thomas Aquinas. With Gilson and Maritain, he teaches that there is such a thing as Christian philosophy. The term, he says, serves "to indicate a Christian way of philosophizing, a philosophical speculation conceived in dynamic union with faith" (§76). It includes important developments of philosophical thinking that would not have happened without the stimulus of the word of God (§76).

The term "Christian philosophy" should not be restricted to the Middle Ages. John Paul II, as I understand him, would find it appropriate for the philosophical writings of the Cappadocian Fathers, Augustine, and other patristic authors, not to mention the Christian thinkers of modern times. Philosophers such as Locke, Leibniz, Malebranche, and others would be unintelligible without reference to their Christian faith.

Although John Paul II accepts the term "Christian philosophy," he warns against certain misunderstandings. The term, he explains, does not mean that the Church has an official philosophy. It might have been thought a century ago that Thomism was the Church's one philosophy, but the present pope avoids taking that position. At the time of Leo XIII, he declares, it seemed that "renewed insistence upon the thought of the Angelic Doctor" was "the best way to recover the practice of a philosophy consonant with the demands of faith" (§57). While encouraging recourse to the wisdom of Aquinas, John Paul II allows for a plurality of systems. Acceptable systems of philosophy, he believes, must share the metaphysical realism of St. Thomas, including his position on the natural knowability of the existence of God (§53). The Angelic Doctor is an authentic model for all who seek the truth and who wish to profit from revelation without demeaning the just autonomy of reason (§78). He evinced an exemplary passion in the search for objective truth (§44) and exhibited admirable courage by tackling new problems and entering into dialogue with the Arab and Jewish thought of his time (§43).[20]

Among the medieval philosophers John Paul II singles out the "great triad" of Anselm, Bonaventure, and Thomas Aquinas (§74). He has words of praise for John Henry Newman, Antonio Rosmini, Vladimir Soloviev, and Vladimir Lossky (§74), all of whom philosophized in the light of their Christian faith without being classifiable as Thomists. Although he does not mention Blondel and Max Scheler by name, he finds merit in the philosophy of immanence and phenomenology (§59). While discountenancing an unprincipled syncretism, he is prepared to learn from alien philosophical movements, even those which he finds dangerous and debilitating. "The currents of thought which claim to be postmodern," he writes, "merit appropriate attention." But they should not be allowed to destroy all certitude and inculcate a total absence of meaning (§91).

In his reflections on Christian philosophy, John Paul II distinguishes between two kinds of benefit that faith confers upon it. The first is an influence on the thinking subject. Faith purifies philosophical reason in a twofold way. On the one hand, it cures philosophy of the pride to which it has at times been subject and with which it was reproached by Paul, Pascal, and Kierkegaard, among others. On the other hand, faith inspires philosophy with courage to tackle certain difficult questions, such as the problem of evil and suffering, that might seem insoluble except for the light cast on them by revelation (§76).

The second influence of faith upon philosophy is objective. Revelation, as already mentioned, assists reason to discover certain truths that are in principle accessible to reason but might never be found in fact without revelation. John Paul II places in this category the ideas

---

20. Romanus Cessario, "Thomas Aquinas: A Doctor for the Ages," *First Things* 91 (March 1999): 27–32, especially at 32.

of creation as the action of a free and personal God; sin as an offense against God; the dignity, freedom, and equality of human persons; and the meaning of history as event (§76).

The pope at one point speaks of reason and faith being interior to each other (§17). The relationship between them, he says, is circular (§73). Philosophy, by offering its specific skills, contributes to the better understanding of revelation. Revelation can assist philosophy by stirring it to explore unsuspected paths and by warning it against false trails.

Because of the intimate connection between philosophy and faith, the ecclesial Magisterium, in its ministry to faith, cannot ignore philosophy. It has a right and a duty to encourage promising initiatives and to warn against aberrations incompatible with the Church's faith. This discernment should not be seen as an intrusion but as a service to right reason and to the philosopher's quest for truth (§§50–51).

Philosophy within Faith

Thus far we have been speaking of philosophy as an independent branch of study, standing apart from theology, even though influenced by it. Before concluding, we must consider philosophy in its third state, in which it functions within theology, which takes its departure from revelation received in faith. Revelation goes beyond reason in the sense that it contains many truths that philosophy cannot discover. These truths are strict mysteries, but they are not conundrums. Revelation, since it comes from the divine Logos, is inherently intelligible (§66). With the help of philosophy, the theologian can achieve a limited but nevertheless very fruitful understanding of such mysteries. Speculative theology makes use of philosophy in its reflection on revealed truths such as the processions of the Trinity, the union of the two natures in the person of Jesus Christ, and the concepts of guilt and atonement that lie at the basis of moral theology (§66).

In connection with dogmatic theology John Paul II refers to the hallowed term *"ancilla theologiae,"* which has a legitimate meaning even though it is subject to misunderstanding. The service rendered by philosophy, he says, is not a matter of servile submission to commands given by theology as a higher discipline. Rather, the term means that philosophy, while holding fast to its own principles, can be fruitfully used within theology (§77). This utilization in no way impairs the proper autonomy of philosophy, for if philosophy were denatured, it could not perform its distinctive service. One of the benefits of sound philosophy is to show that the truth of dogmatic formulas is not tied to any particular time or culture, as some have imagined (§§95–96). Truth is universal by its very nature (§27).

To amplify somewhat the pope's teaching on dogmatic theology, it may be helpful to recall several points of traditional teaching from Thomas Aquinas and the First Vatican Council. Although reason cannot prove the existence or even the possibility of strict mysteries such as the Trinity and the Incarnation, it can expose the errors of those who attempt to demonstrate their impossibility.[21] Philosophical reason, furthermore, can show the analogies between the orders of nature and grace; it can exhibit the internal coherence of the whole supernatural order as disclosed by Christianity, casting light on each revealed truth by manifesting its harmony with other revealed truths and with the goals of human existence.[22] Meditation on the data of revelation can show, finally, that the truths of faith fulfill those aspirations of the human heart which, as Blondel showed, cannot be satisfied by anything within the order of nature.

---

21. Thomas Aquinas, *Summa contra Gentiles,* Book I, chap. 9.
22. Vatican I, Constitution on Catholic Faith, *Dei Filius,* chap. 4 (DS 3016).

The New State of the Question

With reference to the debates of the 1930s, John Paul II's positions do not perfectly agree with any of the positions I have expounded. To the basic question whether there is such a thing as Christian philosophy he answers, against Bréhier and Van Steenberghen, that there is. Against Blondel, he holds that such philosophy is Christian in its substance and content, not simply in its orientation. Against Gilson, he holds that there can be a valid philosophy that is not influenced by revelation, and that the Christian philosopher need not be a theologian. And finally, against Maritain he contends that Christian philosophy can be practiced in a variety of styles, and is not necessarily Thomistic. On the whole, the pope's positions coincide most closely with those of de Lubac, who sought to mediate between Blondel and Gilson.

Even if John Paul II had done nothing more than sort out what is and is not acceptable in the earlier positions, his encyclical would be sufficient to establish a new state of the question. But he also takes a positive step forward. In the encyclical and in several of his unofficial writings before and after he became pope, he expresses his view that personalist anthropology must stand at the center of Christian philosophy today. The philosophy of consciousness, developed according to phenomenological method, can throw new light on the subjectivity of the person, which stands at the basis of culture, civilization, and politics.[23] Biblical revelation has taught Christian philosophers such as Gabriel Marcel and Jewish philosophers such as Martin Buber and Emmanuel Lévinas that the whole of human existence is a coexis-

23. Karol Wojtyła, "The Task of Christian Philosophy Today," in *The Human Person,* ed. G. F. McLean, *Proceedings of the American Catholic Philosophical Association* 53 (1979): 3–4.

tence in dialogue, and that the primary dialogue partner is the God of our faith.[24]

Personalist phenomenology, practiced according to the principles of the Lublin school of Thomism, can contribute to a much-needed renewal of metaphysics (§83).[25] The forms of metaphysics that were still flourishing in the 1930s are languishing today. The battle is no longer between Cartesian rationalists, German idealists, and Catholic neo-Scholastics. Many contemporary philosophers, proclaiming the "end of metaphysics" (§55), are embracing agnosticism, relativism, and consequentialist pragmatism, or devoting their energies to purely formal questions concerning language and hermeneutics (§§5, 47, 81–82). Theology, for its part, all too often evades the challenge of truth. Falling into fideism or sheer positivism, many theologians limit themselves to sociological, linguistic, and historical studies of the Bible and Church teaching (§§48, 55, 61, 94). Both disciplines are therefore in need of conversion. They must alike regain their sapiential dimension.

The encyclical is a pressing appeal for faith and philosophy to "recover their profound unity which allows them to stand in harmony with their nature without compromising their mutual autonomy" (§48). Once the distinction of goals and methods is in place, the intimate association between the two disciplines can be restored. Understood no longer as closed systems but as inquiries aimed at ultimate truth, they can be seen not as rivals or enemies, but as allies. The old debates about the turf belonging to each discipline and about their

24. John Paul II, *Crossing the Threshold of Hope* (New York: Alfred A. Knopf, 1994), 36–37.

25. Ibid. In §83 the pope explains that by metaphysics he does not mean any particular school of thought, such as Hegelianism, but the conviction that true and certain knowledge is not restricted to the realm of the empirical.

respective preeminence need not greatly trouble us today. The current need is for dialogue and mutual support.

Faith and reason, as described by John Paul II, are united like the two natures of Christ, which coexisted without confusion or alteration in a single person. Christian wisdom, similarly, involves a synthesis of theology and philosophy, each supporting and benefiting the other. The pope also uses an analogy from Mariology. Just as Mary, without impairment to her virginity, became fruitful by offering herself to the Word of God, so philosophy, he says, can become more fruitful by offering itself to the service of revealed truth (§108).

Integral Christian wisdom, which sometimes goes by the name of philosophy or theology, draws on the full resources of reason and revelation alike. It is exemplified by the intellectual projects of Augustine, Bonaventure, and Thomas Aquinas, who sought to achieve a universal wisdom by synthesizing the totality of knowledge under the auspices of faith.

Vatican II taught that "faith throws a new light on everything," thus making it possible for the believer to reflect not simply on the word of God but on the whole of life from the perspective of the word of God (GS 11). In particular, the mystery of the human person takes on new meaning in the light of Christ, who is the key, the focal point, and the goal of all human history (GS 10).

Fides et ratio begins with the statement that faith and reason are the two wings on which the human spirit soars to the contemplation of truth. The entire encyclical is an inspiring summons to the pursuit of a wisdom in which theology and philosophy are harmoniously integrated to the advantage of both and the detriment of neither.

The program set forth in the encyclical is radical and bold, especially in view of the troubled climate of the academic world today. Philosophers and theologians who wish to implement the pope's vision must resolutely struggle against mighty odds. But a measure of success is attainable, especially in universities that stand within the Christian and Catholic tradition. A revitalized Christian philosophy could reinvigorate our nation and our culture. This revitalization is also a key element in John Paul II's strategy for the new evangelization. By reestablishing the harmony between faith and reason, it can help to prepare for the new springtime of faith that is envisaged as Christianity enters upon its third millennium.

THE CHALLENGE TO METAPHYSICS
IN *Fides et ratio*

JOSEPH W. KOTERSKI, S.J.

There is a tremendous irony at work in *Fides et ratio:* the pope, the very symbol of faith, is busy defending reason against unreason. A century ago we would have found the pope defending faith against reason—or at least against the vast claims made in the name of reason to test the reasonability of any claim made by faith and to dismiss any faith-claim that was deemed unreasonable according to the standards of the day. But reason has fallen on hard times in this era of postmodernism and so now reason finds itself in need of some defense.

An image from the *Divine Comedy* may prove helpful. Vergil, the very symbol of reason, makes a fine guide through Hell, but he becomes more of Dante's fellow pilgrim on the climb up Mount Purgatory, and then he yields his place as guide entirely to Beatrice, the embodiment of grace, during the heavenly ascent. Although Vergil knows hell and its tricks and deceits very well, he has never seen the sights of Purgatory before; and so it is not his place to determine their itinerary in Purgatory, or to dismiss what strange things they encounter in Purgatory as infernally unreasonable, that is, as unreasonable in terms of what passes for being reasonable in hell. Rather, Vergil's task is to join Dante in believing that Lucia and Beatrice and Blessed Mother have prepared a salvific journey for Dante and, as reason incarnate, to help Dante discover the meaning already latent in each experience. Reason without faith would eventually lose its way here; but unless there were a basic confidence in reason's capacity to recognize any truth at all, Dante would never have escaped the beasts that corner and terrify him in the dark wood at the beginning of the poem.

With the help of this image, let us consider *Fides et ratio* in three different contexts: country, church, and college. In each of these three contexts there are some beasts prowling around and threatening to scare reason off, and it is to meet these adversaries that the pope seems to be so interested in bucking up reason's courage. Let us consider each of these three contexts and their respective beasts in turn, beginning with the summons that *Fides et ratio* issues about the truths necessary for country, especially for a free democratic country. The three beasts that frighten Dante at the very start of the *Comedy* are a lion (pride), a leopard (lust), and a she-wolf (avarice). If Dante were to stand for the life of the mind at the beginning of the twenty-first century, those three beasts (I think) might well stand for nihilism, relativism, and what the pope calls "those undifferentiated and pluralistic philosophical systems" that have rendered suspect the trust that the mind can achieve any kind of truth. It is the she-wolf—not so much of simple avarice but of indiscriminate power, especially the power of the all-encompassing and ever-intrusive state—that threatens here. The very image which the pope uses to describe the pathology of contemporary philosophy (when he calls it an abyss) echoes the texts of Dante:

The need for a foundation for personal and communal life becomes all the more pressing at a time when we are faced with the patent inadequacy of perspectives in which the ephemeral is affirmed as a value, and the possibility of discerning the real meaning of life is cast into doubt. This is why many people stumble through life to the very edge of the abyss without knowing where they are going. (§6)

In such earlier documents as *Veritatis splendor* and *Evangelium vitae* as well as in this passage from *Fides et ratio* (with its talk of the need of "a foundation for personal and communal life"), one gains a deep sense of the pope's conviction that life in free modern societies requires a certain moral consensus as its foundation. But what is needed is not just any kind of consensus, a consensus of mere convention, a consensus by which all the parties to some social contract agree to hold certain conventions as valid merely so that life together can go on peaceably. Rather, what is needed for free democratic societies to survive and prosper is respect for certain norms that are the non-negotiable supports for human dignity, that is, norms that are not decided upon by anyone, not chosen by any consensus, but available to be discovered—in short, certain important truths about the human person that are true independently of any social contract agreement and are there to be discerned, however much smog and fog propaganda may throw up, and however much a sense of nihilistic abyss may threaten.

In his various encyclicals and speeches the pope repeatedly speaks of basic human rights as a way to get across his points about the human dignity that comes from being made in the image of God. He freely makes use of the language of liberal political philosophy in doing so. That he uses such language at all makes some people wince; but, in fact, he always uses the language of human rights far more deeply than the pragmatic liberalism of contemporary jurisprudence does when it treats rights merely as matters of procedural fairness or of legislative power (as if rights were actually conferred by the state rather than discerned and to be protected by the state). In a fundamental continuity with the natural law tradition, which takes rights to flow from duties (the duties one has to God, to one's neighbor and one's society, and to self), and takes duties to flow from the nature of the person, the pope (it seems to me) has been arguing for all of his academic and ecclesial life for a dignity that flows from the nature of the human person, whether in encyclicals like *The Redeemer of Man (Redemptor hominis)*, in catechetical lessons like *The Original Unity of Man and Woman*, or in such philosophical tomes as *The Acting Person* and *Love and Responsibility*. Further, he always makes his case for rights *not* in the context of atomistic individualism, but with a mindfulness of human solidarity.

Let me try to sketch a bit of the background to the emphasis on human solidarity in John Paul's social thought by considering it as but the latest installment of an incredibly consistent tradition of papal social teaching offered over the last hundred years from *Rerum Novarum* on. The popes have tended to see social ethics against the dual problematic of the modern state and the industrial revolution. Ever since the time of the French Revolution, popes have identified this pair of concerns as the proper matrix of social thought. In a long series of encyclicals they have developed a consistent analysis of the nature of the problem, but its resolution has remained perplexing. This has been so especially since the demise of even the vestiges of the old "Christendom" with the fall of the last Christian kingdoms by the end of the First World War, together with the steady obliteration of those social and cultural forms in which Christian solidarity had traditionally been embedded, the mediating institutions called for by the principle of solidarity. The development of the modern state has been a kind of revolution from above that has generated a social atomism in which individuals are more isolated, deprived of the support of many of the older mediating institutions, and thereby kept relatively weaker before the power of the state. The industrial revolution, on the other hand, has been a kind of revolution from below, for it has made possible a mass society of unprecedented size, yet without the protections that had organically grown up for social charity.

One can trace what appear to be zig-zags in papal policy for the last century and a half and thus find a policy that sometimes criticizes the state for exercising too much power but sometimes chides the state for not using enough of its power to remedy social ills. But however much zig-zag there has been in suggested papal solutions, the recurrent papal analysis of the problem that is in need of solution has been both accurate and consistent, for it has objected to the trend in modern regimes to make public the things that deserve to be private and to privatize the things that ought to be public. These trends have been the result of a basic error: the repudiation of any natural or supernatural good in favor of a view of the political common good as merely a creation of the human will. This extremely clever fiction championed by social contract theory holds that the social order, like the political order, is only an instrument for satisfying the interests of the contracting parties.

The resolution of the problem, however, is another matter. Pope John Paul II has been continuing to develop the opening which Pope Pius XII made toward considering the previously suspect notion of constitutional democracy as *a* (but not *the*) legitimate means for social order. Relying on the distinction worked out by Jacques Maritain between the instrumentalist and substantive conceptions of the state, John Paul II's *Centesimus annus,* with its focus on the transcendent dignity of the human person as the primary subject of rights, tried to enunciate a vision of the social order that would weaken the power of the state by progressively expanding the chain of social solidarity.

Whether this new vision will in fact take hold remains a question for future historians to judge.

The inclusion within *Fides et ratio* of concerns so prominent in the trio of John Paul II's social encyclicals and so very important in *Veritatis splendor* and in *Evangelium vitae* is not then simply a matter of the pope's own personal history, but it does reflect the long struggle of his own people for freedom against a totalitarian regime. The struggle he personally witnessed certainly did sharpen his conviction that democratic forms of government have a special ability to protect and defend the dignity of human persons—hence the need to challenge tendencies which destroy or weaken such regimes. There are, I suppose, days when we may grow sour about the prospects of the great American experiment in democracy and when we are tempted to ask what to do if the jig's really up. But the pope's own recurrent advice is directed at recalling our attention to the project of ending the erosion of moral consensus that is imperiling the social order of free societies, that is, restoring a true consensus rather than being resigned about the end of a noble experiment. I do not take his remarks at §89, for instance, to be a simple broadside aimed at pragmatism in a technical philosophical sense, so much as a comment on the beast of undifferentiated power, on the view that power and not truth is decisive, and thus on the practical effect of pluralistic philosophies that render any confidence about getting to moral truths suspect. His recommendation of what to do about it is to resume thinking about the true nature of the human person in the best traditions of anthropology and metaphysics:

No less dangerous is pragmatism, an attitude of mind which, in making its choices, precludes theoretical considerations or judgments based on ethical principles. The practical consequences of this mode of thinking are significant. In particular, there is growing support for a concept of democracy which is not grounded upon any reference to unchanging values: Whether or not a line of action is admissible is decided by the vote of a parliamentary majority. The consequences of this are clear: In practice, the great moral decisions of humanity are subordinated to decisions taken one after another by institutional agencies. Moreover, anthropology itself is severely compromised by a one-dimensional vision of the human being, a vision which excludes the great ethical dilemmas and the existential analyses of the meaning of suffering and sacrifice, of life and death. (§89)

Although these remarks are crafted with the whole world in mind, one can readily see their application to a free democratic society like our own. There are tensions in our own constitutional history between freedom and equality that have emerged when we have taken "freedom" to refer merely to doing as one likes without being restrained and when we have treated equality as if it meant an identity oblivious of differences. Earlier in our national history there was a wider consensus about certain moral values that were seen as necessary in order to have a democratic form of government at all and that permitted such a regime to be the best place to defend freedom and human dignity. But the calling into question of the very category of moral truth and the undifferentiated celebration of tolerance and diversity has shifted the whole matter to a discussion of power. This is easily seen, for instance, in the infamous phrase from the *Casey* decision about the absolute right to determine the meaning of one's own existence, a view that presumes that the only meaning which really exists is the meaning we construct or choose. Or, to take an example from a different sphere of morality, there has been an uncritical extension of the notion of discrimination from the arena in which anti-discrimination laws were enacted (namely, the legitimate purpose in distributive justice to rectify the historical disadvantages to the black community from generations of the actual injustice of slavery) to many other arenas simply in the name of diversity. The reduction of the whole issue to questions of the empowerment of minority groups has removed the cogency of justice claims and made the issue seem merely a matter of a power scramble. This relocation of the question from truth to power has generated untold resentment and evacuated the original meaning of tolerance—namely, the toleration of something recognized as evil but permitted by authorities in those cases where physically or legally uprooting it would cause more social damage than the evil itself. Toleration in this sense of the word retains the important notion of shame and social disapproval to discourage what law could not eliminate without doing tremendous collateral damage to freedom and the common good. Finally, this illegitimate extension of anti-discrimination laws has prevented the country from devising even yet an effective solution to the case for which anti-discrimination laws and policies were first devised, namely, the perpetuation of an underclass on racial lines.

But, to return from meditation on our current situation back to our papal Vergil: a consensus determined by the least common denominator will only be a consensus of convention, not an agreement that comes from the truth. And where such pragmatism falls short, there is need

for a philosophy of *genuinely metaphysical* range, capable, that is, of transcending empirical data in order to attain something absolute, ultimate and foundational in its search for truth. . . . I do not mean to speak of metaphysics in the sense of a specific school. . . . I want only to state that reality and truth do transcend the factual and the empirical, and to vindicate the human being's capacity to know this transcendent and metaphysical dimension in a way that is true and certain, albeit imperfect and analogical. In this sense, metaphysics should not be seen as an alternative to anthropology, since it is metaphysics which makes it possible to ground the concept of personal dignity in virtue of the spiritual nature of human beings. (§83)

A second context is church, and here the beast that is most prominently threatening is the leopard—I do not so much mean the spots

of lustful lechery that mark the beast of Dante's *Comedy* (although
we are sadly mindful of these spots too) but the lust for spiritual
good feeling and the concomitant phenomenon of the contemporary
version of fideism, a readiness to believe just about anything. One all
too often runs into people who are deeply hungry for spirituality but
who are indifferent to real faith and to questions about the truth of
religious claims. While there have been ages when skepticism was the
great problem, the pope seems to me to have a different diagnosis for
our age: one might almost call the problem gullibility, rooted in a
kind of nihilism—whether the formal nihilism of despair that marks
much of Europe where the faith is dead but superstition is widespread, or the American version of nihilism, or just the nothingness,
the absence of content, that has often marked the pulpit when its
content is restricted to vapid moralizings about the social gospel.
Clearly, the pope's point is not to denigrate questions of social justice
or social charity—for we saw earlier his tremendous concern for
social thought and his sense of the real demands that justice and
charity make.

But John Paul II finds equally pressing a need for intellectual rigor
and serious reflection in matters of faith, lest religion and true spirituality turn into mere superstition and mythology. Speaking of faith
and reason, he says:

Each without the other is impoverished and enfeebled. Deprived of what
revelation offers, reason has taken sidetracks which expose it to the danger
of losing sight of its final goal. Deprived of reason, faith has stressed feeling and experience, and so run the risk of no longer being a universal
proposition. It is an illusion to think that faith, tied to weak reasoning,
might be more penetrating; on the contrary, faith then runs the grave risk of
withering into myth and superstition. By the same token, reason which is
unrelated to an adult faith is not prompted to turn its gaze to the newness
and radicality of being. (§48)

There are various insights here. One might think, for instance, of the poverty of contemporary catechesis: a whole generation and more that has not been adequately taught the faith and so is prone to believe all sorts of spooky things—willing to believe (for instance) what the media says that religion holds—willing to believe (as my freshmen often inform me) that all religions are the same, for they are quite innocent that the law of an eye for an eye and a tooth for a tooth is not the same as the law about turning the other cheek. This is not to deny that even the *lex talionis* was a great advance over vengeance codes, but simply to note the huge difference between talion and true forgiveness.

At another level, when one gets to that stage in life when one has a greater hunger for spiritual fullness, the virtual nihilism of intellectually contentless religion abandons people to the attractions offered by various forms of feel-good religion. Except for the fact that God does not need the worship that He asks us to give, I would say "Poor God!"—for His divine identity seems constantly to get re-fashioned in light of our feelings of need and desire—in the long American tradition of Ben Franklin, the Lord gets turned into the slave of our self-help techniques and retains little of the reality to which the mysteries of the Faith point.

At still another level, the above quotation is a comment on the excessively abstract nature of theology nowadays. We will need to return to the question of theology again in the third context on colleges, but some comment is appropriate here. One sees this phenomenon, for instance, in the dislocated philosophical rationalism that is often taught in academic theology courses, a theology that is soteriologically neutral instead of a theology designed somehow to strengthen the efforts at the proclamation of the Gospel by serious intellectual reflection on the mysteries of the faith, not mysteries seen as myth or as projections of the consciousness of the individual author or of the redactional community, but mysteries as genuine revelations of the transcendent God: all Scripture is given to us for salvation. The pope sheds a certain light on this metaphysical focus needed in theological discussion when he writes:

The word of God refers constantly to things which transcend human experience and even human thought; but this "mystery" could not be revealed nor could theology render it in some way intelligible were human knowledge limited strictly to the world of sense experience. Metaphysics thus plays an essential role of mediation in theological research. A theology without a metaphysical horizon could not move beyond an analysis of religious experience nor would it allow the *intellectus fidei* to give a coherent account of the universal and transcendent value of revealed truth. If I insist so strongly on the metaphysical element, it is because I am convinced that it is the path to be taken in order to move beyond the crisis . . . and to correct certain mistaken modes of behavior now widespread in our society. (§83)

I take his point here to be that there is desperate need for such often shunned metaphysical categories as the natural and the supernatural, sin and grace, immortality and transubstantiation if theological analysis is to bring us beyond the admittedly important analysis of religious experiences, that is, bring us to questions about the authenticity of religious experience, the real efficacy of the spiritual practices to which we might be attracted, and to the validity of the truth claims made on religious issues. In the Jesuit tradition, we might translate this into the discernment of spirits: separating out what comes to us from the good spirit as opposed to what is coming to us just from within ourselves, let alone what comes from the other guy.

A third area of the pope's special concern in this encyclical on faith and reason is the college. The threat here comes from the beast which Dante calls the lion of pride—for us, the near arrogance and presumption so prevalent in academia. The remedy, of course, is humility, properly understood. The long section of this encyclical devoted to the Wisdom Literature of Israel makes the point in one way, for that literature teaches us, above all, that fear of the Lord is the beginning of wisdom. Another of the pope's heroes, St. Bernard of Clairvaux, does it in his own way when he teaches us in *De gradibus humilitatis* that humility is "reverent love for the truth"— meaning, I think, that humility is not equivalent to humiliation, but is intrinsically linked to love of truth: if there is something good and praiseworthy, to delight in it with proper gratitude; if there is something weak, deficient, or blameworthy, respectfully to acknowledge the fact and then to work prayerfully for correction or reparation or renovation. The pope takes up the theme of humble reason in the passage where he distinguishes between two possible roles for reason in theology: the humble role of reason in the search for intelligibility that is captured by the time-honored motto *fides quaerens intellectum*, versus the presumptuous role which the Enlightenment assigned to reason, of passing judgment on the reasonability of the faith, and frequently rendering a negative judgment on faith-claims when they seem to have failed to conform to the measure of the human mind:

Reason in fact is not asked to pass judgment on the contents of faith, something of which it would be incapable, since this is not its function. Its function is rather to find meaning, to discover explanations which might allow everyone to come to a certain understanding of the contents of faith. . . . The intellect must seek that which it loves: the more it loves, the more it desires to know. Whoever lives for the truth is reaching for a form of knowledge which is fired more and more with love for what it knows, while having to admit that it has not yet attained what it desires. . . . The desire for truth, therefore, spurs reason always to go further; indeed, it is as if reason were overwhelmed to see that it can always go beyond what it has already achieved. It is at this point, though, that reason can learn where its path will lead in the end. . . .

The fundamental harmony between the knowledge of faith and the knowledge of philosophy is once again confirmed. Faith asks that its object be understood with the help of reason; and at the summit of its searching, reason acknowledges that it cannot do without what faith presents. (§42)

The task of reason is not to assess what is "reasonable" according to the standards of the day any more than the task of Vergil is to object to the wonders that he discovers in Purgatory that they are unreasonable by the standards of infernal logic. Rather, it is to trust in the truth of what revelation and tradition proffer, to inquire about what the truths of faith genuinely mean, and thereby to draw the inquirer closer and closer to God Himself. In the course of commenting on the proper interaction between philosophy and theology, and implicitly correcting a false freedom which many theologians have claimed for their discipline, the pope writes:

Divine truth, "proposed to us in the Sacred Scriptures and rightly interpreted by the Church's teaching," enjoys an innate intelligibility so logically consistent that it stands as an authentic body of knowledge. The *intellectus fidei* expounds this truth, not only in grasping the logical and conceptual structure of the propositions in which the Church's teaching is framed, but also, indeed primarily, in bringing to light the salvific meaning of these propositions for the individual and for humanity. From the sum of these propositions, the believer comes to know the history of salvation, which culminates in the person of Jesus Christ and in his Paschal Mystery. Believers then share in this mystery by their assent of faith. (§66)

For reason to accept revelation as a second source of genuine knowledge is to practice a deep humility against the temptation to pride. It thus need not be at all humiliating, but enriching—a reason not for jealousy but truly for joy.

On this point we might turn to a figure like St. Margaret Mary Alacoque for an interesting example of the importance of the difference between humble reason and arrogant reason. Humble reason seeks to discover the meaning in the truths of the faith, while arrogant reason is inclined to dismiss the claims of faith for failing to be adequately reasonable. The devotion to the Sacred Heart which the Saint received in her visions seems entirely outside the pale of acceptability to reason operating in the one sense: it is not just that the art associated with the devotion seems overly sentimental (a tremendous challenge for the artists of our day) but that for such a rationalistic mind the doctrine of the Incarnation has to be pared back to a pittance—one thinks of Roger Haight's *Jesus the Symbol of God,* which simply cannot countenance any affirmations of Our Lord's divinity and (hard as it is to believe) argues that the Gospel of John, the Nicene Creed, and the formula of Chalcedon all need to be re-interpreted in light of our experience, in short, that Jesus must be a human person in whom the fullness of God is symbolically manifest for us. To reason operating in the other sense, the devotion to the Sacred Heart presents to us a doctrine that is part of the deposit of faith and summons us to re-examine any limits we may have placed on our thinking about what God can do. Assuming that there is a truth of faith and trusting it, this use of reason seeks to remain open to this truth and to plumb its significance in ways our limited imagination might never have suspected (see John 3:16). In this way even Vergil and reason may someday get to the eternal light, a light not of their own making, as a profitable return many times over for the hard work of bringing us poor scared Dantes out of the clutches of the beasts of the darkness by the light that is proper to reason in its own sphere, and thus eventually making possible a journey into eternal light.

PERSON AND COMPLEMENTARITY
IN *Fides et ratio*

PRUDENCE ALLEN, R.S.M.

The philosophy of the person contained in Pope John Paul II's most recent encyclical *Fides et ratio* is remarkable for its dynamism, its depth, and its call. This encyclical reaffirms the ontological priority of persons over systems of thought, individual experiences in faith, and arguments of discursive reason. For purposes of analysis this essay will consider the human person in relation to three areas of discourse: reason and faith, philosophy and theology, and philosophers and theologians.[1] Each area of discourse has its own parameters, yet reason, philosophy, and philosophers operate in one order of knowledge, while faith, theology, and theologians operate in relation to another order of knowledge (§§9, 16).

John Paul II defends a complementarity theory of interrelation between the two components for each of these areas of discourse. In the present context, we understand "complementarity" to mean "two

---

1. I am grateful for suggestions for revision of this chapter by Joseph Koterski, S.J., Jorge Rodriguez, John Hittinger, Mary Judith O'Brien, R.S.M., and Rita Rae Schneider, R.S.M.

factors of equal value when interacting create something more than either factor can achieve alone." Thus, we can consider how faith and reason can be complementary, philosophy and theology can be complementary, and philosophers and theologians can be complementary. When two factors are complementary, they are considered to be of equal worth and dignity at the same time that they have significant differences. They may also become synergetic when joined in cooperative yet differentiated union. Complementarity always operates in a field of creative tension. If one aspect is given dominance while the other is dissolved, then the creative tension ceases. Therefore, when the difference between reason and faith—or that between philosophy and theology, or between philosophers and theologians—fades, a serious imbalance occurs in the search for truth.

This essay stresses philosophical approaches to the person and introduces theological approaches by way of comparison. However, genuine complementarity of the two approaches depends upon philosophers and theologians articulating for one another their different paths to truth. Therefore, a more thorough approach would necessitate development by theologians.

1. Reason and Faith

In *Fides et ratio,* the person is described as a conscious being who questions his or her own existence. This capacity to question is a mark of human intelligence which leads the person to insight, raising further questions, leading to greater insights. The human person engages in the world, wondering "why?" and desiring to know the truth about the self in relation to things and events in the world. Desire is an inclination toward a good not yet possessed, and it is caused by the love of this good as absent. The desire to know the truth about oneself is a craving for an absent good. This desire is preceded by love, which may initially be a form of self-love. The desire for truth about the self, then, is a movement of the human person toward something not yet possessed.[2]

The human person's desire for truth about the self generates a momentum which John Paul II likens explicitly to a journey and implicitly to a pilgrimage. On this journey the person is accompanied step by step by the believing community, the Church. The search for truth is not described as a disembodied mental exercise or even a contemplative gift distinguished from personal identity. On the contrary, John Paul II describes it as "humanity's shared struggle to arrive at truth" in which "every truth attained is but a step toward that fullness of truth which will appear with the final revelation of God" (§2). As on any pilgrimage, there are persons who interact along the way,[3] there are horizons which change as progress is made, and there are shared moments of struggle and loss, love and joy. Thus, the human person, and not just the human mind, is the one on the way.

Fides et ratio traces a journey of the human person who begins with the dynamic desire to know the self and who moves toward the fulfilment of this desire by discovering God as the Truth. The docu-

2. See Thomas Aquinas, *Summa theologica* (Westminster, Md.: Christian Classics, 1981), 5 vols., Vol. II, Pt. I– II, Q. 30, art. 1, rep. obj. 1. In the *Summa theologica* Thomas describes this movement of desire for truth as propelling the person, who seeks a higher good, into action: "The craving for wisdom, or other spiritual goods, is sometimes called concupiscence; either by reason of a certain likeness; or on account of the craving in the higher part of the soul being so vehement that it overflows into the lower appetite, so that the latter also, in its own way, tends to the spiritual good, following the lead of the higher appetite, the result being that the body itself renders its service in spiritual matters . . .".

3. *Fides et ratio* gives attention to the charisms of bishops, priests, deacons, and Christian philosophers who collaborate along the path of this pilgrimage. Due to the constraints of this essay it will not be possible to indicate here the various distinctions made concerning the different ways persons in these categories interact with someone on the pilgrimage of truth. It bears noting, however, that reference to *Fides et ratio*'s particular forms of collaboration provides a rich amount of material for future reflection on formation of students in catholic universities, seminarians, and the missions of other kinds of Catholic educational institutions, hospitals, medical clinics, and organizations.

ment describes the dynamic process of a person coming to know and to love God. Using such metaphorical images as 'resting in the shade within a particular horizon,' section 107 summarizes it this way:

> . . . the grandeur of the human being . . . can find fulfilment only in choosing to enter the truth, to make a home under the shade of Wisdom and dwell there. Only within this horizon of truth will people understand their freedom in its fullness and their call to know and love God as the supreme realization of their true self.

One discovers God through confronting such questions as "Why?" and "Who am I?"

A cyclical movement starts with the human being who seeks truth about the self by reason, who encounters the Truth by revelation, and who only then comes to know the full truth about this self. This is vividly depicted in the salutation to *Fides et ratio:*

> Faith and reason are like two wings on which the human spirit rises to the contemplation of the truth; and God has placed in the human heart a desire to know the truth—in a word, to know himself—so that, by knowing and loving God, men and women may also come to the fullness of truth about themselves.

This cyclical movement exists within a person who exercises reason and faith in seeking and responding to truth. The movement takes place in the context of interpersonal relation, i.e. persons drawn out of the self by the very action of seeking God in communion with others. John Paul II's emphasis on the substantial being or person who has faith and reason, rather than upon faith or reason as separated mental states, derives from his Christian personalism. Human activity must be understood in relation to the person, not the person in relation to the activity. Faith and reason depend upon the human person in order to exist; they do not exist as some mysterious force or spiritual wave in the cosmos. The human person is both the vocal and the silent witness to acts of faith and reason which lead to the full actualization of the person.

Fides et ratio §28 teaches: "One may define the human being, therefore, as *the one who seeks the truth*."[4] A definition distinguishes the essence of a thing. Following this definition we could conclude that human essence involves a dynamic movement toward something which is (or someone who is) the truth. John Paul II develops his innovative interpretation of the human person in relation to truth by reflecting on his methodology in §33:

Step by step, then, we are assembling the terms of the question. It is the nature of the human being to seek the truth. This search looks not only to the attainment of truths which are partial, empirical or scientific; nor is it only in individual acts of decision-making that people seek the true good. Their search looks towards an ulterior truth which would explain the meaning of life. And it is therefore a search which can reach its end only in reaching the absolute. Thanks to the inherent capacities of thought, man is able to encounter and recognize a truth of this kind. Such a truth—vital and necessary as it is for life—is attained not only by way of reason but also through trusting acquiescence to other persons who can guarantee the authenticity and certainty of the truth itself. There is no doubt that the capacity to entrust oneself and one's life to another person and the decision to do so are among the most significant and expressive human acts . . .

From all that I have said to this point it emerges that men and women are on a journey of discovery which is humanly unstoppable—a search for the truth and a search for a person to whom they might entrust themselves. Christian faith comes to meet them, offering the concrete possibility of reaching the goal which they seek.

In this wonderful dynamic of a person seeking the God who comes to meet him, John Paul II develops the insight of the Second Vatican Council as expressed in *Gaudium et spes* 19.1 and quoted in Part I, Section I, Chapter 1 of the *Catechism of the Catholic Church:*

4. For a further discussion of this theme in *Fides et ratio* see Francesco Viola, "The human person as seeker of truth," *L'Osservatore Romano*, no. 37 (September 15, 1999): 9–10.

The dignity of man rests above all on the fact that he is called to communion with God. This invitation to converse with God is addressed to man as soon as he comes into being. For if man exists, it is because God has created him through love, and through love continues to hold him in existence. He cannot live fully according to truth unless he freely acknowledges that love and entrusts himself to his creator.[5]

The human person has a desire and a capacity for God which is released in his or her search for truth about the self; and God comes to meet the human person through the revelation of Jesus Christ, who in an historical event became man and dwelt among us.

Fides et ratio develops certain implications of the dynamism of this kind of relation in §34:

This unity of truth, natural and revealed, is embodied in a living and personal way in Christ, as the Apostle reminds us: "Truth is in Jesus" (cf. *Eph* 4:21; *Col* 1:15–20). . . . What human reason seeks "without knowing it" (cf. *Acts* 17:23) can be found only through Christ: what is revealed in him is "the full truth" (cf. *Jn* 1:14–16) of everything which was created in him and through him and which therefore in him finds its fulfilment (cf. *Col* 1:17).[6]

The struggle for the unity of truth is not just for the sake of knowledge and understanding. It is for that solace experienced in coming to know oneself as a person in union with truth—a truth which frees both the self and others who share the same journey.

Pope John Paul II teaches that relation with other human persons and with the Divine Persons is necessary for a man to fulfil his essence. One searches for truth in repeated acts of entrustment to the One who is the Truth. This journey passes by way of encounter with and entrustment to Jesus Christ. It leads to an eventual complete ful-

5. *Catechism of the Catholic Church* (New York: Image, 1995), #27.
6. It is this relational understanding of the identity of the human person that David Schindler captures in the title of his recent article on *Fides et ratio,* "God and the End of Intelligence: Knowledge as Relationship," *Communio* 23 (1996): 510–40.

filment for the person who discovers his or her true self along the way.

A person seeks the truth through acts of faith and reason. Faith is an act of personal assent of intellect and will to the encounter with God. More precisely, faith is the personal act of assent to the revelation of Jesus Christ who comes to encounter us. Reason is stirred by this interpersonal encounter. Each person wants a personal relation with God who is the Truth and who reveals the truth to the self.

Sections 13–14 of *Fides et ratio* describe characteristics of a personal response to the revelation of Jesus Christ. In exercising reason one searches to a greater depth and uses signs to reach hidden truth. By seeking to know absolute truth, one is impelled to extend the range of knowledge. The potentiality of taking full and harmonious possession of one's life is actualized by following this truth. God's revelation appears as a gratuitous gift which stirs thought and seeks acceptance as an expression of love. God guarantees faith's truth which the intellect receives as a pure gift. In an act of entrustment to God by believing this truth a person fully exercises freedom of will. This response of faith is set within a unique and irreducible history, and it anticipates a full and joyful contemplation of God at the end of time.

How the revelation of Jesus Christ relates to one's response of faith and reason is beautifully described in Bishop Rino Fisichella's analysis of *Fides et ratio* in *L'Osservatore Romano:*

The truth which *Fides et ratio* examines, then, finds its starting point in the Revelation of Jesus Christ. As if to say: truth is not a theory or a mere speculative exercise; it is articulated, instead, on the basis of an historical event. Here God reveals the definitive truth about himself, man and the world, and indicates a path to be taken so that truth can be expressed in a full and complete way.[7]

7. Rino Fisichella, "Reason finds in Revelation the possibility of being truly itself," *L'Osservatore Romano,* no. 2 (January 13, 1999): 10.

Bishop Fisichella considers the "truly innovative element" in the Church's understanding of the way reason and faith work when the human person encounters the revelation of the Divine Person Jesus Christ.

To summarize our previous reflections: the person is affected in two ways through the complementarity of faith and reason. First, faith and reason are both understood as responses to the revelation of Jesus Christ coming to encounter the human person who is seeking the truth (§7). Second, the response of the human person by faith and reason to the stirring of this encounter is by acts of intellectual assent and by acts of wilful entrustment, acts of love, releasing further questions (§§13–15). The response of faith is likened to one wing and the response of reason to the complementary wing.

The preaching of Christ crucified and risen is the reef upon which the link between faith and philosophy can break up, but it is also the reef beyond which the two can set forth upon the boundless ocean of truth. Here we see not only the border between reason and faith, but also the space where the two may meet. (§23)

Faith and reason can gain momentum from directly encountering the revelation of Jesus Christ. Reason is set free (§§20 and 22) and faith is strengthened. In these two kinds of human response to revelation, the foundation for a true complementarity can begin to be worked out within a person. When reason becomes weary or strained, faith reaches forward (§21). When faith is undergoing a dark night of the soul, reason can guide the person beyond a reef of doubt into the ocean of truth.

Faith helps reason, and reason helps faith to become ordered, healed, and set free. John Paul also describes the converse. When faith and reason become separated,

... each without the other is impoverished and enfeebled. Deprived of what Revelation offers, reason has taken sidetracks which expose it to the danger of losing sight of its final goal. Deprived of reason, faith has stressed feeling and experience, and so run the risk of no longer being a universal proposition. It is an illusion to think that faith, tied to weak reasoning, might be more penetrating; on the contrary, faith then runs the grave risk of withering into myth or superstition. By the same token, reason which is unrelated to an adult faith is not prompted to turn its gaze to the newness and radicality of being. (§48)

The Holy Father then asserts the fundamental principles of complementarity:

This is why I make this strong and insistent appeal—not, I trust, untimely—that faith and philosophy recover the profound unity which allows them to stand in harmony with their nature without compromising their mutual autonomy. The *parrhesia* of faith must be matched by the boldness of reason. (§48)

The prior discussion might imply that faith and reason are simply parts of a human person and that the complementarity between them would be fractional. This would mean that faith and reason work together toward a common goal, shown numerically as $\frac{1}{2} + \frac{1}{2} = 1$. However, the complementarity of faith and reason is more like an integral complementarity which goes beyond adding up to a single integer. The following example will help to develop this point. John Paul describes faith as an act not of part of the person, but rather of the whole person. In an address to university students and professors at Mass for the opening of the academic year 1999 he states:

The act of faith is not simply an intellectual adherence to the truths revealed by God, but neither is it merely an attitude of confident entrustment to God's action. Rather it is the synthesis of both these elements, because it involves both the intellectual and the affective realm, as an integral act of the human person.

These reflections on the nature of faith have immediate consequences on the way of working out, teaching and learning theology. If, in fact, the act of faith that leads to man's justification involves the whole of the person, theological reflection on divine Revelation and on the human response cannot but take due account of the multiple aspects—intellectual, emotional, moral and spiritual—which intervene in the relationship of communion between God and the believer.[8]

Drawing upon themes expressed in his earlier philosophical text *The Acting Person,*[9] John Paul II explains his view that faith involves the whole person:

The act of faith considered in its integrity must necessarily be expressed in concrete attitudes and decisions. In this way it becomes possible to overcome the apparent antithesis between faith and action. Faith understood in the full sense does not remain an abstract element, uprooted from everyday life, but involves all a person's dimensions, including the existential contents and experiential aspects of his life.[10]

The practical reason of the human person provides the root for existential contents, experiential aspects, and various kinds of human action.[11] It is the whole person who thinks, the whole person who believes, and the whole person who acts. Thus, the full horizon of faith and reason opens for the pilgrim journeying toward the truth,

8. John Paul II, "Faith involves the whole person," in *L'Osservatore Romano,* no. 42 (October 20, 1999), 1. See also Javier Prades, "The Search for the Meaning of Life and Faith," *Communio* 26 (1999): "Faith's response to God's gratuitous invitation brings about in inter-personal communication in which reason is impelled to open itself to the deepest meaning of this dialogue. The act of faith involves the believer's whole person," 635.

9. Karol Wojtyła, *The Acting Person,* trans. Andrzej Potocki (Dordrecht and Boston: D. Reidel, 1979).

10. John Paul II, "Faith involves the whole person," *L'Osservatore Romano,* no. 42 (October 20, 1999), 1.

11. Msgr. Livio Melina describes the actions of practical reason in his article on *Fides et ratio* entitled "The 'Truth about the Good: Practical Reason, Philosophical Ethics, and Moral Theology'" *Communio* 26 (Fall 1999): 640–61.

and truth's profound personal and interpersonal dimension is revealed.

II. Philosophy and Theology

In *Fides et ratio* John Paul II posits that philosophy is part of the natural human being. His first reason for this sweeping classification follows his noting that persons ask questions about the meaning of existence (§3):

Born and nurtured when the human being first asked questions about the reason for things and their purpose, philosophy shows in different modes and forms that the desire for truth is part of human nature itself. It is *an innate property of human reason* to ask why things are as they are, even though the answers which gradually emerge are set within a horizon which reveals how the different human cultures are complementary. [Italics added]

Upon this basis he argues that all human beings are philosophers. As soon as a person begins to ask fundamental questions, he begins to do philosophy.

John Paul II repeats this argument in section 30:

The truths of philosophy, it should be said, are not restricted only to the sometimes ephemeral teachings of professional philosophers. All men and women, as I have noted, are in some sense philosophers and have their own philosophical conceptions with which they direct their lives. In one way or other, they shape a comprehensive vision and an answer to the question of life's meaning; and in the light of this they interpret their own life's course and regulate their behavior.

A basic philosophy goes beyond just asking questions; it also formulates answers to the fundamental questions about the meaning of life. These answers are organized into a comprehensive vision or world view which orders the person's actions and behaviors.

Further evidence offered by John Paul II that philosophy is a universal phenomenon includes the development of national and international legal systems (§3) and implicitly shared principles of logic (non-contradiction, finality, and causality) (§4). In addition, there is, in different cultures, a common concept of persons as free and intelligent and sharing certain moral norms. The Holy Father suggests in #4 that human beings from different cultures and different times recognize some common philosophical principles: "It is as if we had come upon an *implicit philosophy,* as a result of which all feel that they possess these principles, albeit in a general and unreflective way."

John Paul II mentions in §1 of *Fides et ratio* the philosophical questions raised by wise men in different cultures:

These are the questions which we find in the sacred writings of Israel, as also in the Veda and the Avesta; we find them in the writings of Confucius and Lao-Tze, and in the preaching of Tirthankara and Buddha; they appear in the poetry of Homer and in the tragedies of Euripides and Sophocles, as they do in the philosophical writings of Plato and Aristotle. They are questions which have their common source in the quest for meaning which has always compelled the human heart. In fact, the answer given to these questions decides the direction which people seek to give to their lives.

Thus, the incorporation of everyone into the momentum of philosophy provides a dynamic foundation for the appeal to grow in philosophical skill and wisdom by doing better what human beings by their very nature are enabled to do.

Some men and women have engaged in sustained speculation about the fundamental questions. They have learned the skill of a "rigorous mode of thought, and then in turn, through the logical coherence of the affirmations made and the organic unity of their content, [they have produced] . . . a systematic body of knowledge" (§4). Taking the natural instinct of human reason these philosophers ask questions and develop extensive skills of thinking, reasoning, and observation to provide sophisticated answers to the questions

posed. They teach others their philosophical methodologies and conclusions by writing and by oral teaching.

In *Fides et ratio* John Paul II names individual philosophers. This
suggests that philosophy is not primarily a field of abstract systems of
thought. Rather philosophy is portrayed by John Paul II as composed
of individual men and women struggling to articulate the fundamental principles of life using methodologies based on observation of the
senses, raising intelligent questions, reasoning from accepted data and
principles, and properly generating conclusions according to "right
reason."

Philosophers have an obligation to compare their particular theories with the universal core of truths which emerge in different times
and cultures. In section 4 the pope claims that professional philosophers ought to test the correctness of their conclusions by comparing
them with commonly held philosophical principles:

Although times change and knowledge increases, it is possible to discern a
core of philosophical insight within the history of thought as a whole . . .
Precisely because it is shared in some measure by all, this knowledge should
serve as a kind of reference point for the different philosophical schools.
Once reason successfully intuits and formulates the first universal principles
of being and correctly draws from them conclusions which are coherent
both logically and ethically, then it may be called right reason or, as the
ancients called it, *orthos logos, recta ratio.*

The Holy Father notes how the philosophical schools of Stoicism,
Epicureanism, Platonism, and Aristotelianism critically encountered
the Christian mind at certain moments in western history: St. Paul in
ancient Greece (§§36–38), St. Augustine in Italy and Africa (§§39–
41), St. Anselm in France and England (§42), and St. Albert and St.
Thomas in France, Germany, and Italy (§§43–44). Christian philosophy and theology began to emerge as intertwining fields of study
within the works of these great thinkers. By the time of Thomas

Aquinas, the autonomous and complementary methodologies of philosophical and theological investigation were well differentiated and became integrated into Christian education.

By the thirteenth century, institutional structures evolved to allow the development of theology and philosophy as separate academic disciplines (§45). The University of Paris developed four separate faculties: an undergraduate Faculty of Arts which taught philosophy and three graduate faculties of Theology, Medicine, and Law.[12] This provided the model for other educational programs. An institutionalization of reason in academic philosophy and institutionalization of faith in academic theology evolved.

Immediately struggles ensued between the Faculty of Theology and the Faculty of Arts involving disagreements about the relation of reason to faith.[13] Certain propositions of philosophy were condemned as incompatible with Christian theology, and the Faculty of Arts "promulgated a regulation (which said that) no master or bachelor of arts was to determine or even to dispute a theological question. . . . Should he do so, . . . he was to be removed from the faculty forever unless he retracted within three days."[14] The two academic fields of philosophy and theology grew in separate directions. John Paul II summarizes in *Fides et ratio* §45:

Although they insisted upon the organic link between theology and philosophy, St. Albert the Great and St. Thomas were the first to recognize the autonomy which philosophy and the sciences needed if they were to perform well in their respective fields of research. From the late Medieval peri-

---

12. See Hastings Rashdall, *The University of Europe in the Middle Ages,* 3 vols. (London: Oxford University Press, 1958), and Gordon Leff, *Paris and Oxford Universities in the Thirteenth and Fourteenth Centuries: An Institutional and Intellectual History* (New York: John Wiley and Sons Inc., 1968).

13. See John F. Wippel, "The Condemnations of 1270 and 1277 at Paris," *Journal of Medieval and Renaissance Studies* 7 (1977): 169–201.

14. Ibid., 184.

od onward, however, the legitimate distinction between the two forms of learning became more and more a fateful separation. As a result of the exaggerated rationalism of certain thinkers, positions grew more radical and there emerged eventually a philosophy which was separate from and absolutely independent of the contents of faith. Another of the many consequences of this separation was an ever deeper mistrust with regard to reason itself.

Two recent articles on *Fides et ratio* document the stages in which this institutional separation of theology and philosophy evolved.[15] These authors trace the steps through which philosophy and theology lost a complementary harmony and balance. When philosophy and reason dominate, as they did with European rationalism, a kind of polarization ensues which results in the marginalization of theology. In this movement philosophy attempts to replace theology. In more recent times, in some places where the field of theology has dominated, an ensuing fideistic polarization renders philosophy equally useless (§55).

In contrast to imbalanced polarities when either philosophy or theology dominates Catholic intellectual life, John Paul II describes in §99 ways in which the two fields can move toward greater cooperation:

Philosophical enquiry can help greatly to clarify the relationship between truth and life, between event and doctrinal truth, and above all between transcendent truth and humanly comprehensible language. This involves a reciprocity between the theological disciplines and the insights drawn from the various strands of philosophy; and such a reciprocity can prove genuinely fruitful for the communication and deeper understanding of the faith.

15. See Giovanni B. Sala, "The Drama of the separation of faith and reason," *L'Osservatore Romano*, no. 13 (March 31, 1999): 9–10, and Avery Dulles, "Can Philosophy Be Christian?" *First Things*, no. 102 (April 2000): 24–29; see also the first essay in the present volume.

The need to strengthen philosophy and theology has been well summarized by Robert George as the need for "Harmonious Partners."[16]

John Henry Newman considered the evolving historical relation between theology and philosophy in his classic *The Scope and Nature of University Education.*[17] While in the thirteenth century theology was the dominant organizing field in universities and philosophy served primarily as preparation (or handmaid to the queen of the sciences), today we find theology marginalized in most universities while philosophy may dominate intellectual life or be devalued as well. The marginalization of theology has become so extreme that it is even being relocated from a humanities to a social science department as a form of religion whose experience should be evaluated on par with other religions.[18]

In an effort to strengthen theology in the contemporary world, Yves M.-J. Congar wrote *A History of Theology,* tracing the relation of the two fields through six different eras.[19] In *Fides et ratio* John Paul II echoes Congar's analysis when he again states that theology "calls upon" philosophy (§77). He argues that theology needs philosophy in order to have its own reason "formed and educated to concept and

16. Robert P. George, "The Renaissance of Faith and Reason," *Crisis* (January 2000): 19–22.

17. John Henry Cardinal Newman, *The Scope and Nature of University Education* (New York: E. P. Dutton, 1958).

18. See a recent article on this topic by Daniel Cere, Director of the McGill Newman Center, Montreal, Quebec, Canada: "Newman, God, and the Academy," *Theological Studies* 55 (1994): 3–23. In particular, "The effective marginalization of a major discourse such as theology or ethics narrows the range of inquiry and leads to 'bias.' The discipline of theology ensures that there is a substantive debate about the question of the supreme good within the academy," 18; and "When theology is marginalized, the question of God and the complex issues surrounding the God question fade into academic oblivion. This not only narrows but actually distorts academic discourse about religion. A methodological atheism is imposed on scholarly interpretation of religious experience," 20.

19. Yves M.-J. Congar, *A History of Theology* (Garden City, N.Y.: Doubleday and Company, Inc., 1968).

argument . . . and as a partner in dialogue in order to confirm the intelligibility and universal truth of its claims" (§77).

The Holy Father is hesitant to use the traditional metaphor of philosophy as the handmaid or servant of theology lest it seem that he subordinates philosophy to theology: "The term can scarcely be used today, given the principle of autonomy to which we have referred, but it has served throughout history to indicate the necessity of the link between the two sciences and the impossibility of their separation" (§77). He suggests the attractive metaphor of faith and reason as the two wings on which the human spirit rises to contemplate the truth. Because it is the whole person who thinks or believes, the numerical formula $1 + 1 = 2$ captures better than $\frac{1}{2} + \frac{1}{2} = 1$ this kind of complementarity. The same conclusion can be reached for the complementarity of the autonomous fields of study, philosophy and theology, within an academic institution. When each field has its proper autonomy and place within the institution of higher learning, together they build up the complementary orders of knowledge.

John Paul II emphasizes the interpersonal nature of this interaction. Academic disciplines are composed of persons, theologians and philosophers, who work within them, of students who learn from them, and, in a Christian institution, in relation to the Divine Persons in the Holy Trinity:

In short, Christian revelation becomes the true point of encounter and engagement between philosophical and theological thinking in their reciprocal relationship. It is to be hoped, therefore, that theologians and philosophers will let themselves be guided by the authority of truth alone so that there will emerge a philosophy consonant with the word of God. (§79)

Only when theology and philosophy situate themselves in mutual relation with the revelation of Jesus Christ, Word made flesh, will they be enabled to maintain the appropriate tension of their complementary search for and proclamation of the truth. Analogous to the first horizon of faith and reason, the second horizon of theology and philosophy is opened to the one journeying toward the truth; both horizons reveal a profound personal and interpersonal dimension.

While *Fides et ratio,* a papal encyclical, is addressed to the universal Church through bishops, its application to different cultures varies. Particular needs of institutional philosophy and theology in American culture are evident today. In the past century there have been three periods in academic philosophy; each period had a different goal and method for teaching philosophy in Catholic universities and seminaries. For purposes of this presentation, the time periods may be identified as: (1) traditional scholastic, (2) revolutionary secular, and (3) new evangelizing contemporary.

In the first period, lasting until the late 1960s Catholic philosophy was typically taught in seminaries in America primarily by secondary source Latin texts in scholastic philosophy.[20] Principles and conclusions were abstracted from St. Thomas Aquinas and Thomistic commentators; the student was often expected to commit them to memory. The texts covered logic, natural philosophy, cosmology, philosophical psychology, metaphysics, ontology, natural theology, and ethics. The subtitle of one popular work by Farges and Barbedette *Ad mentem S. Thomae Aquinatis esposita et regentioribus scientiarum inventis aptata necnon instructa contra Kantismum et Modernismum,* indicates that the authors demonstrated how Thomistic philosophy may refute Kantianism and Modernism.[21]

---

20. At St. Thomas Seminary in Denver, the two-volume text for undergraduate philosophy in the 1940s was A. Farges and D. Barbedette, *Philosophia Scholastica* (Paris: Baston, Berche, and Tralin, 1918). The first volume covered logic, cosmology, and philosophical psychology; the second volume was on metaphysics, ontology, natural theology, and ethics. Theology used a similar four-volume Latin text in dogmatic and moral theology. I am grateful to Msgr. Jerome Murray, class of 1949, for this information.

21. For seminarians at The Catholic University of America during the years 1943–45,

During the first period described here, the professors and students of philosophy had a rigorous formation through a common core of abstracted Thomistic principles summarized systematically in the Latin language. While lectures in seminaries could be in English, those at universities were often in Latin. Examinations could occur in either language. The students gained confidence that they had learned what is objectively true about the world from the perspective of reason and philosophical argumentation, but they did not enter into a dynamic of philosophical questioning or engage in direct learning of secular authors. A complete separation of philosophy from theology gave a clear focus to each stage of education, yet it mitigated against a student's discovery of the genuine complementarity of these two pathways to truth.

Two momentous events delineate the second period of education: the revolution in academic programs of nearly all universities, Catholic and non-Catholic, which occurred in Europe and North America between 1961 and 1969, and the Second Vatican Council, 1962 to 1965. In the 1960s the traditional scholastic phase of Catholic education was dramatically overturned by a revolutionary secular orientation. In such secular American universities as Berkeley, San Francisco State, Columbia University, Cornell University, Harvard University, and the University of Colorado at Boulder, radical student movements relentlessly attacked the notion of a traditional common core in education. They used both non-violent and violent means to

---

the main text was the two-volume Josephus Gredt, O.S.B., *Elementa Philosophiae: Aristotelico-Tomisticae* (Friburg: Herder, 1926) supplemented by the three-volume J. S. Hickey, O. Cist, *Summula Philosophiae Scholasticae in usum Adolescentium* (Boston: Benzisser Brothers, 1933). I am grateful to Rev. Robert V. Nevans from Greeley, Colorado, class of 1949 for this information. Since the seminary in Rome was closed because of the war, Catholic University served as the meeting point for seminarians from across the United States. Another similar text also used was the three-volume work by Henry Grenier, *Cursus Philosophiae* (Laval, Quebec: Le seminaire de Quebec, 1944).

achieve their objectives.[22] Within one decade, protests had increased so dramatically that educational systems were under seige all across North America. The result was that by the 1970s a spirit and practice of educational anarchy permeated both the secular and the Catholic academic curriculum. There was no consensus on what constituted a common core of texts, philosophy and theology lost their places of preeminence in Catholic institutions of higher learning, and social sciences such as sociology, anthropology, and political science began to become more central.[23]

What was the effect of this anarchy in secular education on Catholic educational institutions? San Francisco State College in California and the Sorbonne University in France, both Catholic institutions at their founding, were at the center of the violent demonstrations. Across the United States many Catholic educational institutions began to follow the model of the major Protestant institutions such as Harvard, Yale, Princeton, and William and Mary, which had been founded with a strong Christian identity, but had over time become increasingly secularized.[24] In the secular model of education the

22. This sequence of assaults is well documented by the philosopher Sidney Hook in *Academic Freedom and Academic Anarchy* (New York: Cowles Book Company, 1970). He states that by 1969, "Wherever American educators meet today, there is one theme of overriding concern that shadows their deliberations even when it is not on the agenda of discussion. This is the mounting wave of lawlessness, often cresting into violence, that has swept to many campuses," 232.

23. See Allan Bloom, *The Closing of the American Mind* (New York: Simon and Schuster, 1987). Bloom, professor of philosophy from the University of Chicago, described the effect of this revolution on the student of the 1980s: "The university now offers no distinctive visage to the young person. He finds a democracy of the disciplines. . . . This democracy is really an anarchy, because there are no recognized rules for citizenship and no legitimate titles to rule. In short there is no vision, nor is there a set of competing visions, of what an educated human being is. . . . There is no organization of the sciences, no tree of knowledge," 337.

24. See George M. Marsden, *The Soul of the American University: From Protestant Establishment to Established Nonbelief* (New York: Oxford University Press, 1994). Marsden, a professor of history from the University of Notre Dame, documents the way in which various

fields of philosophy and theology are fragmented, isolated in separate areas of the university, even sometimes in different academic faculties, i.e. social sciences and humanites.

The Second Vatican Council in its 1965 document *Gaudium et spes* asked the Church to engage directly with the modern world in the field of education. One section of the document identified "faith and culture" as an urgent area of concern: "Those involved in theological studies in seminaries and universities should be eager to cooperate with men versed in other fields of learning by pooling their resources and their points of view."[25] The areas of the social sciences and sciences were noted explicitly in this context. In addition, the turn from the almost exclusive use of Latin in liturgy to vernacular languages opened the way for the devaluation of Latin and the simultaneous insertion of non-Latin texts in other areas of Catholic life. In addition, most modern and contemporary philosophical texts not in Latin were from the secular traditions. Consequently, philosophical education even in Catholic universities and seminaries began to be based on non-scholastic vernacular texts. These texts, not fully compatible with Catholic theology, were often supplemented by social science texts. Catholic theology began to "float" in the ranges of opinion, popular views, and will of the majority, rather than on solid philosophical foundations of objective truth and reality. Complementarity between the fields of theology and philosophy was generally lost in this second phase of education.

In the third period in Catholic education, the period of new evangelization, some Catholic philosophy programs found new ways to

---

Protestant denominations played unique roles in founding these major universities and how these affiliations have lost their place. One wonders if most Catholic universities, are now, by their identification with the American secular model of education, going down the same path.

25. *Gaudium et spes,* in *Documents of Vatican II,* Austin P. Flannery, ed. (Grand Rapids, Mich.: Eerdmans, 1984), #62.

establish philosophy on solid vernacular foundations, open both to the ancient Greek and medieval traditions and to new developments in modern and contemporary philosophy.[26] This new evangelization (§103) of Catholic philosophical formation demands attention not only to philosophy itself, but also to the relation between philosophy and theology. This provides a constructive guide for the third period of educational orientation following upon the traditional scholastic and revolutionary secular periods described above. In the period of new evangelization, philosophers and theologians need to engage directly with one another in establishing curriculum and structure of their educational programs. It is to the principles of this third period of education that our analysis will now turn.

III. Philosophers and Theologians

We come now to the final phase of our pilgrimage-like journey. *Fides et ratio* is directly addressed to "theologians and philosophers whose duty it is to explore the different aspects of truth . . ." (§6). His joining together of theologians and philosophers here is not accidental, for theologians and philosophers are called not just individually, but also in relation to one another. Each group is called to place its professional gifts at the service of the another. Theologians and philosophers are invited by the Holy Father to find concrete ways to work for a genuine complementarity in mutual, but differentiated, explorations of truth.

W. Norris Clarke, in his commentary on *Fides et ratio* entitled "The Complementarity of Faith and Philosophy" notes that

26. The School of Philosophy at the Catholic University of America, The Faculty of Philosophy at the Catholic University of Lublin, the Dominican House of Studies in Ottawa, and Thomas Aquinas College in Santa Paula, California, present evidence of this new trend.

... to develop properly, philosophy needs a *community of persons,* and especially the experience of *trust between persons,* since so much of what we know and take as data for understanding must come from trust in what others tell us. This is especially true with respect to the philosophical understanding of the person and interpersonal relations . . .[27]

Furthermore, theologians and philosophers need to develop interdisciplinary communities of persons. This is a daunting task when institutional structures so often mitigate against natural and regular discourse. Philosophers are often located in different physical spaces from theologians in universities and on different campuses in minor and major seminaries. There are Catholic professional societies and interdisciplinary programs or institutions which offer new possibilities for dialogue which philosophers and theologians should be encouraged to actively engage.[28]

Among the professional philosophers there are some who have excelled in contribution to humanity. "In different cultural contexts and at different times, this process has yielded results which have produced genuine systems of thought" (§4). John Paul II identifies several in *Fides et ratio.* In this act of naming he accentuates the unique contributions, especially in respect to the fruitful interaction of reason with faith, of the following professional philosophers: Plato, Aristotle, Augustine, Anselm, Bonaventure, St. Albert the Great, St. Thomas

27. W. Norris Clarke, "The Complementarity of Faith and Philosophy," *Communio* 26 (1999): 562–63.

28. For example, The Studium du Séminaire de Paris of the Ecole Cathédral in Paris integrates theologians, philosophers, and scholars of other disciplines in their seminars. The Fellowship of Catholic Scholars in the United States fosters interdisciplinary dialogue around a common topic selected each year. Lonergan University College, Concordia University, Montreal, Canada had for many years a core interdisciplinary seminar incorporating philosophers, theologians, scientists, and others into a study of a given thinker such as Galileo, St. Teresa of Avila, Foucault, Darwin, during each academic year. Some seminaries such as St. John Vianney Theological Seminary in Denver have theologians and philosophers regularly giving invited lectures in one another's courses.

Aquinas, Blaise Pascal, Kierkegaard, and Francisco Suarez. He notes further:

> the courageous research pursued by more recent thinkers, among whom I gladly mention, in a Western context, figures such as John Henry Newman, Antonio Rosmini, Jacques Maritain, Etienne Gilson and Edith Stein and, in an Eastern context, eminent scholars such as Vladimir S. Soloviev, Paval A. Florensky, Petr Chaadaev and Vladimir N. Lossky. (§74)

Indicating a deep gratitude for the work of these and other "masters" of thought, the Holy Father hopes that professional philosophers will gather momentum from previous philosophers in "both the search for truth and the effort to apply the results of that search to the service of humanity" (§74).

There is a dynamic interpersonal connection among professional philosophers, particularly among those who have produced systematic bodies of knowledge and genuine systems of thought. The Holy Father correctly observes that philosophers can gather momentum from one another. Not all momentum is good, however. Critical and self-critical attitudes toward philosophical systems have always been a central aspect of the professional philosopher's work.

Just as Thomas Aquinas took a critical attitude toward the philosophy of Aristotle and Islamic philosophy, contemporary philosophers are asked by the Holy Father to take a critical attitude toward modern and contemporary secular philosophy. This critical attitude is not to be a rejection of a philosopher's thought, but rather a sifting of what is true from what is false in a particular system of thought (§43). Karol Wojtyła's own work on the philosophy of Kant is another good example of this principle. Modern philosophers have positively brought careful attention to the identity of the self (§5).

> Modern philosophy clearly has the great merit of focusing attention upon man. From this starting point, human reason with its many questions has

developed further its yearning to know more and to know it ever more deeply. Complex systems of thought have thus been built, yielding results in the different fields of knowledge and fostering the development of culture and history. Anthropology, logic, the natural sciences, history, linguistics and so forth—the whole universe of knowledge has been involved in one way or another.

Contemporary teachers of philosophy have an obligation to become familiar with the foundations of modern philosophy in order to evaluate and cite its positive contributions to the philosophy of the person and to all the other fields noted above.

Not only do teachers need to understand the truths contained in the works of various modern philosophers, they also need to learn where the philosophers fall into error. This serves as a direction signal for systematic and ideological errors of thought. "Rather than make use of the human capacity to know the truth, modern philosophy has preferred to accentuate the ways in which this capacity is limited and conditioned" (§5). Here is another kind of momentum than the one identified above—the momentum of erroneous philosophical theories which have brought into the contemporary educational culture an enormous challenge for teachers of philosophy. *Fides et ratio* identifies several "wrong ways" for philosophers to travel on their pilgrimage to the truth about the self and the world. When an erroneous philosophy is widely dispersed, it becomes detached from the original philosopher who proposed it. Through the rampant errors in philosophical systems today the human being has lost confidence in his or her capacity to know the truth about the self, about God, and about the world: "Hence we see among the men and women of our time, and not just in some philosophers, attitudes of widespread distrust of the human being's great capacity for knowledge" (§5).

When the work of professional philosophers is detached from the fundamental questions of life it can permeate the minds of men and women and weaken a confidence in their own natural desires for truth. This effect can be so damaging at times that it undermines the very identity of the human being as the one who seeks the truth. "A philosophy which no longer asks the question of the meaning of life would be in grave danger of reducing reason to merely accessory functions, with no real passion for the search for truth" (§5). As a result, teachers of philosophy today are challenged by John Paul II to uncover healthy foundations which will enable the natural philosophical temperament of men and women to flourish once again.

Fides et ratio §5 clearly identifies some of the "charged" effects of new secular philosophies: human beings are now at the mercy of caprice; they judge persons often only by pragmatic criteria; they thus lose a capacity to contemplate truth; they abandon the investigation of being and give in to agnosticism and relativism, "yielding to an undifferentiated pluralism," and lose their "way in the shifting sands of widespread scepticism." In §81 we read further that persons are falling into a crisis of meaning, being weighed down by the fragmentation of knowledge and overwhelming amounts of data, tending toward attitudes of indifference and nihilism within an immense expansion of technology.

John Paul II presents three specific calls to professional philosophers who teach today. Each call aims to uncover a solid foundation within a particular context of difficulty. The first requirement for philosophers is to recover philosophy's proper focus to search for the ultimate meaning of life. In the context of a society driven by utilitarianism and functionalism, where a 'utility principle' or 'calculus' uses other human beings, the philosophy teacher is to stimulate "philosophy to conform to its proper nature" (§81) which is to treat persons as ends worthy of love. The second requirement for philosophers is to verify the human capacity to know objective truth in a society which has lost confidence in the human being's capacity to find the truth because of the erroneous teachings of relativism and phenomenalism. The third requirement for philosophers is to discover a genuinely metaphysical range of thought which provides absolute and ultimate foundations. This principle addresses a culture which limits analysis of experience or phenomena and remains within narrow confines of linguistic analysis or hermeneutics. From the perspective of the philosophy of the person, "it is metaphysics which makes it possible to ground the concept of the person's dignity in virtue of the person's spiritual nature. In a special way, the person constitutes a privileged locus for the encounter with being, and hence with metaphysical enquiry" (§83). John Paul II argues that the proper way for philosophers to work on this principle is to develop "a close relationship of continuity between contemporary philosophy and the philosophy developed in the Christian tradition" (§86).

The Holy Father stresses that Christian philosophers have a vocation to help young people who have no valid points of reference because "the ephemeral is affirmed as a value and the possibility of discovering the real meaning of life is cast into doubt." In this context of no objectively valid points of reference, there are also no clear foundations for personal and interpersonal or communal life (§6). He lays partial blame for this situation directly on philosophers who are not living their true vocation well:

This is why many people stumble through life to the very edge of the abyss without knowing where they are going. At times, this happens because those whose vocation it is to give cultural expression to their thinking no longer look to truth, preferring quick success to the toil of patient enquiry into what makes life worth living. With its enduring appeal to the search for truth, philosophy has the great responsibility of forming thought and culture, and now it must strive resolutely to recover its original vocation. (§6)

In section 56 he sends out a call for philosophers to their full actualization:

> I cannot but encourage philosophers—be they Christian or not—to trust in the power of human reason and not to set themselves goals that are too modest in their philosophizing. The lesson of history in this millennium now drawing to a close shows that this is the path to follow: it is necessary not to abandon the passion for ultimate truth, the eagerness to search for it or the audacity to forge new paths in the search.

Returning to the broader theme of complementarity in the search for truth, we reflect upon the way that theologians can help philosophers live the full integrity of their vocation in the contemporary world. Philosophers may learn humility and courage by close proximity with theology:

> As a theological virtue, faith liberates reason from presumption, the typical temptation of the philosopher. St. Paul, the Fathers of the Church and, closer to our own time, philosophers such as Pascal and Kierkegaard reproached such presumption. The philosopher who learns humility will also find courage to tackle questions which are difficult to resolve if the data of revelation are ignored—for example, the problem of evil and suffering, the personal nature of God and the question of the meaning of life or, more directly, the radical metaphysical question, "Why is there something rather than nothing?" (§76)

The virtues of humility and courage, which release a person from vain presumption and fear, are important benefits indeed!

A benefit that theologians offer philosophers is the Word of God as a proper subject of study. Sections 73–74 of *Fides et ratio* describe how philosophical reflection on theology's source enriches the philosopher's work by stirring his or her reason to discover "new and unsuspected horizons" and to "explore paths" the philosopher alone would not have anticipated. The Word of God, the starting point for theologians, can open the range of thought for philosophers in dynamic ways. The Word of God can ground philosophers in a "uni-fied and organic vision of knowledge" about God (§85). Without this gift of God, enhanced by the study and elaboration of theologians, philosophers may offer disintegrated, fragmented, and increasingly narrow contributions to society.

In section 108 of *Fides et ratio* John Paul II draws an analogy be-tween Mary and philosophers. This sets the direction for the future relations between philosophers and theologians:

For between the vocation of the Blessed Virgin and the vocation of true philosophy there is a deep harmony. Just as the Virgin was called to offer herself entirely as human being and as woman that God's Word might take flesh and come among us, so too philosophy is called to offer its rational and critical resources that theology, as the understanding of faith, may be fruitful and creative. And just as in giving her assent to Gabriel's word, Mary lost nothing of her true humanity and freedom, so too when philoso-phy heeds the summons of the Gospel's truth its autonomy is in no way impaired. Indeed, it is then that philosophy sees all its enquiries rise to their highest expression.

Philosophers must respond to the encounter with revelation of the Gospel by offering "entirely" our rational and critical resources to theologians. We will not lose our autonomy; rather our search for truth will be elevated "to [its] highest expression." The two wings of reason and faith work together in philosophers and theologians to enable them in a community of persons to rise together to a fuller contemplation of truth.

When we consider the other side of the task, *Fides et ratio* lists the complementary gifts of philosophers to theologians. Two areas of general philosophical expertise are the philosophy of culture and the philosophy of history. Philosophers can help theologians not to "be swayed uncritically by assertions which have become part of current parlance and culture but which are poorly grounded in reason" (§55).

Philosophers can also help theologians overcome the "risk of doing philosophy unwittingly and locking themselves within thought structures poorly adapted to the understanding of faith" (§77). Theologians need philosophers to form and educate their reason to concept and argument; philosophers are thus partners of theologians in dialogue "to confirm the intelligibility and universal truth" of their claims (§77).

The Holy Father notes how philosophers with expertise in particular areas of study may be of service to theologians who also have a particular specialty. In paragraphs 64–71 of *Fides et ratio* the following connections are made: philosophers of knowledge, communication, and language may help theologians in biblical studies; philosophers of language, relations, human person, world, and being may assist dogmatic theologians; philosophers of ethics (moral law, conscience, freedom, responsibility, guilt and decision making), human nature, and society may aid moral theologians; and philosophers of knowledge, God, language, and meaning may cooperate with fundamental theologians.

The above areas are sketched as possible new and open spaces of collaboration for the complementary work of philosophers and theologians. John Paul II leaves particular initiatives to the philosophers and theologians. He clearly sounds an admonition and a call. The admonition is that if philosophers and theologians refuse to collaborate the price will be very high both for them and for society at large. In the contemporary world the call is addressed to philosophers as a dramatic initiative to engage together, in appropriate complementarity with theologians, to lead the world forward in new evangelization. He challenges philosophers to be true to the integrity of their vocation (§106):

I appeal also to *philosophers,* and to all *teachers of philosophy,* asking them to have the courage to recover, in the flow of an enduringly valid philosophical tradition, the range of authentic wisdom and truth—metaphysical truth included—which is proper to philosophical enquiry. They should be open to the impelling questions which arise from the word of God and they should be strong enough to shape their thought and discussion in response to that challenge. Let them always strive for truth, alert to the good which truth contains. Then they will be able to formulate the genuine ethics which humanity needs so urgently at this particular time.

The Holy Father calls for a common work of philosophers and theologians in the company of other members the Church for the greater good of the world. Bishop Angelo Scola emphasizes this dimension of call: "John Paul II with *Fides et Ratio,* far from wanting to fix limits and, in some way, to bring a close to the inquiry, has cleared the field for genuine philosophical and theological research. The Encyclical *Fides et Ratio* does not represent an end, but a beginning."[29]

A passage from *Fides et ratio* §103 describes how the complementary challenges of theology and philosophy can serve the new evangelization:

A philosophy which responds to the challenges of theology's demands and evolves in harmony with faith is part of that "evangelization of culture" which Paul VI proposed as one of the fundamental goals of evangelization (*EN* 20). I have unstintingly recalled the pressing need for a *new evangelization;* and I appeal now to philosophers to explore more comprehensively the dimensions of the true, the good and the beautiful to which the word of God gives access. This task becomes all the more urgent if we consider the challenges which the new millennium seeks to entail, and which affect in a particular way regions and cultures which have a long-standing Christian tradition. This attention to philosophy too should be seen as a fundamental and original contribution in service of the new evangelization.

29. Angelo Scola, "Human Freedom and Truth," *Communio* 26 (1999): 492. This dimension of call is also picked up by the Reform theologian Martin Bieler, in "The Future of the Philosophy of Being," where he says: "The encyclical opens important horizons for *future development." Communio* 26 (1999): 459.

The response to this call to evangelize anew as philosophers and theologians is ours to actualize.

The call to evangelize anew through the cooperation of philosophers and theologians leads to a further dynamic of complementarity which is creatively synergetic in its effects. Here, the result of the complementary interaction goes far beyond the numerical balance captured in the formula $1 + 1 = 2$. A numerical formula for this kind of complementarity needs to be something more like $1 + 1 \rightarrow 3$. When philosophers and theologians interact in an integral complementarity as called for by John Paul II in *Fides et ratio* we synergetically generate something far greater than the simple addition of our contributions.

Conclusion

It is good to step back and reflect briefly on the way that the three identified areas of complementarity interact. A fundamental challenge of contemporary secular culture is its increasing fragmentation. *Gaudium et spes* (§10) notes that the human person feels divided within the self, and the separation of faith from reason and of reason from faith participates in this fact of contemporary discord.[30] The new evangelization of culture and education focuses on the human person as an integral whole being, whose acts of faith and acts of reason express decisions of the whole person. When faith and reason enter into a relationship of complementarity within the person, they are in

30. The full passage from *Gaudium et spes* §10 is as follows: "The dichotomy affecting the modern world is, in fact, a symptom of the deeper dichotomy that is in man himself. He is the meeting point of many conflicting forces. In his condition as a created being he is subject to a thousand shortcomings, but feels untrammeled in his inclinations and destined for a higher form of life. Torn by a welter of anxieties he is compelled to choose between them and repudiate some among them. Worse still, feeble and sinful as he is, he often does the very thing he hates and does not do what he wants. And so he feels himself divided, and the result is a host of discords in social life."

service to each other to lead the person to union with God and to communion with others.

The academic fields of philosophy and theology are wounded in contemporary secular culture by their fragmentation and isolation. Students immersed in fragmented secular educational environments may erroneously conclude that it is not possible to develop an integral and harmonious intellectual, spiritual, affective, human life. The new evangelization needs to focus on educational structures and programs so that complementarity within the interdisciplinary operations of philosophy and theology may find a new and energetic center of activity. A contemporary model of complementarity between philosophy and theology, built up by persons who are seeking to integrate a complementarity of reason and faith, may help bring a renewal to interdisciplinary studies.

Philosophers and theologians interacting with one another will set the pace for the new evangelization that *Fides et ratio* calls forth. Without these initiatives the academic structures will remain inordinately pressured by the secular values which surround them. Each of the three kinds of complementarity (reason and faith, philosophy and theology, philosophers and theologians) can enhance the others, so when a decision is made to work toward complementarity in one area, a synergy will likely affect the new evangelization in another area. This is the dynamic power of the new evangelization. This is the call to heed into the third millennium.

Philosophari in Maria: Fides et ratio AND MARY AS THE MODEL OF CREATED WISDOM

DAVID VINCENT MECONI, S.J.

1. Introduction

In the middle of the eighteenth century, on the Feast of the Purification, John Henry Newman held Mary up as the perfect model of theological wisdom. In a sermon addressed to the students of Oxford, Newman names Mary the exemplary theologian because she is the "pattern of Faith, both in the reception and in the study of Divine Truth. She does not think it enough to accept, she dwells upon it; not enough to possess, she uses it; not enough to assent, she develops it; not enough to submit the Reason, she reasons upon it."[1] Newman saw in Mary's *fiat* the vocation of the theologian because she not only embraces God's Word but explicates this reception in rational discourse. At the close of the twentieth century, Mary is once again held up as an intellectual model. This time, however, it is not the theologian she guides, but the philosopher.

---

1. *Sermon XV* (1843) as in *Fifteen Sermons Preached Before the University of Oxford Between A.D. 1826 and 1843,* ed. Mary Katherine Tillman (Notre Dame: University of Notre Dame Press, 1997), 313.

John Paul II concludes *Fides et ratio* by invoking Mary as the model of philosophy because, as he writes, her "life itself is a true parable illuminating the reflection contained in these pages."[2] He goes on to state that because of this "deep harmony" between "the vocation of the Blessed Virgin and the vocation of true philosophy," all should *"philosophari in Maria."*[3] Whereas Newman saw in Mary's "yes" the vocation of the theologian, John Paul sees in Mary the task of all philosophers: "Just as the Virgin was called to offer herself entirely as human being and as woman that God's Word might take flesh and come among us, so too philosophy is called to offer rational and critical resources that theology, as the understanding of faith, may be fruitful and creative" (§108). As John Paul's thinking goes, Mary receives Christ, *the* supernatural reality, and spends the rest of her life contemplating this mystery to which she freely assented. Mary thus becomes the model of created wisdom. She represents humanity's supreme openness to reality as well as a subsequent life of meditation upon the conditions which this openness demands.

The purpose of this essay is to develop a greater understanding of how John Paul II sees Mary's life paralleling the role of philosophy. Exactly how does her life's vocation manifest a harmony with the vocation of the philosopher? What does the Holy Father mean when he exhorts all to philosophize in Mary? Since Mary is mentioned nowhere except in the final paragraph of the encyclical (§108), her relationship to *Fides et ratio* as a whole is not all too clear. At first

2. §108. All citations from *Fides et ratio* come from the Daughters of St. Paul edition (Boston, 1998); henceforth the section numbers will simply be included in the body of the essay.

3. The earliest available reference of the phrase *philosophari in Maria* appears to come from Odon, Benedictine Prior of Cantebury and Abbot of Battle. In his sermon on the Feast of the Assumption, c. 1200, he states: "Quia igitur philosophari debemus in Maria, videmus quantum nobis sapientiam per interpretationem eius offerat nomen istud Maria." *Bulletin d'information de l'Institut des textes* III (1955): 51–54. See also J. Leclerq, "Maria Christianorum Philosophia," *Melanges de science religieuse* 13 (1956): 103–6.

glance the inclusion of such a Marian invocation may seem artificial if not forced. Far from some perfunctory attachment, however, in this concluding paragraph John Paul relies on Mary to summarize and represent the threefold task of philosophy as he understands it throughout the encyclical: Mary is the *Seat of Wisdom*, the first to offer her whole humanity to the service of Christ, and, consequently, the first to find life's "highest expression" in union with God.

First, Mary exemplifies philosophy's initial task to receive reality and not manipulate it. Unlike some Baconian mastery or Cartesian orchestration of the world, Mary symbolizes the awe of standing before a reality wholly independent of the human mind. As *Seat of Wisdom,* she symbolizes the philosopher's primordial vocation to receive that which is. Second, in Mary we see philosophy's inherent function of offering itself to ultimate, and thus divine, questions. The pope worries that philosophy today has dismissed its inherent directedness toward questions of the highest matter and, as such, needs to give itself to the inquiries of theology. Finally, Mary's life reminds philosophers that the true end of human inquiry is contemplation of the divine, a contemplation of the truth. As *Fides et ratio* makes clear, the human knower's ultimate end is found neither in social activism nor in the assent to partial and fragmentary truths, but in loving union with the fullness of Truth.

II. "How can this be?" (Luke 1:34): Philosophy as Receptive Wonder

Mary's first words to the divine messenger are those of wonder, and it is precisely in the act of wonder that all of philosophy begins. As Socrates instructed Theaetetus, "For this sense of wonder (θαυμάζειν) shows that you are a philosopher, since wonder is the only beginning of philosophy (ἄλλη ἀρχή φιλοσοφίας)."[4] Aristotle simi-

---

4. *Theaetetus* 155d.

larly credited the pre-Socratics with this awareness that the highest vocation of thought lies in admiration about the highest things: "It is through wonder (θαυμάζειν) that men both now begin and at first began to philosophize; wondering originally at obvious difficulties, and then by gradual progression raising questions about the greater matters."[5] Mary's wonder no doubt finds company in the ancients, and in her receptivity John Paul sees the remedy for one of modern philosophy's great ills: methodical doubt.

Mary's reception of reality is a reminder that philosophy is not for the proud. Her openness stands opposed to skepticism. Unlike Zachariah's incredulity before the angel, for which he is struck dumb (Luke 1:18–20), Mary's wonder begins in her humble willingness to receive God's word. According to John Paul, philosophy must be undertaken keeping three "basic rules" in mind. "The first of these is that reason must realize that human knowledge is a journey which allows no rest; the second stems from the awareness that such a path is not for the proud who think that everything is the fruit of personal conquest; a third rule is grounded in the 'fear of God' whose transcendental sovereignty and provident love in the governance of the world reason must recognize" (§18). Within the Christian drama, of course, it is the original sin of pride that rebels against this sovereignty of God, convincing humanity that it can "be like gods" (Gen. 3:5) by creating its own reality. *Fides et ratio* accordingly reaffirms that the human person was never constituted to "discern and decide for himself what was good and what was evil, but was constrained to appeal to a higher source" (§22). Always discovering but never determining God's word, Mary's openness and consequent awe remind all seeking wisdom that receptive wonder is the first step of philosophizing.

5. *Metaphysics* A ii, 982b12–14.

For much of modern thought, however, awe has given way to skepticism. Hegel, for example, maintains that a perplexing confusion *(Verwirrung)* is the beginning of philosophy: "Philosophy must, generally speaking, begin with a puzzle in order to bring about reflection; everything must be doubted, all presuppositions given up . . ."[6] Once Descartes set up doubt as the Archimedean point upon which all human inquiry would pivot, philosophy began to turn away from wonder and the consequent reception of what is to determining what could be allowed. Unlike Mary, who comes to know who she is only by first engaging a reality outside of herself—"And how does this happen to me, that the mother of my Lord should come to me?" (Luke 1:43)—Descartes replaces wonder with doubt and, in so doing, reduces knowledge of self to a static presence of ideas.[7] As John Paul has shown before, "self-knowledge develops at the same rate as knowledge of the world, of all the visible creatures."[8] *Fides et ratio* similarly argues that the human knower has no immediate access to self knowledge; rather, one comes to know through an honest and humble "encounter and engagement" (§70) with what is.

This is precisely why John Paul calls into question any philosophical system "grounded upon doubt." Such skepticism is unable ever to address true human concerns because the human person is the one who by nature *"seeks the truth"* (§28). He therefore looks for an understanding of reason that assists humans in their "unfailing openness to mystery and their boundless desire for knowledge" (§71). Philosophy thus needs to "recover its sapiential dimension as a search for the ulti-

6. *Hegel's Lectures on the History of Philosophy* I, trans. E. S. Haldane (London: Humanities Press, 1955), 406; *Vorlesungen über die Geschichte der Philosophie: Werke in zwanzig Bänden* 18 (Frankfurt: Suhrkamp, 1971), 466–67.

7. See Descartes' *Second Meditation* 24 and *Discourse on Method* 4.32–33; see also James Collins, *A History of Modern Philosophy* (Milwaukee: Bruce Publishers, 1954), 154–64.

8. *Original Unity of Man and Woman,* Oct 10, 1979 as in *The Theology of the Body: Human Love in the Divine Plan,* ed. John Grabowski (Boston: Pauline Books, 1997), 37.

mate and overarching meaning of life" (§81), and to do this, John
Paul invokes Mary as *Sedes Sapientiae.*

The *Seat of Wisdom* is the first image John Paul gives us of Mary. In
so doing, he represents her as the humble dwelling-place, the place
where Wisdom descends. Open to receiving Wisdom, Mary perfectly
accepts the Divine's visitation.[9] In concluding *Fides et ratio* by invoking a feminine vessel which is open to and hence able to receive a
reality outside herself, John Paul draws on a common image, prevalent in classical thought as well as in his own thinking. This feminine
receptivity acts to highlight the first role of the philosopher: the
openness of the soul to a truth not yet its own.

In his apostolic letter *Mulieris Dignitatem* for instance, John Paul
makes a rather bold claim as he argues that woman is the "representa-
tive and archetype of the whole human race" because she best symbolizes humanity's primal vocation to receive God.[10] Therefore, "all
human beings—both women and men—are called through the
Church, to be the 'Bride' of Christ. . . . In this way 'being the bride,'
and thus the 'feminine' element, becomes a symbol of all that is
'human.'"[11] In casting all human persons as feminine *vis-à-vis* a mas-

9. This image of the Mary as *sedes* corresponds to the angelic θρόνοι described by
Dionysius the Areopagite: "The title of the most sublime and exalted thrones conveys that
in them there is a transcendence over every earthly defect, as shown by their upward-bear-
ing toward the ultimate heights, that they are forever separated from what is inferior, that
they are completely intent upon remaining always and forever in the presence of him who
is truly The Most High, that free of all passion and material concern, they are utterly available to receive the divine visitation, that they bear God and are ever open, like servants, to
welcome God." *The Celestial Hierarchy* 205D as in *Pseudo-Dionysius: The Complete Works,* ed.
Paul Rorem (New York: Paulist Press, 1987), 162. Although Mary as the *Seat of Wisdom* is
a commonplace in the Fathers, she began to be invoked liturgically as such only in the
eleventh century; see M. O'Connell, *Theotokos: A Theological Encyclopedia of the Blessed Virgin Mary* (Wilmington, Del: M. Glazier Press, 1982), 368–69.

10. *Mulieris Dignitatem* §4; *Theology of the Body,* 447.

11. *Mulieris Dignitatem,* §25; *Theology of the Body,* 480. John Paul's Wednesday Addresses between 1979 and 1984 were very reliant upon this imagery. For example, he poses this
question when examining the Sermon on the Mount: Does not Christ "feel the need to

culine source which acts upon and in the human soul, John Paul relies on a classic metaphor: the true seeker of wisdom is impregnated from above, conceives truth within himself (e.g., Gal. 4:19), nurtures it, and then brings it forth into the world.

This identification of the feminine with the role of the philosopher, perhaps most notably exemplified in Boethius' "Lady Philosophy," finds its origin in Plato. In the *Symposium,* for example, woman becomes the archetype of the philosopher. Socrates uses the prophetess Diotima to explain the way to true beauty. The philosopher is the one who "has given birth (γενέσθαι) to true virtue and nourished it, and if any human being could become immortal, it would be he."[12] This line of thought is evidenced in the *Republic* as well. There the philosopher is the one who, "getting near what really is and having intercourse with it and having begotten (γεννήσας) understanding and truth, he knows, truly lives, is nourished and—at that point but not before—is relieved from the pains of giving birth."[13] The ancients anticipate Mary as the model of philosophy by holding up the dynamics of impregnation, parturition, and suckling the truth as the paradigms by which the human knower comes to know what is.

This maternal imagery emphasizes philosophy's need to be open to all of reality. True philosophy can never pre-formulate expectations of what could and could not be the case. John Paul sees the ultimate challenge to this openness in the death of God. Can one's way of thinking embrace the unthinkable? All philosophical systems

---

impregnate them with everything that is noble and beautiful?" *Blessed are the Pure of Heart,* Oct., 29, 1980; *Theology of the Body,* 168.

12. *Symposium* 212a; trans. Alexander Nehamas & Paul Woodruff (Indianapolis: Hackett Publishing, 1989), 60.

13. *Republic* 490b; trans., G. M. A. Grube (Indianapolis: Hackett Publishing, 1992), 163–64. Notice how the entire vocation of the philosopher is defined by Socrates as paralleling the midwife's role: "My art of midwifery is in general like theirs; the only difference is that my patients are men, not women, and my concern is not with the body but with the soul that is in travail of birth" (*Theaetetus* 150b).

must be ready to incorporate the "radical newness" (§101) of history. "The true keypoint which challenges every philosophy, is Jesus Christ's death on the Cross. It is here that every attempt to reduce the Father's saving plan to purely human logic is doomed to failure" (§23). Or as Jesuit theologian John Michael McDermott understands this, "Because freedom and being are mysteries, philosophy has to be open to novelty in history. History is constituted by the encounter of divine and human freedoms. No philosophy can reduce reality to a rational, necessary system entirely determined by human thought."[14] In the *Pietà,* we see a human knower able to embrace reality as it comes; with no preconceived notions of how reality should be, we see Mary's receptivity at its most challenged. The crucified Lord resting in Mary's arms reveals the place where human and divine freedom perfectly intersect.

Such reception brings wonder, the true mark of the philosopher. In Mary we see the first instance of Christian awe, the first Christian philosopher who stands before the ultimate reality and seeks to understand through assent. Her wonder must however give way to her oblation; she does not stand paralyzed before reality but gives herself to it. Let us now turn to Mary's *fiat,* to the offering she makes of herself.

III. "Behold, I am the Handmaid of the Lord. May it be done to me according to your word" (Luke 1:38): Philosophy as the Handmaid of Theology

John Paul next uses the person of Mary to represent how philosophy must offer itself to theology. Mary exemplifies the perfect oblation every human thinker must make to the Divine. Here lies the central concern of *Fides et ratio:* to reunite philosophy and theology by

14. John M. McDermott, "Dogmatic theology needs philosophy," *L'Osservatore Romano* (5 May 1999), 9.

reminding philosophers of both the inherent majesty of their vocation and that human reason is always directed toward a truth which
transcends it (§5). Like Mary, philosophy's end lies not in resting content in itself, but in presenting itself to concerns of the highest kind.
This reunion between philosophy and theology is not only the focal
point of the encyclical but a key theme of this pontificate.[15] John
Paul's confidence in philosophy is rooted not only in his "trust in the
power of human reason" (§56) but also in a humility which recognizes how human reason is not sufficient unto itself.

John Paul accordingly argues that philosophy has an inherent tendency toward theology and in this symbiosis, each form of inquiry is
enriched. "I have judged it appropriate and necessary to emphasize
the value of philosophy for the understanding of the faith, as well as
the limits which philosophy faces when it neglects the truths of revelation. . . . [E]ach influences the other, as they offer to the each other
a purifying critique and a stimulus to pursue the search for deeper
understanding" (§100). Philosophy disregards its inherent eros for
divine truths at its own peril. As the history of ideas has shown,
when philosophy begins to mistrust revealed truths, it soon begins to
mistrust human reason itself. This "crisis of rationalism" (§45) has
come about because philosophers have dismissed the truths of revelation as either "myth or superstition" (§48) or, at best, unimportant.
Quoting from Clement of Alexandria (d. 215), the pope provides
what he sees as the proper understanding of the nature of human
reason and its relationship to divine truth: "Since philosophy yearns
for the wisdom which consists in rightness of soul and speech and in
purity of life, it is well disposed toward wisdom and does all it can to

15. Even John Paul's understanding of religious education, for example, pivots precisely on this issue: "Religious faith itself calls for intellectual inquiry; and the confidence that
there can be no contradiction between faith and reason is a distinctive feature of the
Catholic humanistic tradition as it has existed in the past and as it exists in our own day."
Catholic Higher Education as in *Origins* (1 Oct. 1987), 269.

acquire it. We call philosophers those who love the wisdom that is creator and mistress of all things, that is knowledge of the Son of God"[16] (§38). This insight helps us to understand better why Mary is the model of the offering philosophy must make of itself.

Mary's *fiat* challenges claims made against the Catholic understanding of philosophy. Unlike many Moderns whose aim is "to elaborate a purely human wisdom in accord with the teachings of the faith but apart from all theological schools and all influence of revelation,"[17] John Paul sees in the Lord's handmaid a way to help mend that "fateful separation" (§45) between faith and reason which holds such a powerful sway over today's intellectual milieu.

The criticism against the idea of a "Christian philosophy" is that philosophy loses its autonomy and becomes nothing more than a theological lackey. The most noted instance of this debate is the exchange in the early twentieth century.[18] After the publication of Leo XIII's *Aeterni Patris,* critics such as Pierre Mandonnet, Léon Brunschwicg, and Emile Bréhier argued that Christian philosophical systems such as those that developed during the Middle Ages were not the products of unaided human reason but of dogmatic Churchmen only cloaking revealed truths within standard philosophical terminology.[19] In 1928 the Sorbonne's Emile Bréhier delivered three lectures entitled *Is There a Christian Philosophy?* His conclusion was an unequivocal *no.* Any philosophy that would call itself Christian, so went Bréhier's argument, abdicates its reliance on human reason

16. *Stromata* VI, 7, 55, 1–2; *Patrologia Graeca* IX, col. 277 as at *Fides et ratio* §38.

17. James Collins, *God in Modern Philosophy* (Chicago: Regnery Press, 1959), 58–59.

18. See *Bulletin de la Société française de philosophie* 31 (1931) and *Journées d'études de la Société thomiste* 2 (1933).

19. The secondary literature covering the events and persons of this period is extensive. See Maurice Nédoncelle, *Is There a Christian Philosophy?* trans. Illtyd Trethowan (New York: Hawthorn Books, 1960); Gerald McCool, *From Unity to Pluralism: The Internal Evolution of Thomism* (New York: Fordham University Press, 1989); Leo Sweeney, *Christian Philosophy* (New York: Peter Lang, 1997).

alone and instead relies on pre-formulated doctrine.[20] This position only inspired such thinkers as Jacques Maritain and Etienne Gilson to show how, in fact, there is such a thing as a Christian philosophy: "Thus I call Christian *every philosophy which, although keeping the two orders formally distinct, nevertheless considers the Christian revelation as an indispensable auxiliary to reason.*"[21] John Paul likewise calls for a way of philosophizing which never confuses the truths accessible by human reason with those necessarily revealed but which, nonetheless, stays open to the reality of those supernatural truths. He therefore maintains that it is in the nature of all philosophy *qua* philosophy to yearn for the truths of revelation; this dynamic is not something idiosyncratic to Christian philosophy. Hannah Arendt has likewise stated that "it remains undeniable that the notion of divinity antedated any Christian revelation, and that means that there must be a mental capacity in man by which he can transcend whatever is given to him, transcend, that is, the very factuality of Being."[22] Thus what is proposed in *Fides et ratio* is not the Christian usurpation of reason but the honest awareness that all human thought tends toward the divine, and in so doing, is enriched *precisely as human thought.*[23]

To emphasize this point, the encyclical makes a crucial distinction between human reason's autonomy and its self-sufficiency. Philosophy's autonomy, its principles and methods, must always be respected

20. For Emile Bréhier's position and argument, see his *Historie de la philosophie, vol. I: l'Antiquité et le moyen âge* (Paris: Alcan, 1927); "Y a-t-il une Philosophie Chrétienne?" *Revue de Métaphysique et de Morale* (April–June, 1931); *La philosophie du moyen âge* (Paris: Albin Michel, 1949).

21. Etienne Gilson, *The Spirit of Medieval Philosophy* (New York: Charles Scribner's Sons, 1940), 37.

22. Hannah Arendt, *The Life of the Mind* (New York: Harvest Books, 1971), 129.

23. This elevation and fulfillment of the human has been a touchstone of this pontificate and is evident in every aspect of John Paul's teaching. In *Dies Domini*, for example, the Holy Father offers us this image even when defending the sanctity of the Sabbath: "Time given to Christ is never time lost, but is rather time gained, so that our relationships and indeed our whole life may become more profoundly human" (§7).

and never coerced: only *as* philosophy can it offer itself to theology's needs. In Mary's *fiat,* John Paul therefore stresses, she never loses anything of her humanity; she offers herself *both as human and as woman* to the Father. However, like Mary, philosophy is called to offer itself to believers who philosophize "in dynamic union with the faith" (§76). This union has two aspects.

The first fruit of the union between philosophy and theology is faith's purification of reason's inherent pride. With other critics of rationalism, John Paul knows that when philosophy is left to itself, it tends toward hubris, "the typical temptation of the philosopher" (§76). The human intellect needs revelation to guide its inquiry and to temper its misleading presumption toward self-sufficiency. By continuously seeing itself alongside the truths of faith, philosophy is reminded that human knowledge must always be at the service of the Good; reason comes to see itself as the handmaid of God. This is not to imply that philosophy has a "purely functional role with regard to theology" (§77), but the pope is insistent that human reason can never become an end in itself; for when that happens, philosophy loses its ability to question and be questioned (§79).

The second aspect of the union between philosophy and theology becomes apparent when one considers how the truths of revelation influence the philosopher's concerns. Revelation introduces certain truths that philosophy might otherwise never see: e.g., the difference between person and substance, a personal God, the reality of human fallenness, the inherent dignity of the human person, and history as a free event (§76). Herein lies the boon of the Christian philosopher. Christian dogma "broadens reason's scope" (§76) with the result that philosophy actually becomes richer and more insightful through its engagement with the truths of revelation.

As philosophy needs theology, the converse is true as well. Theology stands in constant need of philosophical reflection "as a partner in dialogue in order to confirm the intelligibility and universal truth of its claims" (§77). In defending the autonomy of human reason, the Holy Father obviously worries about a creeping fideism: dogmatic positions which fail "to recognize the importance of rational knowledge and philosophical discourse for the understanding of faith, indeed for the very possibility of belief in God" (§55). Two common dangers which he highlights are biblicism and various forms of speculative theology exhibiting "fideistic tendencies." These positions—a biblical exegesis ignorant of its own philosophical presuppositions and a theology based simply on its own authority—dismiss the essential interplay between a proper reading of sacred Scripture, valid philosophical and theological traditions, and the guidance of the Church's Magisterium.[24] The pope thus concludes that humanity's search for veracity and authenticity comes from a mutual reciprocity between each of these fonts of truth.

Therefore, as philosophy comes to give itself more and more to theological matters, it will recover its true goal of contemplation. Philosophy does not terminate in opinion or action. Instead, as Cardinal Ratzinger has noted commenting on *Fides et ratio:*

> When philosophy completely extinguishes this dialogue with the thinking of faith, it ends up—as Jaspers once formulated it—in an 'empty seriousness.' In the end, philosophy will feel forced to renounce the question of truth, that is, to relinquish its very nature; for a philosophy which no longer asks about who we are, about why we exist, about whether God and eternal life exist, has as philosophy, abdicated.[25]

John Paul senses that much of philosophy has chosen to abandon its terminus in the divine because fallen intellects find it all too easy to

24. With this, John Paul here joins other critics of the extremes of rationalism and fideism by navigating a middle position between the two. One can hear him say along with Blaise Pascal: "If we submit everything to reason our religion will be left with nothing mysterious or supernatural. If we offend the principles of reason our religion will be absurd and ridiculous." *Pensées* §173.

25. Joseph Cardinal Ratzinger, "Culture and Truth: Reflections on the Encyclical," *Origins* (25 February 1999), 630.

run from the truth when they realize its demands (§28). In neglecting ultimate concerns, much of modern philosophy has lost its purpose and has forgotten that its final task is contemplation of truth. With Mary, the philosopher can never be one who rests simply in doubting, nor even one who aims his thinking toward action; rather, he must be one whose goal it is to know and love the truth of things.

IV. "And his Mother kept all these things in her heart" (Luke 2:51): Philosophy as Contemplation

Mary is therefore depicted as the model of humanity's finding its "highest expression" in communion with God. She acts as a guide to those who seek to know; acts to remind philosophers that their end is contemplation of God. This is why she is invoked as the one "who, in giving birth to the Truth and treasuring it in her heart, has shared it forever with the world" (§108). Philosophy's openness and offering can be completed only by its resting in God. By treasuring God's Word in her heart, Mary reminds philosophers that the proper end of intellectual inquiry is nothing short of the contemplation of the truth.

John Paul fears that much of the modern mind has forgotten this contemplative dimension of philosophy. Without adoration of the truth as the attainable end of human searching, the human person is forced "to live in a horizon of total absence of meaning, where everything is provisional and ephemeral" (§91). This in fact is the very problem Arthur Schopenhauer saw with the entire Enlightenment project: "It is perhaps the best description of Kant's shortcomings if one says: he did not know what contemplation is."[26] Without contemplation as the end of human inquiry, modern philosophy becomes a way of manipulating the truth instead of seeing ultimate truth as the

26. *Early Manuscripts* I.13 as quoted in Rudiger Safranski, *Schopenhauer and the Wild Years of Philosophy* (Cambridge: Harvard University Press, 1987), 113. This is precisely

final object of human contemplation and adoration *(speculari)*. Was it not Descartes who wanted to replace "the speculative philosophy taught in the schools" with a wholly practical knowledge able to make us the "lords and masters of nature"?[27] It is precisely this *knowledge as power* which John Paul sets out to contest at the end of *Fides et ratio*.

Under the catchword *postmodernity*, John Paul examines five philosophical positions that have rejected philosophy's contemplative end (§§86–90). The first is *eclecticism* and is marked by a disregard for the coherence or context of an idea. Any philosopher who randomly picks and chooses ideas and terms simply to make his point without any regard for the sources from which he borrows, does not advance the human search for ultimate meaning. "Such manipulation does not help the search for truth and does not train reason—whether theological or philosophical—to formulate arguments seriously and scientifically" (§86). Whereas eclecticism disregards the pertinent historical and cultural context of a philosophical position, *historicism* stresses the historical to such a degree that certain "truths" which may have been considered true at one point in time are no longer considered to be so: "What was true in one period, historicists claim, may not be true in another" (§87).

The next threat is what the Holy Father calls *scientism*. This position maintains that only the so-called positive sciences are believed to discover what is. Truth by definition is now that which is demonstrable and repeatable, "relegating religious, theological, ethical and aesthetic knowledge to the realm of mere fantasy . . . to the realm of

Augustine's critique against the pagan schools of philosophy: without "contemplation of immaterial light through participation in God's changeless immortality," the human search for truth is cyclical and thus meaningless; *De civitate Dei* XII.21.

27. *Discourse on Method* 6.62 as in *The Philosophical Writings of Descartes* I, trans. John Cottingham, Robert Stoothoff, Dugald Murdoch (Cambridge University Press, 1985), 142–43.

the irrational or imaginary" (§88). How did such a fissure come about? Princeton's Robert George provides this answer: "The positivism at the heart of scientism was devised by philosophers as part of their philosophical position—reason itself in the critique of what were perceived to be the pretensions of reason. By instrumentalizing reason—viewing it as, in Hume's famous phrase, the mere 'slave of the passions'—it reconceived philosophy not as the search for wisdom, what the Pope calls the pursuit of sapiential knowledge, but as a purely analytic enterprise."[28] In other words, in impoverishing human knowledge, scientism takes philosophical inquiry away from its proper end and settles for partial and disconnected answers which will always be less than ultimate, less than satisfying.

The fourth threat to a philosophy intent upon contemplation is *pragmatism*. Like scientism, pragmatism attempts to develop philosophical solutions in the absence of ethical demands. John Paul sees this thinking supported in political democracies which are grounded not in the unchanging truths about the nature of the human person and society, but, rather, in vacillating public opinion. Pragmatists think they must do away with eternal questions in their search for practical solutions. John Dewey, for example, poses this question:

Would not the elimination of traditional problems permit philosophy to devote itself to a more fruitful and more needed task? Would it not encourage philosophy to face the great social and moral defects and troubles from which humanity suffers, to concentrate its attention upon clearing up the causes and exact nature of these evils upon developing a clear idea of better social possibilities; in short, upon projecting an idea or ideal which, instead of expressing the notion of another world or some far-away unrealizable goal, would be used as a method of understanding and rectifying specific social ills?[29]

28. Robert George, "The Renaissance of Faith," *Crisis* (January 2000) 20.
29. John Dewey, *Reconstruction in Philosophy* (New York: New American Library of World Literature, 1950), 107.

Finally, *nihilism* best describes the postmodern position. It is characterized not only by the dismissal of any possibility of attaining final truth but by putting a "destructive will to power" or some "solitude without hope" in its place (§90). One cannot help but think of Nietzsche and Sartre lurking behind the pope's warning here: without an objective truth independent of the human mind and popular opinion, the human knower is doomed to solving moral dilemmas and philosophical problems through arrogated power and strength, and, in no time, the human person finds himself abandoned to a life without meaning or purpose. Karol Wojtyła understands better than most how such a position of despair can be justified after "the terrible experience of evil which has marked our age." He is quick to point out, however, that this is no "temptation to despair" (§90)[30] and therefore calls for philosophers to reclaim the majesty of their vocation, to rediscover how their search, properly understood, can reach its end "only in reaching the absolute" (§28).

In his classic work *Leisure: The Basis of Culture,* Josef Pieper likewise argues that once philosophy forgets its contemplative *telos,* it is no longer philosophy in the full sense. It is the nature of philosophy, emphasizes Pieper, to transcend the world of work. It never acquires "its legitimacy from its utilitarian applications, not from its social function, not from its relationship to the 'common utility.'"[31] Rather, while philosophy can lend its insights and critical apparatuses to temporal concerns, it can never become subordinate to the state or to some other external force. Philosophizing is possible only insofar as

---

30. Germane to our study of Mary's connection with the philosopher's pursuit of truth, George Weigel again and again recounts how Mary played a significant role in John Paul's thinking as he poised himself to face Communism in his native Poland: "and he thanked Mary, Queen of Poland, 'for all those for whom truth has become strength'—the truth that triumphed over lies." *Witness to Hope: The Biography of John Paul II* (New York: Harper Collins, 1999), 610.

31. Josef Pieper, *Leisure the Basis of Culture* (South Bend, Ind.: St. Augustine Press, [1948] 1998), 74.

it is able to pursue its goal of pure speculation or contemplation. The philosopher can never be at the service of some agenda or program, regardless of its noble intent; he must, rather, be left to discover his vocation's inherent need for *theoria.*

The end of human inquiry is contemplation of truth in its fullness. Partial and participatory truths leave the intellect wanting. Similarly, action and service likewise can never become the end of the philosopher's search. As philosophy seeks ultimate answers, it will simultaneously reclaim its contemplative dimension. If this does not happen, philosophy will be not merely impoverished, but unfaithful to its vocation: "A philosophy denying the possibility of an ultimate and overarching meaning would be not only ill-adapted to its task, but false" (§81). Philosophy must therefore "choose the better part" (Luke 10:42) and exist solely to know and adore the truth.

v. Conclusion

Mary's inclusion at the end of *Fides et ratio* acts as a recapitulation of the project as a whole. It is anything but some spurious or pious addendum. In concluding his defense of natural reason and its relationship to the truths of revelation, John Paul holds up Mary as the model of every philosophical inquiry. Her life reminds all who seek to know that the first posture of the philosopher is one of humble receptivity. Philosophy must be content with an initial wonder before what is. Receptive, philosophy must make itself available to questions of the highest kind. In offering itself to the concerns proposed by theology, philosophy seeks the nature of God and the deepest meanings of the world and of the human person. This offering is the only option between an inhuman rationalism or a spurious fideism. Finally, John Paul calls for philosophers to reclaim their contemplative purpose. Truth exists to be known, and only knowledge can lead to love. Philosophy can never be judged by its practical goals or its ability to ameliorate social ills but in its ability to know what is.

Not too long ago, the metaphysician Hilary Putnam called for a new way to understand human interaction with an externally objective world. He wanted an ontology able to stress free interaction and interpersonal subjectivity—what he named a *realism with a human face*.[32] In ethics, Emmanuel Levinas has likewise brought attention to the human face: the symbolic representation of the *wholly other* who always comes into my purview anew and thus represents the demands of human love and responsibility.[33] In the realm of theological speculation, Hans Urs von Balthasar sees in the face the beginning of humanity's recognition of our inherent worth and status as *imagines Dei*.[34]

Fides et ratio too desires to recover the face of truth. In Christ, "the Eternal enters time, the Whole lies hidden in the part, God takes on a human face" (§12). Thus while the eternal face of Christ is the answer, Mary's is our guide. The human search for meaning does have a face, a human face. It is not the face of a monk or a scholar, it is not even the face of an angelic doctor; it is the face of a mother, the Virgin of Nazareth. Mary beckons all humans to know the truth of things: to open themselves up to what is, to give themselves to the direction of the Divine, and to rest in the loving knowledge of God. In this, Mary becomes, for all who yearn to know, the perfect model of created wisdom.

32. Hilary Putnam, *Realism with a Human Face* (Cambridge: Harvard University Press, 1990); see also his *Paul Carus Lecture* published as *Many Faces of Realism* (Lasalle, Ill.: Open Court, 1987).

33. Emmanuel Levinas, *Totality and Infinity: An Essay on Exteriority*, trans. Alphonso Lingis (Pittsburgh: Duquesne University Press, 1969), 187–219.

34. Hans Urs von Balthasar, *Theo-Drama III: Dramatis Personae: Persons in Christ* (San Francisco: Ignatius Press, [1978] 1992), 292ff.

IMPLICATIONS

THE NEW EVANGELIZATION AND THE TEACHING OF PHILOSOPHY

BISHOP ALLEN VIGNERON

Introduction

That philosophers suffer no indignity in being implicated in the practical, indeed, that it is impossible for philosophers to be purely philosophical, are lessons Plato has Socrates teach us in the *Apology*. A philosopher is not a god but a citizen—more than just a citizen, but never not a citizen. The knowledge of the philosopher is by nature the highest theoretical excellence. As such it transcends the flux of human affairs, but never leaves the philosopher an alien to his culture, never divorces him from the unfolding of human history. Quite the contrary. When Plato displays the distinction between theory and practice by the device of foiling Socrates against the Sophists, we see that if one attempts to be a philosopher apart from his city—apart from practical affairs, he lapses into sophistry. Yes, the theoretical life is not the same as the practical. But were the philosopher to attempt to be only theoretical, only a philosopher, he could not be a philosopher. He would only seem to be philosophical, with that seeming which is the proper antithesis of the philosopher's true being.

91

In making clear to us that philosophers cannot be aliens in the city, Plato helps us see that being a teacher is not a betrayal of being philosophical. Indeed, in *The Republic* Socrates seems most clearly himself, *presents himself most clearly as a philosopher,* when he educates Glaucon. This teaching of the young is always a "mixed activity"—at once political action and contemplative act. How could such teaching not be political, when to philosophize with the young has such a deep impact on those upon whom the city pins its hopes for the future? And for the *paideia* of the next generation to display less than the truth of being at which contemplation aims would seem satisfactory to civic leaders only if they wanted to appear responsible while, in fact, they betrayed their sacred trust. The necessity of the being together of the theoretical and the practical in a philosopher being a teacher is a further profile of their necessary togetherness in a philosopher just being himself. So, for Socrates to teach the brightest and the best of the young Athenians, far from demeaning philosophy, contributes to his excellence as both philosopher and citizen. Being a philosophy teacher, then, blends naturally with being a philosopher.

Long ago—at least as early as St. Justin Martyr, if not already when Paul cited Greek thinkers in his preaching on the Areopagus—the Church recognized that membership in the communion of saints does not disqualify one from membership in the fellowship of philosophers. Not only is a philosopher always also a citizen, further he is called to be a saint. So, with the revelation of Christ we find a new form—being a believer—which is able to blend with being a philosopher. And this new manifestation of the philosopher, as a *Christian* philosopher, means that he can be a new kind of teacher. In the context of being in the world, the philosopher serves his city by teaching citizens-in-waiting, without breaking trust with his genius. In the context of being in the world *now-revealed-as-created,* he can serve the Gospel by teaching saints *in fieri* with no loss of integrity.

I offer these remarks about the pedagogical dimension of being a philosopher to validate the choice of my topic from the side of philosophy. In what follows I want to look at the encyclical letter *Fides et ratio* to see what direction we can find there for the work of teaching, which constitutes the principal act of piety we offer to philosophy. And more specifically, since our teaching is done so often in the context of the Christian faith we share with our students, I will inquire about the kind of philosophical pedagogy we should be giving to the next generation of believers.

Now, to narrow my topic even further, I will discuss the implications of *Fides et ratio* for the teaching of philosophy specifically as these follow from the encyclical's missionary or apostolic aim. As the final end of the work, this purpose informs both the document as a whole and in particular the wisdom we can draw therefrom about our teaching of philosophy.

I look to Aristotle to account for the rightness of the move I am making. He points out that leading a community is not the same as controlling the life of a herd or a hive.[1] Directing common actions, while not totally different from controlling a herd's movements, is not identical to it either. The difference lies in the capacity for *logos* possessed by the members of a human community, their capacity for speech and reason, for meaning and persuasion, which is not present in a hive. The community's leader leads by helping the members understand; he reads the various potentialities latent within the circumstances of their past and present. And from that presentation, he moves them on—whether by showing or by command, i.e., through rhetoric or authority—to common action. He informs them of what can or should be, so that together they can impose upon their future the form that is best for the common good.

1. *Politics* I: 2, 1253a, ll. 5ff.

Pope John Paul II is our leader, or more accurately, our shepherd, and his aim in *Fides et ratio* is to give his authoritative understanding of the relationship between faith and reason so that he can move the People of God on to a common action—the action to which He has given the summary name "The New Evangelization for the Third Christian Millennium." The renewal of philosophy is an important strand in that common action, and Christian philosophy professors are central players in accomplishing that part of the bigger strategy the Holy Father has in mind. We do not only contemplate, and we do not only strengthen the city, but we are agents in the Christian missionary task. Spending some time thinking about where the pope would lead us and why, will—I believe—help us better to work along with him in accomplishing our share of the mission.

So then, I will attempt three things in what follows: (1) I will try to place the missionary aim of *Fides et ratio* within the context of the whole program of Pope John Paul II's papacy, to see how this *goal* then takes on the character of a *means* to an even more ultimate *end*. (2) Then I will move to offer my own interpretation of that program, an interpretation that I will do my best to see is well-informed philosophically. (3) And from that interpretation, I will go on to draw out implications for our work as teachers of philosophy.

II. The Aim of *Fides et ratio:* A Means toward the New Evangelization

In the first pages of *Fides et ratio,* the pope makes it clear that his aim in writing the encyclical is to offer the Church's support to philosophers, by clarifying the nature of their work, so that they can excel at it: "I wish to reflect upon this special activity of human reason [viz., philosophy]. I judge it necessary to do so because at the present time in particular, the search for ultimate truth seems often to be neglected"(§5). Philosophers have lost their way, and on behalf of

the Church the pope offers them her guidance. The pope makes this
offer, not for the sake of philosophy itself, but for the sake of those
who need the truths voiced by philosophers, as well as for the sake of
the Church's articulation of the truths she knows through revelation.[2] His aim is religious, not philosophical. At the end of the intro-
ductory chapter, the Holy Father links these religious aims to the
overall program of his pontificate:

> With its enduring appeal to the search for truth, philosophy has the great
> responsibility of forming thought and culture; and now it must strive res-
> olutely to recover its original vocation. This is why I have felt both the need
> and the duty to address this theme so that, on the threshold of the third
> millennium of the Christian era, humanity may come to a clearer sense of
> the great resources with which it has been endowed and may commit itself
> with renewed courage to implement the plan of salvation of which its his-
> tory is part. (§6)

For the Holy Father, helping philosophy find its way through the
confusion that has hobbled it, so that it can take up its true task with
renewed vigor, is a necessary part of the new evangelization.

This new evangelization, the goal the pope held up to the Church
from the first days of his pontificate, must always, he insists involve
the "Evangelization of Culture"—which, when viewed from the other way around, is also called the "Inculturation of the Gospel."[3] The
first step to accomplishing this evangelization of culture is to find
points at which the Christian life and civic life intersect, that is to
identify ways in which revealed truth and the convictions and values

---

2. "On her part, the Church cannot but set great value upon reason's drive to attain
goals which render people's lives more worthy. She sees in philosophy the way to come to
know fundamental truths about human life. At the same time, the Church considers philosophy an indispensable help for a deeper understanding of faith, and for communicat-
ing the truth of the Gospel to those who do not yet know it" (§5).

3. On this topic see the Pontifical Council for Culture, *Toward a Pastoral Approach to
Culture* (Boston: Pauline Books and Media, 1999).

imbedded in a community's life are complementary. Then, grace purifies and elevates what is authentic in those naturally occurring goods,
while, at the same time those goods newly express what God has
shared with us in revelation.

I want to offer an additional comment about the purification that
goes on in the contact of the Gospel with a community's convictions
and the societal structures which form the "sediment" of these convictions. I maintain that this process has some similarity to the purification of *doxa* that occurs when philosophical minds seek to move to
the level of *episteme*.[4] In the movement from opinion into knowledge,
if the doxic convictions are sound, no new truth is gained, but the
same truth is gained in a new way. It is re-gained, but now with clarity about its necessity. The doxic element that cannot stand up against
investigation because it contradicts the first things must be transformed or discarded.

Analogously, in that purification of a culture's convictions and values which goes on in the evangelization of culture, the doxic elements are likewise regained on a new foundation; however in this
case it is not the foundation of necessity disclosed to the philosopher; rather, revealed truth is the foundation here. The values and
convictions of a culture are measured against Christ and the implications of his teachings. Those doxic elements that are authentic have
traditionally been termed *semina verbi,* "seeds of the word," fragments
of meaning which come to fruition by being taken up into the Word
who is Christ, the Meaning of all meanings, and thereby purified of
any meaningless dross.

To speak of the "New Evangelization of Culture for the Third
Christian Millennium" implies that while new, this project is not a

---

4. On the distinction between *doxa* and *episteme,* the thumbnail sketch s.v. "doxa" in F.
E. Peters, *Greek Philosophical Terms: A Historical Lexicon* (New York: New York University
Press, 1967) provides a useful introduction.

novelty. It is a new turn on the road that has already become quite familiar, viz., the road of the first two Christian millennia. In some sense, our task in the new evangelization of culture is to do again what our forebears did: to identify and purify the *semina verbi* of our culture's fundamental attitudes, beliefs, and values—specifically, values about the dignity of the human person—and incarnate them into a "Gospel culture."

As was the case in the first two Christian millennia, this monumental task cannot be accomplished without the resources of philosophy. And it is at this juncture that our work of teaching philosophy becomes so important: the Church cannot succeed in this audacious project of the new evangelization without leaders—both clergy and lay. And they will be incapable of that leading unless we give them, while they are our students, a sound philosophical training, one that particularly equips them for the part the pope is calling them to play in the new evangelization of culture.

The New Evangelization and the Next Christian Culture

A. A PRECEDENT: THE FIRST EVANGELIZATION AND THE CULTURE OF CREATION

As I mentioned above, the new evangelization of culture for the third Christian millennium is not a novel project. It is in some sense a "recapitulation"—a project at once new and old—a recapitulation of the last 2000 years of Christian history; and understanding that history offers us light for making our way into the future.

It is easy to see how the "old evangelization" was a process of inculturation, yielding its fruit in what most often goes by the name "Christendom." On the basis of one of the highest achievements of this evangelization, I would suggest that it might more aptly be called a "culture of creation." As a result of the preaching Christ to the Hellenistic world, the basic truth that only one being is not a creature became the touchstone for measuring the soundness of all that ancient world's convictions and institutions. This "creation culture" went through various stages and achieved notable benchmarks. To give you some idea of how I would map that process, I will identify several stages in the establishment of this "creation culture" and some paradigmatic achievements that serve as landmarks for progress along the way. These are offered not with the intent of painting a picture complete in every detail, but as points from which we can plot the outlines of history's course.

From among the stages in that process of evangelizing Hellenism that results in the "creation culture," here I will single out the Apostolic, the Patristic, and the High Medieval.

At the very inauguration of what I have called the Apostolic period—Pentecost Day, the first act of the Twelve taking up their worldwide mission was marked by a sign that their message was destined to be incarnated into the culture of the age: "Each one heard [the Apostles preaching] in his own language" (Acts 2:6). This intuition was definitively ratified at what has come to be known as the "Council of Jerusalem." At that gathering of the Apostles and other disciples, it "seemed good to the Holy Spirit and to [them]" not to require the Gentile believers to accept the prescriptions of the Mosaic Law (Acts 15:28). That is to say: Acceptance of Jesus as the Savior foretold to the Jews does not demand taking on the culture and way of life of the Jews. Thus, it was determined that the saving revelation of Jesus Christ could legitimately be incarnated into the Hellenistic culture through its acceptance, its embodiment, in the lives of the Gentile converts who were members of that society and who shared in the *doxa* of its members.

We can look to the ministry of the Apostle Paul for two paradigmatic examples of the inculturation of the Gospel revelation into Hellenism: his preaching on the Areopagus (Acts 17:22–34) and his

teaching at the beginning of the Letter to the Romans (Rom 1: 18–
32). In the first Paul, without obscuring the differences, establishes
some points of intersection, some identities, between the Christian
revelation and the religious (Acts 17:23) and cultural (Acts 17:28) heritage of the Greeks. In his sermon he further clarifies that the ground
for this identification is the identity of the God who has created all
men and disclosed Himself to them thereby, with the God who has
revealed Himself definitively in Jesus Christ (Acts 17:26–27, 30–31).
In the first chapter of the Letter to the Romans, St. Paul gives
the classic formulation to the same teaching about the identity of the
Creator and the Revealer, which serves as the foundation for the
incarnation of the revealed word into the *doxa* of Hellenistic society.

The work of inculturating the Gospel begun by the Apostles
reached a full flowering in the time of the Fathers.[5] Outstanding
minds of creative genius—men like Clement of Alexandria and Origen, Basil of Caesarea and Gregory of Nyssa, Augustine and Leo the
Great—argued persuasively that there are *semina verbi* in the Hellenistic culture, and they took it in hand to identify them. From there they
moved on to the all-important work of both analyzing the degree to
which these *semina verbi* required purification in the light of the Gospel, and synthesizing the purified "seeds" with the revealed word in
order to give birth to the culture that would become Christendom.

For purposes of illustrating the success of the Patristic Period in
reshaping the *doxa* of the Hellenistic age, the teaching of the first
four ecumenical councils (Nicea, 325; Constantinople, 381; Ephesus,
431; Chalcedon, 451) is of primary importance. The clarifications
achieved in these gatherings built upon the efforts of the Christian
thinkers who had prepared for them and gave a new and more solid

5. For a brief overview, see Enrico dal Covolo, S.D.B., "The Encounter of Faith and
Reason in the Fathers of the Church," English Edition of the *L'Osservatore Romano,* no. 11
(17 March 1999), 9.

platform upon which the Fathers could subsequently pursue the agenda of inculturation. The councils defined that Jesus Christ is *homoousios* ("consubstantial") with the Father, one person—the Second of the Three Divine Persons of the Holy Trinity, with both a human nature and a divine nature. This doctrine, while enfleshed in a form of expression borrowed from the philosophical culture of Hellenism, fundamentally reshaped what it used, so that the borrowed is purged of that culture's tacit assumptions about the antithetical relationship between time and eternity, between the divine and what is not divine. That is to say, the doctrine, while presenting the revelation in terms that appeared to be so thoroughly Greek, refashioned those elements to such a degree that they present an insight about the relationship of God to the world that overturns Hellenistic *doxa* in this regard.[6] Now the world is recognized as created, with God present to it in a way beyond that which the Greeks had been able to imagine.[7] By this move the Church of the Patristic period advanced the work begun by the Apostles, and gave a definitive reconfiguration to the very foundation upon which she incorporates the Hellenistic heritage into a new cultural synthesis—what we know as "Christendom."

On the foundation lines set out in this understanding of the relationship of the world to God, St. Augustine, in his master work, *The City of God,* moved to tease out the relationship between God's city and man's—a distinction unheard of by the ancients, but now comprehensible in the light of recognizing the world as created. In so

6. On this process of refashioning Greek philosophical categories and doctrines in the light of revelation, see Walter Kasper, *Jesus The Christ,* trans. V. Green (London: Burns and Oates, 1976), 179, 181. See also his *The God of Jesus Christ,* trans. Matthew J. O'Connell (New York: Crossroad, 1984), 178–87.

7. Robert Sokolowski, in *The God of Faith and Reason: Foundations of Christian Theology* (Notre Dame, Ind.: Notre Dame University Press, 1982), offers a full-length study of the strategic significance of the new Christian distinction between God and the world. See especially the chapter "The Incarnation and the Christian Distinction" (pp. 31–40) on the connection between orthodox Christological doctrine and the God-world distinction.

doing, St. Augustine supplies important elements for the blueprint to be used in the construction of Christendom in the millennium that was to follow.

Just about a century short of that thousand year mark, the Church once again confronted in a dramatic way the issue of the suitability of incorporating elements from Greek civilization into its life and thought. In the thirteenth century, Christian thinkers had to face this problem specifically in regard to the work of Aristotle: Are there *semina verbi* in Aristotle? If yes, what are they? And to what degree do they require purification before incorporation into an evangelized culture?—all vexing questions in the light of Aristotle's doctrines on the eternity of the world and the unicity of the intellect.[8]

Continuing in the trajectory stretching back to the Jerusalem of the Apostles, Thomas Aquinas was able to recognize the identities and differences at play between Gospel truth and Aristotelian wisdom. Out of that labor he fashioned a new synthesis—what we can call a "metaphysics of creation," wherein *ens commune* is recognized as a participation in *Ipsum Esse Subsistens*.[9] Taking ontology as the highest expression in a culture about what is most ultimate and final (the "all"), we are surely justified in regarding Aquinas's synthesis of Ancient and Christian truth about God and the world as the paradigmatic blossoming of that inculturation of the Gospel begun with the gift of tongues at Pentecost—the full flowering of the culture of creation.

8. For a panoramic view of this period, see Fernand Van Steenberghen, *Aristotle in the West: The Origins of Latin Aristotelianism,* trans. Leonard Johnston (Louvain/New York: Nauwelaerts/Humanities Press, 1970).

9. Van Steenberghen's *Thomas Aquinas and Radical Aristotelianism,* trans. D. J. O'Meara, J. F. Wippel, and S. F. Brown (Washington, D.C.: The Catholic University of America Press, 1980), is a highly readable guide to this work of transformation accomplished by Aquinas.

OUR TASK: A CULTURE OF COMMUNION

This "creation culture," achieved through the inculturation of Christian faith into the wisdom of Ancient reason, was something like a "volatile" or unstable compound. From its flowering into an expression at the metaphysical level in the life's work of St. Thomas, it quickly began its devolution into what we call "Modernity."[10] The breakdown of the synthesis achieved by St. Thomas is already seen in the rise of Nominalism, and comes to full expression in the seminal writings of thinkers such as Machiavelli and Hobbes.

Modernity is marked by a worldview (both in ordinary conviction and at the highest levels of theory) made up of a mixture of elements—some elements taken from the patrimony of the culture of creation, other elements inimical to the Gospel. The fundamental axioms of this Modern world had to do with the autonomy of the self, what is classically referred to as "the turn to subjectivity." This highlighting of the self was a residue from the creation culture. However, withdrawn out of that context, the self becomes the "anti-creature," not receiving existence as a created participation in divine Being, but existing over against God, competing with, if not usurping, his ultimacy. And in the name of this newly discovered autonomous self, the force of Christian belief in Western culture is gradually eroded.

A benchmark of this passage from Christendom to Modernity, perhaps the definitive benchmark, was the French Revolution. This event clearly exemplified the rejection of the incarnation of the Gos-

---

10. While acknowledging the many senses for the term, I am using "Modernity" here as the name for that period in the history of Western Civilization that extends from the Renaissance to World War I, from Machiavelli to Hegel. Although these centuries are by no means a homogeneous reality, there are sufficient common elements to justify treating them as a coherent whole.

pel which is Christendom. In the name of achieving the "liberty, equality and fraternity" which are the goals of the autonomous self, the heritage of faith had to be eradicated. For about two hundred years the reaction of the Church to this watershed event was to attempt to undo this modern culture by means of censure and correction, in order to restore the prior synthesis, and in this way safeguard the revealed truths embodied in that synthesis.

In the papacy of Pope John Paul II we find a clear articulation of a new strategy. What the Holy Father is calling for in summoning the Church to a new evangelization is precisely to evangelize Modernity, the world after the French Revolution, the culture of liberal democracy, with its emphasis on the emancipation of the self.

The Second Vatican Council was precisely the "New Pentecost" we prayed for, because it marks a definitive turn, the inauguration of this new strategy, a fresh beginning in the task of inculturating the Gospel. Almost two thousand years ago, Peter and the rest of the Apostles came out of the Cenacle and began to evangelize the known world. The fruit of this effort was the achievement we know as Christendom. In 1965, the pope and the bishops came out of the Council *aula* and began a new evangelization, and this, too, must give birth to a new Christian culture. The Council Fathers made the judgment that even this modern culture, birthed to supplant Christendom, contains *semina verbi,* which the Church, in fidelity to her mission, must identify, purify, and incorporate into a new inculturation of the Gospel.

This move was epitomized in the rejection of confessional states as the only possible form of Christian culture. Rather the liberal democratic culture, with its center on the free self, possesses material for a new incarnation of the Gospel. The agenda of Pope John Paul II's ministry is to advance this bold strategy, a strategy of millennial importance. Yes, the liberation of the self was the fulcrum point on which the Moderns tipped the Christian culture of the first two millennia off its foundation. Nevertheless, again and again, and yet once more again, the Holy Father holds up the dignity of the human person as the cornerstone of the inculturation of the Gospel into Modernity. The human person is the focal point for so much of the *doxa* of our modern culture, and its convictions and attitudes on this central theme are the cache containing the *semina verbi* which will blossom during this new evangelization of culture.

The Church's work for the next millennium—this finding and purifying the *semina verbi* in the culture—is the latest act in the drama that goes all the way back to the Children of Israel despoiling Egypt (Exod. 12:35–36). And reading the Bill of Rights along with Sacred Scripture, while it is as daring as reading Homer or Plato or Aristotle alongside the Bible, is no less imperative if the Church is to be faithful to her mission and to give her Lord the glory he deserves

I view this present stage in the Church's efforts to evangelize culture as roughly analogous to the experience of the first generations of the Fathers, as they took up the work of inculturating the Gospel into the Hellenistic world. Now, as then, the task is to articulate the basic intuitions of the culture and to explore where these intuitions harmonize with the Gospel and where they need to be corrected by it. Ours, as was theirs, is a time of ferment and creativity.

Pope John Paul II, in his service as one of the Fathers of this new evangelization, has focused the Christian mind on such themes as: the necessity of solidarity for the survival of the self (*Solicitudo rei socialis* and *Centesimus annus*); the impossibility of free persons apart from a transcendent moral order *(Veritatis splendor);* the incoherence of subjectivity that is not a dative for receiving the disclosure of truth *(Fides et ratio).*

All the basic leitmotivs of Pope John Paul II's Magisterium identified immediately above find their grounding in communion as their first principle, the principle of a one which cannot not be a many. I will hazard to predict, then, that if there is to be an evangelized culture in the third Christian millennium, it will be a "culture of communion." As the inculturation of the Gospel in the first two millennia required the reshaping of all convictions and values in the light of the first principles that eventually emerged in creation metaphysics, the convictions and values of the culture needed for the next Christian millennium will rest upon the metaphysics of communion. Thomas taught us that *ens commune* exists as a participation in *Ipsum Esse Subsistens, ens commune* has *esse,* but is not *esse.* Could we not look for the day when we will see that "to be," whether subsistent or by participation, cannot not be "to be with"? That sort of metaphysics would be the highest achievement of a culture of communion, the *episteme* for all the many elements that would constitute its *doxa.*

iv. The Philosophical Education of the Leaders in the New Evangelization

Given what I have called my "read" on the state of the Church's mission as she passes into the next millennium, what, then are some important qualities we should cultivate in our philosophical instruction. I will mention two that I would characterize as "formal," and one that concerns content, or the "material" side of our pedagogy.[11]

In the formal column, first, I would underscore the need to cultivate in our students a "wide-mindedness," a readiness to stretch themselves beyond the usual boundaries of their intellectual capital. This habit will enable them to appreciate truth wherever they find it. It is the opposite of sectarianism, the contrary of a partisan spirit. It is a species of boldness and a kind of justice. "Boldness," since it pushes

---

11. On a related topic, for the essential elements and qualities the Church requires in the philosophical instruction of seminarians, see *Optatam totius,* no. 15; *Pastores dabo vobis,* no. 52; The Letter of the Congregation for Education, *The Study of Philosophy in Seminaries* (20 January 1972).

them beyond their comfortable reach; "justice," since it requires that insight be given its due, no matter what the source.

Second, I believe we need to train our students in the skill of intellectual discernment. They must develop a ready disposition to separate out the wheat from the chaff. This skill is really the fruit of a quality which from the first has been a hallmark for the philosophical enterprise: rigorous thinking which systematically lays out the points of coherence and incoherence in the positions under investigation. It is the habit of "thinking down to the roots," to the causes and first principles. Such rigor and ultimacy in thinking is indispensable, for without the moderating influence it provides, our students' wide-mindedness will be nothing more than eclecticism on its way to intellectual promiscuity.

In effect, what I am highlighting are the habits of mind which make fruitful dialogue possible. These are the habits that make our students sure footed as they move from dialectic to insight. Further, they are ingredients in that "loving veneration of truth," to which Pope John Paul II invites future priests in their study of philosophy. This "cult of truth" means acknowledging that truth is not a product, but a treasured gift from God, who is supreme Truth.[12] Not only seminarians but all our students must be wide-minded, because God has sown the seeds of His truth everywhere, and authentic piety demands that no truth should be ignored. They must be discerning because that same piety forbids them to mistake the counterfeit for His genuine gift.

In order to identify a thematic or content element that should be found in our pedagogy, I want to take my starting point once more from the new evangelization and its goal of inaugurating a culture of communion.

---

12. *Pastores dabo vobis*, no. 52.

It seems to me that to elaborate the theoretical support upon which we can erect this culture of communion, we cannot escape the demand that we give a reasonable account of our corporeality. I read the *Republic* as Plato framing with limpid clarity the problem that the ancient metaphysics had with the body: How can the city flourish when the citizens are animals? How is it possible for those who are irreducibly singular because of their bodies to fulfill their duty of acting for the common good? Or, to come at the question in Aristotelian terms: How can matter, the very principle of individuation, as the not-the-form, how can matter by its very definition not be the antithesis of the common? How can the body not be an irreducible problem for communion and never an aid?[13]

I believe the Holy Father has made a highly original step toward solving this dilemma in his theology of the body.[14] To say that the spousal meaning of the human body is inscribed in one's very flesh is to discover that matter is a resource rather than an obstacle to communion. Therefore, for our philosophy instruction to be adequate for building a culture of communion, while it may not be able to discover this spousal meaning of the body, it must at least leave room for it. A metaphysics incapable of seeing the worth of the body for the good of communion is not what we need. And more, given the complementarity of the created order with the order of grace, I believe we ought to be on the lookout for a metaphysics which, while dependent on theology for discovering the body's value for communion, can later establish independently that corporeality is a particularity which is capable of transcending itself to embrace the

13. On human communion as a metaphysical question, see Kenneth L. Schmitz, "Community, the Elusive Unity," *Review of Metaphysics* 37 (1983): 243–64.

14. One can find the text for the 130 general audience addresses in which the pope expounds his teaching in John Paul II, *The Theology of the Body* (Boston: Pauline Books and Media, 1997). For a summary account, see George Weigel, *Witness to Hope: The Biography of Pope John Paul II* (New York: HarperCollins Books, 1999), pp. 334–43.

whole without negating its very particularity. We need a metaphysics that grounds not only the capacity but also the necessity of the whole existing in the part.

Building on what I find in the Holy Father's thought, I want to suggest that we can push even farther. By faith we know that in the order of grace the body is not a principle hostile to communion; even more wonderfully, we encounter in the Eucharist a body—the Body of the God-Man—that is the very cause and principle of the most perfect communion possible for man. *A fortiori,* Christian philosophy, then, must discover a metaphysics that allows us to assert this conviction without fear of rational incoherence. And, again on the basis of the relation of nature to grace, I have a not-unreasonable hope that this most Catholic doctrine can point philosophy toward an insight about being, an insight it otherwise might never have imagined, but one which, once gained, can be explicated by the light of reason.

So, our philosophical pedagogy would have to meet this litmus test, if I am correct: a certain friendship for, or at least benignity toward, the Church's teaching on human sexuality and her doctrine on the Holy Eucharist. Establishing this friendship with a view to contributing to the mission of the new evangelization is not of the perennial essence of philosophy, but it is essential to our work as Christian philosophers in the new Christian millennium.

THE IMPLICATIONS OF *Fides et ratio*
FOR CATHOLIC UNIVERSITIES

DAVID RUEL FOSTER

Character and Intended Audience

Fides et ratio is destined to be seen as the intellectual capstone of this most academic of popes. It is at once provocative in its account of philosophy and theology, harmonious with tradition, and engaging in its style. It is that rare text that will engage faculty across the country in fruitful discussion—not just arguments. Its importance for Catholic higher education, however, has as yet been under-recognized.

The initial interest from the press was significant, and although the encyclical is no longer news, I believe it will attract a growing readership. In fact, *Fides et ratio* will have a major impact on Catholic higher education and higher education in general because it will be widely read, and that because it is so intrinsically interesting and provocative.

For most of the academic community, who are unfamiliar with Church documents, the encyclical will be novel reading. Still, many professors will find its arguments heartening because it expresses something that they sensed was amiss but had not yet been able to articulate.

Fides et ratio reaches out to a broad audience by using the common philosophical nature of the person as a common ground for discussion. It recalls the fundamental questions that we all ask about who we are, where we have come from, and what we can hope for. It frequently uses images from Greek philosophy and invokes Greek poets and playwrights. It even notes St. Paul's similar practice recorded in Acts 19.

As an encyclical letter the document has the traditional salutation from the Pope to his "Venerable Brother Bishops," but the contents indicate that scholars are the primary audience. When the address is explained in section 6 the bishops are mentioned first, then theologians and philosophers, and finally all those who search. It is evident, however, from the text that the pope is speaking directly to scholars. The apostolic constitution *Ex corde Ecclesiae* is addressed "especially to those who conduct Catholic Universities," and then to their respective academic communities, and finally to all those who have interest in them, from bishop to laity.[1] In contrast to *Ex corde,* which is directed to administrators, *Fides et ratio* is directed to faculty. It is helpful to read the documents with this in mind.

The primary dialogue partners are Catholic theologians and philosophers, but included as well are all scholars in both secular and religious schools. Some secular scholars will find in *Fides et ratio* a champion for their convictions; others, a clear statement of a position worthy of consideration.

Fides et ratio will ultimately engage the faculties of Catholic universities[2] more than *Ex corde Ecclesiae.* Although *Ex corde* has engendered much discussion among Catholic faculties, it is *Fides et ratio* that will

1. *Ex corde Ecclesiae* #9.
2. All institutions of Catholic higher education are meant to be included.

speak to their heart. The importance of *Ex corde* is that it caused a significant amount of self-examination on the part of Catholic colleges, but its weak affirmation of academic freedom aroused suspicion. In contrast, *Fides et ratio* provides the principles for a robust affirmation of academic freedom.

This essay will consider five important implications of *Fides et ratio* for Catholic universities: (1) the fundamental principle that speaks to the heart; (2) an answer to the question "Can the Church engage in authentic dialogue?" (3) the principles for a defense of academic freedom; (4) the rights of the academic community; (5) a critique of curriculum and the distinction between types of pluralism.

The Principle That Speaks to the Heart

Fides et ratio's vision of the person as one who can know the truth, especially the truth about persons, is as refreshing as admitting the emperor has no clothes. This will win it a wide readership because it articulates a position many want to affirm but have difficulty articulating. In fact, I predict that scholars will gradually begin remarking about the numbers of people who are reading *Fides et ratio*. Given the typical readership for encyclicals this may seem an unwarranted claim; yet, the encyclical is timely, and remarkable even among the many splendid encyclicals of this pontiff.

The essence of *Fides et ratio* is not a defense of the compatibility of science and religion, which is now assumed as part of a well-articulated tradition of the Church. Nor is it an argument that faith and reason are compatible, although this position is eloquently restated. The essence of this encyclical is a defense of objective truth and the ability of human reason to know that truth.

The encyclical challenges the postmodern philosophical critique that defines truth out of existence and denies the possibility of knowing the truth if it did exist. The postmodern philosophical critique of knowledge and truth has made this the fundamental question in the philosophy of the human and natural sciences. The encyclical is a vigorous defense of both the existence of truth and our ability to know it, at least in part. By its defense of truth the Church tries to stop higher education from being enervated by a virulent philosophy. The effect of the encyclical's argument will not be on the institution or administration directly, but upon the scholars in common discussion of pressing issues.

It may seem ironic to the prevailing academic opinion makers that at the dawn of the third millennium the Church has emerged as the most prominent defender of reason. Still, despite its less than consistent practice, the Church has affirmed for centuries the value of reason and its harmony with faith. In these times of postmodern skepticism, it is hard to overemphasize the importance of this confidence in human reason and its ability to grasp truth as a bedrock principle of education. This confidence is, nonetheless, compatible with a humility that *Fides et ratio* calls for when it rebukes philosophical pride and affirms the need to always question.

Can the Church Enter an Open Dialogue?

It is not uncommon to hear scholars ask, "How can the Church enter into an authentic dialogue when it claims to have the truth already, and a truth obtained by revelation not reason at that?" Their objection is that the Church is willing to "pontificate" but thinks that she has nothing to learn and therefore no interest in listening.

In *Fides et ratio* the Church explains herself as a fellow pilgrim seeking the truth along the path of life, yet she also claims to know the truth in knowing Jesus Christ. There is a tension caused by competing intentions and a balance that must be kept, yet it is the usual balance between convictions and openness common to human dialogue. The encyclical correctly sees no contradiction here, and its reasoning includes the following four aspects.

I. CHURCH AS FELLOW PILGRIM

The reconciliation of how the Church is both a fellow seeker of the truth and confident that in Jesus she knows the truth is addressed early in the encyclical, and the competing intentions are mentioned together in recognition of the supposed conflict (§2). The Church describes herself as a partner with all humanity in a shared struggle to find the truth, a partner who also, in honest dialogue, must share her reasons for belief that Jesus is the Christ. Speaking of the Church, the encyclical says:

It is her duty to serve humanity in different ways, but one way in particular imposes a responsibility of a quite special kind: the diakonia of the truth. (1) This mission on the one hand makes the believing community a partner in humanity's shared struggle to arrive at truth; (2) and on the other hand it obliges the believing community to proclaim the certitudes arrived at, albeit with a sense that every truth attained is but a step towards that fullness of truth which will appear with the final Revelation of God. (§2)

Note the modesty implied by the qualification that "every truth attained is but a step towards that fullness of truth." Yet, there is no retreat from faith in the defining words of Jesus, "before Abraham was, I Am."

2. THE REAL ENEMY OF DIALOGUE

The pope notes that it is not the conviction of knowing the truth but the lack of respect for the dignity of our dialogue partner that is the true enemy of dialogue. The encyclical reaffirms the Church's desire expressed at Vatican II to dialogue with all who seek the truth. Furthermore it is the opposite, i.e., believing that no truth is knowable, that undercuts human dialogue. Why should we seek the truth together if there is no hope of finding it?

To believe it possible to know a universally valid truth is in no way to encourage intolerance; on the contrary, it is the essential condition for sincere and authentic dialogue between persons. On this basis alone is it possible to overcome divisions and to journey together towards full truth ... (§92)

3. MODES OF TRUTH

The mode of truth about natural phenomenon (i.e., natural sciences) is not the only mode of truth; there is also a mode of truth about persons, which is equally important and often humanly richer. For example, there is a truth we can know about our mother, e.g., her love for us, and in which we may be confident even though we have not submitted her to scientific measurement. The encyclical raises the point because the confidence of the Christian community is based on knowledge of a person, Jesus Christ. The answers to the important questions of life, about origin, nature, and destiny are not fully answerable by natural science (§§30–32). This leads to a last point, namely, the attitude of humility and openness that is proper to authentic human dialogue.

4. ATTITUDE OF OPENNESS

To affirm that in knowing Christ the Church knows the source of truth in a person is not to claim that she knows everything about Him or the world. The knowledge of a person is so rich that it is never exhausted. The encyclical recalls a desire, expressed in *Gaudium et Spes,* to enter into dialogue with everyone, even those who seek to do her harm.

Such a ground for understanding and dialogue is all the more vital nowadays, since the most pressing issues facing humanity—ecology, peace and the co-existence of different races and cultures, for instance—may possibly find a solution if there is a clear and honest collaboration between Christians and the followers of other religions and all those who, while not sharing a religious belief, have at heart the renewal of humanity. The Second Vatican Council said as much: "For our part, the desire for such dialogue, undertaken solely out of love for the truth and with all due prudence, excludes no one, neither those who cultivate the values of the human spirit while not yet acknowledging their Source, nor those who are hostile to the Church and persecute her in various ways".[3]

Another principle for dialogue is a desire to know the truth ever more fully. The Church explains herself as both having a great truth that she wants to share with all humanity, but also ever in need of knowing the truth more completely, and toward that end she is convinced that all humanity can potentially help her.

III. Academic Freedom

Fides et ratio never proposes to defend academic freedom and, in fact, it never mentions the term. But in defending the human person's ability to know by reason, the encyclical provides the principles for academic freedom, as well as a great deal of supporting argumentation. This is particularly important because of the paucity of *Ex corde Ecclesiae's* treatment of academic freedom.

Ex corde Ecclesiae has been a timely and influential document both because of its vision of the university in conversation with the culture and because of the discussions it has engendered among Catholic faculties. *Ex corde* called for Catholic higher education to examine how deeply its Catholicity penetrated its life. The most controversial section calls for the local bishop to oversee the theology faculty. To its credit, *Ex corde* has caused a significant self-examination by Catholic colleges, but it is weak in its description and affirmation of academic freedom. *Fides et ratio* can help fill this gap.

There are four references to academic freedom in the text of *Ex corde:* one in section 12 that affirms that a Catholic University by its

---

3. *Fides et ratio* §104; *Gaudium et spes* §92.

nature guarantees academic freedom, two references in section 29 that affirm academic freedom for scholars in general and for theologians in particular, and one reference in section 37 that asks civil authorities to respect academic freedom. The most complete statement is found in footnote 15, which gives a brief description of what is meant by academic freedom. Each affirmation is notably qualified, so that, while *Ex corde* affirms academic freedom, it is neither robust nor cogent in doing so.

The most frequent criticism of *Ex corde*'s call for a closer relationship between college and bishop is that it endangers academic freedom. There is some historical validity to this concern; in the twentieth century alone we can point to several high profile cases. *Ex corde* does little to address these fears. The respected Church historian Msgr. John Tracy Ellis, in a lecture given at Seton Hall in 1986, reminded his listeners that there were several dozen scholars who suffered in the wake of *Humani generis,* only to be vindicated later, three of the best known being Congar, Daniélou, and Murray. Msgr. Ellis also pointed out that there had been strong statements supporting scholarly freedom, such as the one given by John Henry Newman in his 1854 description of a Catholic university:

It is a place . . . in which the intellect may safely range and speculate, sure to find its equal in some antagonist activity, and its judge in the tribunal of truth. It is a place where inquiry is pushed forward, and discoveries verified and perfected, and rashness rendered innocuous, and error exposed, by the collision of mind with mind, and knowledge with knowledge.[4]

Or in a similar vein, we have the words of John Lancaster Spalding, bishop of Peoria and the leading advocate of founding The Catholic

4. John Henry Newman, *The Idea of a University,* cited from Msgr. John Tracy Ellis' lecture "The Catholic Church and Her Universities," the 1986 Archbishop Gerety Lecture at Seton Hall University. Printed by Immaculate Conception Seminary, Seton Hall University, p. 4.

University of America, when he spoke at the Church of the Gésu in Rome in 1902 on the topic "Education and the Future of Religion."

To forbid a man to think along whatever line is to place oneself in opposition to the deepest and most invincible tendency of the civilized world. Were it possible to compel obedience from Catholics in matters of this kind, the result would be a hardening and sinking of our whole religious life. We should more and more drift away from the vital movements of the age, and find ourselves at the last immured in a spiritual ghetto, where no man can breathe pure air, or be joyful or strong or free.[5]

The contemporary academy, wrongly I think, views the Church as antithetical to academic freedom. But if the Church has in the past both abridged due freedoms and hesitated to champion academic freedom, two matters of historical context help us understand why. First, that those arguing for academic freedom have focused exclusively on individual academic freedom and left the Church feeling compelled to defend a communal academic freedom (which is discussed in the next section). Second, that the Church was in the midst of moving from a more paternal model of relating to the scholarly community to a more fraternal one.

The Church's relationship to European culture stretches back centuries to a time when the culture was young and education rare. Particularly during chaotic times, it fell to Church leaders to assume a more authoritative role for an emerging civilization. The role was not unlike that of a parent who must give explicit direction and who rightfully expects obedience from a child. But time passed and the community matured; the last several centuries compare to the awkward years of transition wherein young adults emerge from rebellious teenagers, and parents must be willing to allow the teenager greater freedom in order to exercise increased responsibility. In like

5. John Lancaster Spalding, *Religion, Agnosticism and Education* (Chicago: A. G. McClure Company, 1902), 175.

manner, Church leaders have had to adjust to a society that no longer accepts Christian principles, a more educated laity that is anxious to exercise a more responsible role, and a more educated and independent clergy. It should be remembered that not so many years ago the whole society reflected a more paternal mode, from our schools to our network television censors. Colleges had a policy of acting *in loco parentis,* including dress codes, parietal hours, and "lights out" time—and those were the state colleges.

That the bishops were quite consciously making this transition is one of the great stories of Vatican II. It was particularly evident in *Gaudium et spes* that the Church wanted to speak to all mankind as brothers and sisters (fellow pilgrims) and to persuade them to examine for themselves the Gospel of Jesus Christ.

Academic freedom is important both because it is in accord with the dignity of the individual person and because it is the best way to aid and safeguard the discovery of truth. Karol Wojtyła is a man who knows firsthand the severe repression of human freedom, including academic freedom. He also knows academic life, having served for many years on a University faculty and having directed his last dissertation from the Vatican.

An important contribution of *Fides et ratio* will be to supply what is missing in *Ex corde.* Although *Fides et ratio* never mentions academic freedom, it does provide clear principles for its defense, notably these four:

1. That there is a dignity of the individual person that requires that the individual's rights be respected; first among these is freedom of conscience.

2. That the distinct academic disciplines have a right to the autonomy of their principles.

3. That reason claims its own rights, and the Church defends the rights of reason.

4. That a scholar must be free to search for the truth because without truth there is no freedom.

The first principle, the dignity of the individual, is a recurring theme in the encyclicals of Pope John Paul II and evident in such Vatican II documents as *Gaudium et spes, Nostra aetate,* and *Dignitatis humanae.* In *Fides et ratio* the reflection on the dignity of the individual is filled out by specific descriptions of the natural orientation of the person toward truth (§28), the ability of the person (by intellect) to seek and find the truth (§§29, 82), the ability of the person (by will) to affirm the truth and choose the good (§33), and in *Gaudium et spes* (§§16, 17, 73) by statements on the duty of the individual to act according to conscience, and the expectation of political freedom to exercise the inner freedom of the will.

The second principle, the autonomy of disciplines, is, according to the encyclical, rooted in reason's orientation to the truth. A philosophy that did not follow reason would be of little use to the Christian community or to anyone else. Thus philosophy must be free to follow its own principles. The fundamental place where the autonomy of the discipline is realized is the individual scholar. Because philosophy must follow its own principles, the Church does not canonize any one philosophy (§49).

The third principle, the intrinsic rights of reason, is based on the existence of an objective truth independent of any human authority, which, in itself, demands respect. This principle, along with the human person's ability to know the truth, is part of the foundation for the Church's recognition of a natural moral law. In making a case for reason, *Fides et ratio* gives a number of arguments that naturally support academic freedom as well, such as, that there is no morality without freedom and no freedom without truth (§§25 and 90).

The fourth principle is the scholar's right to search for the truth. Philosophical and theological studies, indeed the whole of the intellectual life, involve a type of searching. By the very nature of a search, one looks in many wrong places before finding the right place. The encyclical recognizes the importance of this intellectual search and the primacy of philosophical inquiry over any claim to have a complete view of the truth. The ability to speculate is proper to the human intellect. In section 92, the document states that the belief in the objective nature of truth is far from a cause of intolerance but in fact is the essential condition for authentic dialogue. This implies the complementary point that proper tolerance is also a condition for authentic dialogue. When it criticizes "philosophical pride" that presents its own partial and imperfect view as if complete, the Church cannot help but recognize a parallel in theology (with due allowance for the distinct nature of theology). In a similar way, priests recognize in Jesus' sharp criticism of the Pharisees, who mistakenly thought that man was made for the Sabbath, the very sins to which those in religious authority are tempted, and which they must be vigilant to avoid (§4).

iv. The Rights of the Community: Second-Level Academic Freedom

Personalist themes, which are prominent among both theistic and atheistic philosophers of this century (and with the present pope), are evident in the encyclical. For example, *Fides et ratio* says that a person does not understand himself fully except as a person in relation. The first relation he understands is that with other people and especially family. The pope teaches that the richest knowledge we have is about persons and he emphasizes the importance of friendship. One implication is that our search for truth, though personal, is done best in conversation. Another implication is that we have the right to seek the truth together, a right rooted in the freedom of the individual and the natural good we see in community (§§21 and 32).

This insight leads to a practical characteristic of Catholic education—an appreciation for the communal aspect of the search for truth. This in turn leads to an added dimension of academic freedom. The prevalent contemporary view stresses the individual control of one's search for the truth; *Fides et ratio* implies a second level of academic freedom which involves the communal search for truth and the right of the community to speak for itself. The communal aspect of academic freedom does not preclude the individual's right but rather is based on it. It is the individual's right to seek the truth, and with others to form a community that speaks with a common voice according to its principles, while giving due regard to the rights of the individual and the wider society, and within the confines of the truth and the common good.[6]

The first level of academic freedom is that of the individual. It is the foundation for second level or communal academic freedom, which stems from the right of individuals to join together in a community that acts according to its own principles. A metaphor for the two levels is the difference between a one-person sailboat and a tallship. The first allows an individual maximum personal control, the ability to maneuver quickly and to go where one pleases; the larger ship does not steer easily and takes a great deal of cooperation to sail (which is where the authority of the captain comes in), but is safer and faster on long voyages.

The common understanding of academic freedom today emphasizes that freedom of each individual to seek the truth about things and to publish his findings. The individual scholar is the solo sailor, operating with maximum flexibility. Less recognized today is the second or communal level of academic freedom. The Church and Church-related colleges are examples of communities that operate on

6. See *Ex corde Ecclesiae*, fn. 15.

this level. Compared to the individual level the communal pursuit of knowledge seems slow and cumbersome. But there are advantages to the communal level of academic research, just as there are to the large ship verses the small boat. Once under way and beyond the reefs it can go faster and more safely over the vast oceans. A community of scholars can share work among many individuals and can extend over many generations. Furthermore, the principles that the community shares can serve as added tools with which to work. What some might consider an undue constraint, others consider a head start. Much of today's scientific research, for example, is carried out by large teams with clear lines of authority.

The two levels of academic freedom are not mutually exclusive, but rather complementary. To be sure there is a tension between them that must be kept in balance. Much of the debate over academic freedom has lacked an awareness of the rights of communal academic freedom. The debate would be advanced if the parties involved thought of the situation not as an "either . . . or" but as one of finding the proper balance.

Taking political freedom as a parallel, it seems right that individual academic freedom is more fundamental and that communal academic freedom is built upon that of the individuals that belong to it. It is clear that tension can arise between the two levels. Neither level of freedom is absolute; both freedoms can be abused. The main means of preventing excess on either level is the healthy functioning of the other level. Ways can be found to relieve the tension without eliminating the freedom of either level. A community of scholars must make provision for someone who wants to get off the boat, but not be cast into the sea.

The contemporary academy should recognize that there is another level of academic freedom. Catholics should appreciate how vital academic freedom is to the vision of *Ex corde Ecclesiae*. Since there are communities within communities, such as a university community within the larger Catholic community, there are levels within the level of communal academic freedom. And what has been said about the individual in relation to the community can be applied to the relation of the university that stands as a sort of individual in relation to the whole Church.

Keeping with the tallship metaphor, everyone can contribute to the progress of the ship, but not everyone can expect to choose a course any more than a citizen expects to set foreign policy for a nation. Both individuals and community need certain protections. The individual needs to be protected from the arbitrary and excessive exercise of authority, and the community needs to be protected from individuals who, whether maliciously or not, subvert the will of the community.

Some wit might suggest that if the Catholic view were compared to a tallship, that the apt illustration is more the Nina, the Pinta, and the Santa Maria than a modern ship—their point being that the methods and terms are dated, and perhaps this is so. A large community with traditions is often slower to adopt new things. Further, the Church has recently shown that it stands ready to confess its human failings. Yet, at same time, it must be admitted that, even though the ship is old, successful voyages can be completed, as such thoughtful documents as *Gaudium et Spes* and the new *Catechism of the Catholic Church* testify.

It is instructive to recall that the Chinese Communist Party has used a similar sounding argument to explain their lack of individual freedoms. They argue that the Western criticism of a lack of political freedom in China stems from the West's overindulgence of individual rights, whereas the Communist Party emphasizes the rights of the community. In order for the Church's arguments not to have the hollow ring of those of the Chinese Communist Party, the Church must honor in practice the foundational role of the rights of the individual.

v. Implications for Curriculum

The encyclical's most pointed criticisms (e.g. §61) have several implications for the curriculum at Catholic universities. The discussion about the shortcomings of contemporary philosophy is forthright but polite; the sharpest criticism is reserved for Catholic philosophy and theology faculties. This is not surprising since greater intimacy allows greater frankness. The pope expresses frank disappointment about three matters: that theologians and philosophers have been swayed by the current fad to dismiss metaphysics, that they have neglected to pass on the intellectual treasures of Thomas Aquinas, and that they have perpetuated a false sense of pluralism. The first two issues are fairly clear in their meaning and resolution; the third, which takes issue with a common understanding of pluralism, is less so.

A distinction between pluralisms is alluded to several times by the encyclical. It originates in the defense of the proposition that humans have a capacity to know the truth about things, against the attack of certain contemporary philosophies. *Fides et ratio* warns that the contemporary advocacy of pluralism in philosophy (and therefore also in theology) often contains a trap. On the one hand, the pluralism that is appropriate to philosophy and that finds support in the documents of Vatican II is not based on the impossibility of truth but on the impossible richness of truth. A healthy pluralism stems from the depth of being that is never exhausted by our researches. We will never say all there is about love or friendship, but it is true to say that we need friends. The richness of being always leaves us with something more to explore. Our human nature makes misunderstanding possible but does not make understanding impossible.

There is a false pluralism, however, based on a postmodern philosophical critique. Postmoderns call naive any claim for transhistorical truth, as in professing the same faith as our ancestors did. And this is, so they say, because there is no "foundation" upon which such knowledge can be based. Those who seek a foundation are naive or frightened or scheming to keep others in subjection. Philosophy and theology should critically incorporate the valuable insights of the Postmoderns regarding the effect of historical context, the impact of culture and language, and the subjective aspect of all our knowing. Yet, the hidden premises of the postmodern philosophers, about God and man, lead them to extreme conclusions and show them to be not postmodern but ultra-modern. They felt themselves postmodern because they no longer sought a foundation for knowledge as had Descartes, Locke, Kant, etc. They show themselves, however, the children of modern thought by accepting the modern reductions of God to man, of man to beast, and of knowledge to sensation. Given these assumptions, their denial of objective truth and consequent pluralism of "non-truths" is an inevitable outcome of modern philosophy. The essence of *Fides et ratio* is to defend against just such a destructive pluralism.

To conclude, then, the Church, in *Fides et ratio,* expresses her faith in reason and reasons about her faith. This encyclical will ultimately have a greater impact on Catholic Universities than *Ex corde Ecclesiae,* for at least these five reasons:

1. It defends the most basic principle of education by defending the ability of human reason to discover the truth and to recognize it as such.
2. It affirms an openness to authentic dialogue and the Church's belief that through this dialogue the Church comes to deeper knowledge of God.

3. It contains the principles for a robust defense of academic freedom and thus provides an important complement to *Ex corde Ecclesiae.*

4. It provides a living example of a second or communal level of academic freedom, which concerns the right of a community to speak according to its own principles with due regard for the rights of the individual and the wider society, and within the confines of the truth and the common good.

5. Finally, in a frank and personal way, it challenges Catholic faculties to provide a metaphysics open to the full range of reality; to pass on the wealth of wisdom in St. Thomas; and to recognize the difference between a healthy pluralism based on the richness of being and a virulent pluralism based on despair of knowing the truth.

HISTORICAL PERSPECTIVE

Fides et ratio AND BIBLICAL WISDOM LITERATURE

JOSEPH W. KOTERSKI, S.J.

The openness of *Fides et ratio* to the wisdom of philosophical traditions from diverse cultures is a cherished implication of one of the encyclical's main themes: there is no reason for competition between reason and faith, for they both proceed ultimately from the same divine source. Yet, not everything is of equal value in any one of these traditions, and there can be blind spots just as well as insights. Thus, the steadfast openness commended by the pope is by no means an indiscriminate pluralism that accepts all positions as equally valid (§5) but a readiness to sift afresh what is offered as wisdom. Commitment to the capacity of the human mind to discover various truths about even the ultimate questions of human existence forbids any hasty foreclosures and demands a posture at once sympathetic and critical.

One of the things that encourages the hope that such a project is likely to be fruitful is the common stock of questions which different cultures have all asked about the meaning of human life: Who am I? Where have I come from? Where am I going? Why is there evil?

What is there after this life? (cf. §1). Squarely within the list of the wisdom traditions explicitly mentioned as offering valuable advice about the direction which people seek to give their lives are the sacred writings of Israel, and in particular the Wisdom Literature constituted by such books as Proverbs and Job, Sirach and Qoheleth, the Song of Songs, and the Wisdom of Solomon.[1] In comparison to the divine pronouncements that fill the pages of the prophetic books and the direct encounters with God that punctuate the narratives of the Torah, the wisdom books of the Old Testament immediately seem more philosophical. The frequently questioning spirit at play, for instance, in the treatment of the problem of evil in these books manifests the precise phenomenon that warrants Pope John Paul II's inclusion of them in the same list as the Veda and the Avesta, Confucius and Lao-Tze, as well as Tirthankara and the Buddha (§1). The questions that all these texts record "have their common source in the quest for meaning which has always compelled the human heart."

The purpose of this essay will be to reflect on biblical Wisdom Literature in light of *Fides et ratio.* After examining what the encyclical itself says about this portion of the Bible, we will explore some additional themes of a generally philosophical nature important to these writings, and then we will comment on the general question of the relations of faith and reason in light of biblical Wisdom Literature.

---

1. The sacred writings of Israel, the Old Testament, are generally divided into three parts: called Tanak in Jewish scholarship, an acronym for Torah (the "law"—that is, the first five books, Genesis, Exodus, Leviticus, Numbers, and Deuteronomy), Nəvi'im (the "prophets"), and Ktuvim ("writings"). The books that constitute Wisdom Literature are included in this last grouping, but books like Wisdom and portions of books like Daniel that are accepted as belonging to the Bible according to the Catholic understanding do not appear in Hebrew and so are regarded as apocryphal in Jewish and in most Protestant editions of the Bible. On this question, see Joseph T. Lienhard, S.J., *The Bible, The Church, and Authority: The Canon of the Christian Bible in History and Theology* (Collegeville, Minn.: The Liturgical Press, 1995).

I. *Credo ut intellegam*

Nearly all of the discussion of Israel's Wisdom Literature occurs in the second chapter of the encyclical, entitled by a phrase which has been hallowed by thinkers like Augustine and Anselm: *Credo ut intellegam*—I believe so that I may understand.[2] While the sages of ancient Israel did not concentrate on arriving at knowledge about the world through the abstractions of Greek philosophy, the astronomy of Chaldea, or the reflections on death so typical of Egypt, they did generate their own body of sapiential literature. It is often proverbial in character and it regularly displays for us how human reason can seek truth and meaning without making faith in God foreign to the process. In fact, this whole approach to gaining knowledge and wisdom shows how faith in God can readily provide a sort of security and trust within which reason can retain "its own scope for action" (§17). What Augustine and Anselm would later thematize as faith seeking understanding,[3] Israel's Wisdom Literature lived out as a quest to discover the wisdom needed for life.

Chapter two of the encyclical treats the sapiential portion of the Bible under three perspectives: (1) the fundamental human desire for wisdom (§§16–17); (2) what Israel discovered about fruitful and fruitless ways of seeking wisdom by human reason (§§18–20); and (3) the

2. On the importance of this phrase for the history of Christian philosophy, see Etienne Gilson, *The Spirit of Mediaeval Philosophy* (1936; Notre Dame and London: University of Notre Dame Press, 1991).

3. The idea of *fides quaerens intellectum* that is expressed by *Credo ut intellegam* is based, of course, on the Septuagint translation and the interpretive tradition then current that read Isaiah 7:9b as "if you will not first believe, you shall not understand." Modern scholarship reads the Hebrew text differently and thus supports translations of this line that try to capture a certain play on words in the original text. The NEB, for instance, reads: "Have firm faith, or you will not stand firm." For fuller discussion of the point, see *The New Jerome Biblical Commentary* (Englewood Cliffs, N.J.: Prentice Hall, 1990) 15:18 and Hans Wildberger, *Isaiah 1–12: A Commentary* (Minneapolis: Fortress, 1991), pp. 302–4.

indispensable link between faith and reason (§§21–22), a link that the pope finds prominent in the sapiential portions of the New Testament as well as in the Old. Let us consider each point in turn.

Mindful that texts within Proverbs and Job echo some of the queries and insights of Egypt and Mesopotamia,[4] *Fides et ratio* discerns in the inspired writers some of the motivation, the hunger for knowledge, characteristic of all people. Citing Proverbs 20:5 and the portrait of the sage in Sirach 14:20–27, the pope notes the inclination deep-seated in human intelligence everywhere to make good use of the native powers of intelligence to reach "the deep waters" of knowledge.

What is specially distinctive of biblical Wisdom Literature, however, is its great confidence about the contribution that faith in the God of revelation can make to reason's own inquiries. Interpreting, for example, Proverbs 16:9 ("The human mind plans the way, but the LORD directs the steps") to allow that human reason can discover which path one ought to choose in life but that it may well require divine grace to provide sufficient motivation and strength, the pope also discerns in that text the ability of faith to sharpen the mind's vision about the workings of providence in the events of one's life: "with the light of reason human beings can know which path to take, but they can follow that path to the end, quickly and unhindered, only if with a rightly tuned spirit they search for it within the horizon of faith" (§16). Similarly, the pope comments on what Proverbs 25:2 calls "the glory of kings"—namely, to search out what

4. There are many specialized studies of these parallels, but one can find a good summary of what has been discovered in three essays in *Wisdom in Ancient Israel,* ed. John Day, Robert P. Gordon, and H. G. M. Williamson (Cambridge: Cambridge University Press, 1995): "Egyptian Wisdom Literature" by J. D. Ray, pp. 17–29, "Some New Babylonian Wisdom Literature" by W. G. Lambert, pp. 20–42, and "The Wisdom of Ahiqar" by Jonas G. Greenfield, pp. 43–52. By way of example, some thirty of the maxims in Proverbs (22:17–24:22) virtually match the text of the Egyptian *Wisdom of Amenemophis* (c. 1000 B.C.).

God has concealed and thereby to exhibit the nobility of human beings that is manifest when they explore truth within the power of their reason. The famous prayer of Psalm 139 ("How deep to me are your thoughts, O God! How vast the sum of them!") summarizes for Pope John Paul II the yearning of every human heart for a satisfying answer to the ultimate question of existence and the insistence of Israel's wisdom tradition on the profound compatibility of faith and reason, each able to contribute to the knowledge needed for life.

One of the crucial connections between the queries undertaken by reason and by faith for knowledge turns on the theme of epistemological humility or, in biblical terms, the fear of the LORD. Relying on passages about the quest to acquire wisdom such as Proverbs 2 and Wisdom 7, the encyclical identifies three basic rules which reason must observe in order to be true to itself: (1) one must realize that the quest for human knowledge is a journey which in itself is endless and will never permit one to rest content that one has discovered everything that there is to know; (2) on this path one must not be proud or arrogant by supposing all one's achievements to be the fruit of personal conquest; and (3) out of a holy fear of the LORD one must recognize the transcendent sovereignty and provident love of God in the governance of the world. Throughout this corpus of writings, fear of the LORD is again and again called the beginning of wisdom.[5] This should not be misunderstood as a servile fear, of course. Rather, the term refers to a profound reverence similar to but even greater than one might feel toward one's parents, the sort of respect that wants never to disappoint but always to honor the gift received from them by using it well. Throughout the Bible the fear of the LORD is counted the beginning of wisdom, for it entails a deep respect for God's providential order as something we did not create and cannot

5. See, for instance, Proverbs 1:7 and 9:10 or Sirach 1:14.

control and yet something that we must constantly study and watch. For this pattern of docility there is a biblical model in the figure of King Solomon, who is portrayed in Chapters six to nine of Wisdom as he instructs his fellow kings about the prayerful reverence with which he has sought and treasured the gift of wisdom. The reputation he has attained for wisdom, both practical and theoretical, has come not from his natural intelligence but as the gift of God to someone who deeply feared Him and ordered his life to prayer and study.

Ignoring these rules risks making the person foolish instead of wise, like the fool of Psalm 14, who says in his heart "There is no God"[6] and then starts to conduct himself accordingly. Although such a fool supposes himself wise by being acquainted with all sorts of things, the inability to fix his gaze on what really matters all too easily plunges him into a tailspin that leaves him vulnerable even to death. The allusion to this topic in *Fides et ratio* points to an important tale from the opening nine chapters of Proverbs. There we find an innocent youth faced with a choice about whether he will follow Lady Wisdom or Lady Folly. The youth who observes these basic rules and learns the heritage of Israel's proverbial wisdom (Proverbs 10–30) will be rewarded with a virtuous bride (ch. 31), while the young man who yields to curiosity and attempts to satisfy his lusts without regard for fear of the LORD will hazard his own life. The house of Lady Folly turns out to be "the entrance of Hades, which leads down to the halls of death" (Proverbs 7:27).

Various parts of Proverbs warn about arrogance and excessive

---

6. This biblical phrase also has an extensive importance in the history of Christian thought. It is associated especially with Anselm's hypothetical dialogue partner ("the fool") in the *Proslogion,* chapter 4, and was taken up by Gaunilo in his famous reply *Pro Insipiente.* See Anselm of Canterbury, *The Major Works,* ed. Brian Davies and G. R. Evans (New York: Oxford University Press, 1998), pp. 88–89 and 105–10.

curiosity. The proper epistemological humility, however, opens out into the full range of knowledge from which one may draw at one's pleasure. Following out the subtitle given to the whole second chapter of the encyclical ("Wisdom knows all and understands all," a quotation from Solomon's praise of wisdom in Wisdom 9:11), the pope likens the sacred author to those pagan philosophers whose study of the natural sciences constituted most of their philosophical learning. Like the Greek cosmologists, the figure of King Solomon testifies to the ability of the human mind to know the structure of the world and the operations of the elements, the cycles of the seasons and the sky as well as the natures of the animals and plants (Wisdom 7:7–20). From this ability to reason about nature, the human intelligence can philosophize and rise to God, as in the passage which *Fides et ratio* quotes: "From the greatness and beauty of created things comes a corresponding perception of their Creator" (Wisdom 13:5). Now, in the freedom human beings have to use the tools of reason arrogantly, it remains possible to fail to recognize God as Creator of all; but considering the matter positively, the pope finds scriptural warrant for holding the book of nature to be a first stage on the path that leads to knowledge of God. Reason can in this way be valued without being overvalued; the difference involves harmonizing the results which reasoning acquires with the larger order of meaning which faith discloses (Proverbs 20:24).

The final portion of the second chapter of *Fides et ratio* (##21–22) stresses the indispensable linkage of faith and reason that is found both in the Wisdom Literature tradition of the Old Testament and in the sapiential portions of the New Testament. Here the pope focuses in particular on the frustration that reason experiences when it finds itself blocked before mysteries such as evil, death, and the Cross. Commenting, for instance, on the weariness which Proverbs (30:1–6) attributes to someone who has exhausted himself in the effort to understand the mysterious design of God, the pope notes the special aid that faith can bring to reason. Drawing on a passage from Qoheleth (1:13) that also evokes a sense of intellectual strain and exhaustion, the pope finds the sacred author abidingly reliant on the dependable aid of God "who made them inquirers and who gave them the mission to keep searching. Leaning on God, they continue to reach out, always and everywhere, for all that is beautiful, good, and true" (§21).

For Pope John Paul II the sapiential passages of the New Testament are in profound continuity with the Wisdom Literature of the Old Testament on the theme of the nexus between faith and reason. Concentrating at some length on parts of the letters to the Romans and to the Corinthians, he observes the same theme as before, that those who are willing to be open to the knowledge provided by revelation will more easily find reason able to pass safely through blockages that had seemed insuperable.

The first chapter of Romans, for instance, is remarkable in this context for its development of the theme already present in earlier biblical Wisdom Literature that "through all that is created, the 'eyes of the mind' can come to know God" for "through the medium of creatures God stirs in reason an intuition of his 'power' and his 'divinity'" (§22). Thus here we find the theme so prominent throughout *Fides et ratio* that there is a trustworthy capacity in human nature for metaphysical reflection. The Pauline text can serve as a trustworthy warrant for the philosophical claim that our knowledge is not restricted to the sensory data which we receive. When we reflect on this data critically, we can reach the cause which resides at the sources of all sensible reality. Further, the pope takes note of the sorry condition into which the sin of original disobedience has cast us, for Paul affirms that in the divine plan for creation reason should have been able easily to perceive the Creator from contact with creatures. But this ready access to the divine Creator diminished because of the assertion of a "full and absolute autonomy" in relation to the Creator. As in other of his writings on Genesis,[7] the pope expands on Paul's allusion here to the Fall by reflecting on the choice to eat from the tree of the knowledge of good and evil: "The symbol is clear: Man was in no position to discern and decide for himself what was good and what was evil, but was constrained to appeal to a higher source. The blindness of pride deceived our first parents into thinking themselves sovereign and autonomous, and into thinking that they could ignore the knowledge which came from God" (§22).

In the course of history, of course, the story of the Fall has generated various reactions with regard to the consequences for human reasoning. Part of the Protestant tradition, for instance, has tended to see the matter so bleakly as to distrust metaphysics, if not philosophy in general. But the pope sees the consequences of the Fall for human reason more in terms of difficulty and obstacle. The dysfunctional situation is more a matter of deep-seated emotional effects than of some structural failure that would make reasoning impossible in principle: "All men and women were caught up in this primal disobedience, which so wounded reason that from then on its path to full truth would be strewn with obstacles. From that time onward, the human capacity to know the truth was impaired by an aversion to the One who is the source and origin of truth" (§22). Paul, the pope writes, diagnosed the emptiness of human reason as a matter of progressive distortion and inclination to falsehood (Romans 1:21–22) that obscured the eyes of the mind just as chains prevent a prisoner from moving to where one could see clearly. Christ's coming redeemed reason from the weakness that being a prisoner to this world alone had imposed on reason.

7. Pope John Paul II, *Original Unity of Man and Woman: Catechesis on the Book of Genesis* (Boston: St. Paul Editions, 1981).

As one important aspect of the fullness of salvation which Christ's death brought to the world, we may legitimately understand there to be a liberation of reason—not a permission to return to arrogant or willful independence, but an invitation to learn the "wisdom of God" as a replacement to the "wisdom of this world." Pope John Paul II finds the opening of 1 Corinthians to pose the problem of faith and reason quite dramatically: "Where is the one who is wise? Where is the learned? Where is the debater of this age? Has not God made foolish the wisdom of this world? (1 Corinthians 1:20). If every attempt to construe a satisfactory account of the significance and meaning of existence fails where it rests on merely human argumentation, the death of Christ on the Cross offers a completely different approach. This saving event will challenge every philosophy which tries to go it alone or which tries to reduce the Father's saving plan to purely human logic." Rather, "God chose what is foolish in the world to shame the wise. God chose what is low and despised in the world, things that are not, to reduce to nothing things that are" (1 Corinthians 1:27–28). After reflecting on how Paul in great humility came personally to accept this truth ("When I am weak, then I am strong"—2 Corinthians 12:10), the pope repeats the lines about God's choice of what is low and contemptible, a "mere nothing" in terms of anything this world counts as something.

What does this mean? Is *Fides et ratio* simply waxing poetic? Is there any philosophical sense to be made of this? The pope insists that the love which the Cross represents can provide "the criteria of both truth and salvation." In particular, the disclosure of the gratuitous character of God's love revealed in the Cross of Christ has philosophical implications, for the suffering that seems to make no sense to reason when operating alone ("folly to the Gentiles") comes into focus when we lift our gaze to the love of which the Cross is a sign. Put another way, even human altruism tends to remain something of a puzzle to philosophers, for the natural course of our reasoning is to calculate our proper response in love on the basis of the worth of the objects of our love, whether their present goodness or perhaps some expected return.

Now, to accept the universality of God's love for sinners who are, strictly speaking, unworthy of such sacrifice, is a challenge to reason that is like a "reef upon which the link between faith and philosophy can break up" (§23). But it can also be the reef from which "the two can set forth upon the boundless ocean of truth" with tremendous gain for reason if it yields to the wisdom of the Cross. The pope comments: "Of itself, philosophy is able to recognize the human being's ceaselessly self-transcendent orientation toward the truth; and with the assistance of faith it is capable of accepting the 'foolishness' of the Cross as the authentic critique of those who delude themselves that they possess this truth, when in fact they run aground on the shoals of a system of their own devising" (§23). These last comments suggest much broader dialectical application, for instance, against the marxist and state-dominated political philosophies that have produced the twentieth-century totalitarianism. But at a simpler level they may easily be applied to the question of human love that imitates the divine love which pours good into the object of love rather than just tends to draw out advantage or self-satisfaction.

Mindful, then, of the philosophical themes which the pope has selected for *Fides et ratio,* let us turn now in the spirit of his project to consider some important additional philosophical themes within this portion of the Scriptures.

II. Philosophical Concerns in the Wisdom Literature

Biblical Wisdom Literature is full of many of the same concerns that have preoccupied all peoples about how to live life well and that have engaged philosophers from many cultures. Besides the themes discussed above that have emerged explicitly in the treatment of this part of the Bible within *Fides et ratio*, one can also readily discern any number of other philosophical concerns. Running throughout biblical Wisdom Literature, for example, is the steady conviction that wisdom is the mother of the virtues that are needed for living well.[8] But one can also discern a repeated and sustained interest in such philosophical problems as accounting for the presence of evil in the world and dealing with the prospect of death. Examination of each of these points will disclose that reason and revelation are not to be in opposition but should be taken as complementary means by which God engages us.

A. THE QUEST FOR WISDOM AND VIRTUE

The principle that governs the biblical treatment of the relation between wisdom and the virtues is that wisdom is fundamentally a grace which God bestows on those who seek to conform their minds and hearts to him in all things. By the careful scrutiny of the motives, the judgments, the ideas, and the attitudes that inform one's way of life, wisdom can help to fashion the proper use of reason. In turn, reason can cultivate the sort of personal discipline and responsiveness to the stirrings of wisdom that will lead the person to deeper unity with God and peace with one's fellow human beings.

Naturally, there is a profound continuity in this regard with other parts of the Bible. Both the directives throughout the Torah to observe the Law that God has given to Moses[9] and the admonitions

8. The practice of calling wisdom the "mother" of all virtues can be found, for example, at Wisdom 7:12.

9. See, e.g., Deuteronomy 4:1–8, where Moses urges the people: "Keep [the commandments] and do them; for that will be your wisdom and your understanding in the sight of the peoples, who, when they hear all these statutes, will say 'Surely this great nation is a wise and understanding people.' For what great nation is there . . . that has statutes and ordinances so righteous as all this law which I set before you this day?" Passages such as these suggest not only the connection between wisdom and the way of living specified by

in the prophets about obeying God's spoken Word[10] are echoed in the wisdom books, where the value of human reason resides not only in reflecting on the experiences of life but also in taking us to the boundaries of what we can understand for ourselves and in alerting us to the need to pray for the wisdom which will transform our minds and to the need to learn to reason in union with the mind of God.

An examination of the very structure of the Wisdom of Solomon illustrates this point and will prepare for the discussion of the problems of evil and death later in this essay. From its opening lines the book is in the form of an address by King Solomon to his fellow "rulers of the earth." Although the book is presumed to originate in the circles of Hellenistic Jews of first-century B.C. Alexandria, it takes as its spokesman the king who was certainly the patron of the entire Wisdom Literature tradition and who was legendary for his own wisdom from the time when he judged the case of the two harlots disputing over the single living baby (see 1 Kings 3:16–28). The book has three parts: (1) a story about the judgment of the righteous and the wicked in the afterlife; (2) an address by Solomon in praise of wisdom; and (3) a set of examples about wisdom's guidance of God's people from Adam to Moses.

The first five chapters of Wisdom take up the exhortatory theme standard in Proverbs and Sirach in promising reward to the righteous and punishment for the wicked. But where earlier books seem to pre-

---

Torah but also the possibilities opened up by a philosopher's perspective, namely, a comparison between the laws of other nations and one's own laws made in order to assess their relative merits in embodying genuine wisdom. Although Wisdom Literature in general shows an openness to other cultures that counterbalances the tendency to protectiveness of Israel that arises from suspicion against foreigners, Sirach and Wisdom also make a special point of defending Jewish culture by arguing that the wisdom which God has given to His people far outstrips the philosophies produced by other cultures.

10. For a fine discussion on the relation of law and wisdom throughout the bible, see Joseph Blenkinsopp's *Wisdom and Law in the Old Testament: The Ordering of Life in Israel and Early Judaism* (New York and London: Oxford University Press, 1995).

sume that this will take place during life, Wisdom (alert to the problem of the wicked who prosper during life and the righteous who suffer) transforms the theme by promising immortality to the righteous and warning the wicked of judgment to come after death. In particular, the argument of the book proceeds by way of a story about Jews who died for the fidelity to Torah observance and then awaken in the afterlife as the judges of their former persecutors.

Stories from Israel's long salvation history also constitute chapters 10 to 19. Somewhat in the fashion of the *Everyman* genre in that no names are mentioned, the stories are nevertheless clearly recognizable to anyone who knows the heroes of Israel's struggles.[11] The emphasis is placed on the universal applicability of these accounts of divine intervention to protect those who have lived in accord with wisdom and virtue. As we will see in greater detail below, the text makes its case by way of story and example, and yet the author employs terminology and argument deeply resonant of standard philosophical traditions (for example, in the discussion of *immortality* and *incorruptibility*).

But in chapters six through nine the figure of Solomon steps back a pace to reason with the other kings. After praising wisdom and describing both the nature of wisdom and the works for which wisdom is responsible, Solomon leads his fellow rulers in praying for a wisdom to enlighten reason in practical affairs as well as in speculative inquiries. His renown for wisdom, he explains, comes from a divine gift:

11. Reference to the important figures of Israel's history of salvation are much more rare in the Wisdom Literature than in the historical books of the Bible. These figures do become the focus of attention by name in the last part of Sirach (chapters 44 to 50). From a Jewish perspective the catalog of heroes in this portion of Sirach resembles the fascinating stories from other books, especially stories about wise leaders who dealt shrewdly with Israel's enemies, e.g., Genesis, chapters 37–50, Daniel 1–6:29, Esther, Judith, Ruth, and Jonah.

I too am mortal, like all men, a descendant of the first-formed child of earth, and in the womb of a mother I was molded into flesh. . . . No king has had a different beginning of existence; there is for all mankind one entrance into life, and a common departure. Therefore I prayed, and understanding was given me; I called upon God, and the spirit of wisdom came to me. (Wisdom 7:1, 5–7)

The prayer in chapter 9 by which Solomon leads his fellow rulers to ask for the wisdom by which alone they will be guided to govern well hearkens back to the prayer for understanding recorded of Solomon just before the episode with the harlots (1 Kings 3:3–14). His request to God for "an understanding mind" with which to govern the people and to discern between good and evil so pleased the LORD that God gave him not only the discerning mind for which he asked but the long life and riches he had refrained from requesting.

In this portion of the book, wisdom is personified. Like the use of this literary device in such comparable passages as Proverbs 8:22–31[12] and Sirach 24:1–9,[13] the figure of Wisdom (see especially chapters 7 and 8 of the Book of Wisdom) seems meant to inform us that wisdom is not ultimately human but divine and that wisdom was present with God from before He brought creation into existence. In profound continuity with the creation story of Genesis, the theology implied in these passages is based on a notion of creation that is quite open to philosophical appreciation, for it assumes a world that makes sense and has a structure founded upon discoverable laws and principles, as suggested when Solomon is testifying to his fellow kings that

12. In fact, wisdom is personified through the first nine chapters of Wisdom in the story about Lady Wisdom and Lady Folly. See also Wisdom 31:10–31.

13. The brief description in Sirach 24 of wisdom as God's agent in bringing the world into being and as the revelation which God sent to his Chosen People anticipates the full manifestation of God's revelation of eternal wisdom as the Incarnate Word in the prologue to John. See also Colossians 1:15–20. For other such parallels, see the section on biblical Wisdom Literature in Michael Duggan's *The Consuming Fire: A Christian Introduction to the Old Testament* (San Francisco: Ignatius Press, 1991), pp. 393–499.

it is God "who gave me unerring knowledge of what exists, to know the structure of the world and the activity of the elements, the beginning and end and middle of times" and all sorts of other information, from the solstices and constellations to the natures of animals, the powers latent in roots and plants, and the logic of human reasoning (Wisdom 7:17–20). Likewise, there is throughout these passages a clear sense that God is transcendent, that is *over* all creation rather than *within* it, and yet that part of God's self-disclosure comes about through the laws inherent in all the creatures that exist.

The wisdom for which Solomon begs is not just speculative but also deeply practical, and this feature of his discourse to other kings reflects a concern throughout biblical Wisdom Literature with strength of character and moral responsibility. The earnest nature of his plea in chapter 9 arises directly from the charge he has been given to rule Israel and thus from his duty to judge cases and direct common action, but his plea is prefaced by a reminder of the need for good stewardship that belongs to everyone: "O God of my fathers and Lord of mercy, who made all things by thy word and by thy wisdom formed man to have dominion over the creatures thou made and to rule the world in holiness and righteousness and to pronounce judgment in uprightness of soul, give me the wisdom that sits by thy throne" (9:1–4).[14] This prayer invokes the original act by which God entrusted Adam with the power and the duty to govern the world and is consistent with the insistence found throughout Wisdom Literature upon the duty of humanity in general and of each individual in particular to use reason so as to live well.

What is here illustrated with reference to Wisdom takes many forms in the other books of the tradition. Much like the directives

14. For the echoes of Genesis 1:26–31 about human stewardship over the rest of creation, see also passages such as Psalm 8:5–6: only the children of Adam possess in their very being the image of God and exercise dominion over the rest of creation.

about prudent decision making in, say, Aristotle's *Nicomachean Ethics,* the advice given in any number of passages in Proverbs imparts wisdom about handling crisis and stress so as to improve one's practical judgment in decision making. The homey, witty sayings that pack that book do not decide a question in advance, for often the maxims come in contrastive pairs. Rather, the point of the collection seems to be to enhance one's skill in thinking about life's tough questions by studying the pithy sayings that have been deemed wise advice, so that one can ponder one's options with just enough deliberation and just enough urgency to reach a timely but well-considered decision. At the same time there are plenty of proverbs that make clear the individual and social implications of wisdom for questions of justice and righteousness in accord with the commandments that Israel has received as a fundamental moral code. Throughout the collection of proverbs in chapters 10 to 30, one reads of the responsibility of wise parents to teach their children how to think and how to overcome any vulnerability to temptation or deception.

Among other important instances of the virtue of good decision making there is the praise given at Proverbs 31 to the woman who exhibits intelligence, good planning, and diligent industry in providing for her family. Likewise, many of the wisdom psalms feature instructions and encouragement regarding prudent direction of one's life, and the chief virtue needed for conducting one's life with wisdom is fear of the LORD (as discussed in the first part of this essay). Psalms 34 and 112, for instance, sound the theme that fear of the LORD is the most important of all virtues, and Psalm 37 contrasts the life of the virtuous with the life of the wicked. By implication, these texts are insisting that appropriating God's gift of wisdom requires a willingness to obey the truth one has come to know and to exercise the discipline required to live in accord with what one knows. Wisdom will then be more than good ideas—it will settle in the soul.

B. THE PROBLEMS OF EVIL AND DEATH[15]

Although one could focus on many topics within biblical Wisdom Literature on which good advice is readily forthcoming (questions of marriage, friendship, truth-telling, honor, and so on), let us concentrate here on just one pair of topics, evil and death, that not only elicit good advice from the author of these books but also evoke philosophical questioning that leads in the direction of immortality and resurrection. The divine guidance involved in the composition of these books may in this way come to be seen amid the intense human searching for wisdom about very perplexing problems.

It is important to remember here that the hope which Christians have for eternal life with God depends on participation in Christ's victory over sin and death and that, for the most part, divine revelation about the afterlife awaited His coming. The deep consolation that counters the natural fear of death (the promise of the immortality of the soul and the eventual resurrection of the body) began to be made manifest only late in the history of God's revelation of Himself to Israel. But when we consider the relevant passages of the Old Testament in light of Christ's resurrection and His promise that the faithful will also rise on the Last Day, we can readily understand the gradual disclosure of these truths as part of the LORD's careful preparation of His people in the course of revealing everything needed for salvation in Christ. This is a point Pope John Paul II notes in *Evangelium Vitae:*

Revelation progressively allows the first notion of immortal life planted by the Creator in the human heart to be grasped with ever greater clarity: "He has made everything beautiful in its time; also he has put eternity into man's mind" (*Ec* 3:11). This first notion of totality and fullness is waiting to be

15. An earlier version of some of the material in this section appeared in *Catholic Dossier* 2:2 (1996) 44–48 as "The Doctrine of Immortality in the Old Testament."

manifested in love and brought to perfection, by God's free gift, through sharing in his eternal life. (*Evangelium Vitae* 63)

Before the book of Wisdom, biblical hints about post-mortal survival are rare. Psalm 6:5, for instance, is a prayer for deliverance from one's enemies: "for in death there is no remembrace of thee; in Sheol who can thee praise?" If in this cry for help there is any expectation of an ongoing existence, it is muted by the same sense of futility that accompanies the early reference to Sheol as a shadowy region of unknown provenance in Genesis. In Jacob's sorrow over the report that wild animals have slain his son Joseph, he "refused to be comforted, and said, 'No, I shall go down to Sheol to my son, mourning'" (Genesis 38:35).

Those psalms which Christian faith allows us to understand as promises of immortality seem (without the light of Christ) merely to regard death as final and terrible. While the somber tones of Psalm 49, for instance, heap scorn upon those who rely on their own wealth and reaffirm that only trust in God will rescue the just from those who attack them, there is still a constant presumption that this is a protection during one's lifetime and that death is the end: "Even the wise die, the foolish and the stupid alike must perish and leave their wealth to others. Their graves are their homes forever, their dwelling places to all generations" (Psalm 49:10–11). What consolation the psalm offers to the just by promise of divine help in holding off the inevitable fate of death can be seen through the Christian optic to give an ever deeper consolation by the promise of the afterlife: "Man is like the beasts that perish. This is the fate of those who have foolish confidence. . . . Like sheep they are appointed for Sheol; Death shall be their shepherd; straight to the grave they descend, and their form shall waste away; Sheol shall be their home. But God will ransom my soul from the power of Sheol, for He will receive me" (Psalm 49:12–15). The earnest prayers for salvation that appear elsewhere in the book of psalms, however, seem more to envision protection from untimely death rather than to emphasize post-mortal existence, as in Psalm 115: "The dead do not praise the Lord, nor do any that go down into the silence. But we will bless the Lord from this time forth and for evermore" (vv. 17–18; see also Psalm 88:3–6). While faith in the resurrection readily lets us understand them to suggest eternal life with God, the passage can also be interpreted as suggesting that all the dead go to the silence of Sheol but that God will raise up generation after generation forever who will give Him praise.

More explicit revelation about the immortality of the soul and the resurrection of the body surfaces relatively late among the books of the Old Testament, and particularly within biblical Wisdom Literature. The presentation of quite different positions on the problem of death and the mystery of human suffering and death within such books as Proverbs, Job, Qoheleth, Sirach, and Wisdom makes this portion of Scripture resemble philosophical debate in certain respects, even if the culmination of this debate in the doctrine of an "immortal" state for righteous souls and a promise of "incorruptible bodies" is clearly a disclosure of divine revelation that goes beyond the arguments of philosophy and folk wisdom. And yet even the most advanced position on the topic within the Old Testament remains only an anticipation of the fullness of revelation on this point in the resurrection of Christ.

In general, the problem of evil as posed in the Old Testament is a problem of grasping what appears deeply unfair in the relative fortunes of those good people who suffer and die before their time, without children or good name, and of those wicked people who prosper and become famous. But it also raises what has come to be known in philosophical theology as the problem of theodicy: how can the all-just, all-knowing, and all-powerful God allow such things to happen to people who have lived in fidelity and virtue? Although elaborate notions of an afterlife were common in Greece and in other religions of the ancient Near East, the religion of Israel wisely kept its distance from any of the reincarnation myths typical of religions which embraced a cyclic view of time and existence. Mindful of the fact that there was in Eden a tree of *eternal life* (Genesis 3:22–23), Israel never accepted the notion of transmigration of souls and focused instead on this-worldly deliverance of the nation from its enemies, such as the Exodus from Egypt and the return from the Babylonian Captivity. In the prophets we occasionally find apocalyptic scenarios of a cosmic battle on the "Day of the LORD" as a trans-historical solution to Israel's problems, but there is only the smallest hint in the prophetic literature about the concept of personal immortality that comes to mark the later sapiential books.

Proverbs offers a fundamentally optimistic picture about the likelihood of justice being done to the good and the wicked, but it is precisely this sort of optimism that raises the biblical version of the theodicy problem. Many of its proverbs on this point rehearse the basic teachings of Deuteronomy, as in the following: "He who digs a pit will fall into it, and a stone will come back upon him who starts it rolling" (Proverbs 26:27). There is here a highly integrated view of life that promotes a strong connection between a deed and its consequences, with constant exhortation to the young to choose the nobler of the "two ways" that are proposed respectively by Lady Wisdom and Lady Folly (chapters 1–9). By emphasizing that a sinful deed often contains the seeds of its own tragic outcome, the book gives an exhortation by making the point that "Crime does not pay." But in my judgment these relatively optimistic expectations that justice will be done make Proverbs a work of moral advice rather than a metaphysical demonstration that history is such that justice always will be done during this life. Proverbs is not naive about the fact that sometimes the good do suffer and the wicked do prosper. Rather, it explains the link between acts and their consequences according to a law of natural retribution, established at creation and carefully watched over by God, as a principle that any young person thinking about a path for life ought to embrace as a guide to conduct (see chapters 7–8).

Now, sound moral advice about the consequences to expect from one's free choices needs to rest on true accounts about the way the world works, and it is the need to reflect on this correlation that is responsible in part for the philosophical trajectory of other books in the tradition of biblical Wisdom Literature. The moral principle is offered in some striking proverbs. Questions such as "Can a man carry fire in his bosom and his clothes not be burned?" (Proverbs 6:27) admonish us against choosing the way of Lady Folly, who sits in the shadows of the city gate at dusk and entices the unsuspecting with the deadly pleasures of "real living." Lady Wisdom, who discusses the traditional wisdom of Israel at noon in the midst of the town square, tries to show how the way of virtue, community loyalty, and other bonds of morality brings the fruits of life (including the portrait of the ideal wife in chapter 31) for those who make wise choices in regard to marriage and other life questions. There are occasional proverbs (e.g., 3:11–12) about how to endure suffering as parental discipline from the LORD or about not being jealous of wicked people who prosper. They show that it requires genuine wisdom to know how to apply these traditional proverbs to various situations, including the times when we face suffering or untimely death.

Although faith in the resurrection makes it possible to take references to the "life" which righteousness brings as references to an afterlife, there is no direct talk of an afterlife, and it quite possible to read the promise of life (e.g., at 8:35) and of "deliverance from death" (at 10:2) to mean only the reward of a long life (see 9:11), for an early death is regarded as a punishment for sin. The shadowy existence of the dead in Sheol is mentioned as the speedy result of a decision to accept the invitation of Lady Folly (5:23, 7:26–27, 9:18), but the lack of any description, or even promise, of something like "heaven" could well mean that all will end up in Sheol, and so the project at hand is to delay having to go there. Traditionally longevity is seen as the point of observing the Covenant (see Deuteronomy 28:1–14 and Psalm 34:12–14). But the openness of these texts to a deeper meaning about personal immortality is part of the divine pedagogy that gradually prepares a people for the definitive revelation in Christ.

The Book of Job is intensely concerned with the problem of evil in a way that can be taken as a reaction to the optimism cultivated in Proverbs that the just will be rewarded and the wicked punished, but its answer seems to be that there is no theoretical solution to the problem. Rather, there is need to resist the view that, if one is suffering, one must have been guilty of grave wickedness. Likewise, at the practical level, the book is a lesson on combating any desolation that might arise during one's suffering from the thought that God does not protect the just—one sees this especially in Job's cry "I know that my Redeemer lives." Instead, the moral is that one must be faithful to God even amid suffering.

The issue of theodicy is raised by Job's three friends, who operate *as if* the optimistic confidence of the book of Proverbs about the link between acts and consequences and the law of divine retribution *were* an answer at the metaphysical level to the problem of evil. They expect that virtue will be rewarded by prosperity, health, and a long life. This is an expectation that may arise simply from considerations of natural justice (viz., that one should receive what one deserves), or perhaps even from a sense of the justice God dispensed from the time of expelling Adam and Eve from the Garden of Eden. But if it is from this latter source, then these friends are forgetful of the covenant with Noah after the Flood, and in particular of God's promise not to destroy evil in the world again by a massive flood, but thereafter to rain upon the just and the unjust alike.[16] In any case, by their various arguments these friends try to persuade Job that he must have committed some sin, whether by a conscious and deliberate offense (even though they do not know what it is), or perhaps by some unintentional transgression of a ritual law, for they are sure that such suffering as he is experiencing could not be the lot of anyone who is really innocent. If Job is suffering, he must somehow be guilty. Job rejects their judgment categorically. Although exasperated by their stubbornness, he continually seeks to have his suit heard by God. He steadfastly maintains that his innocence would become clear if only he could have his day in court (e.g. 9:32–35; 13:3,16–22; 19:23–29; and 31:35–37).

Although Job does not offer a theoretical answer to the general problem of evil, the dramatic development of the book of Job does seem to propose that the question about evil is being asked in the wrong way and must be put differently (see 21:7–17). The character Elihu, for instance, presumes to speak for God in chapter 32. He may show great piety, but he is in error to think that he understands the divine plan enough to discern who is righteous and who is unrighteous by measuring Job's suffering and chastisement. His bombast is shattered by God's own whirlwind (chapter 38). This dramatic divine appearance both asserts God's utter sovereignty and declares Job "not guilty." No human wisdom can comprehend God's mind sufficiently to answer the question about God's justice, for wisdom is beyond any creaturely understanding (chapter 28). Job is right to keep silence, except to praise the unfathomable mystery of God's majesty (42:1–16) and to plead for his friends, who suddenly seem guilty of presumption in God's court.

16. See Genesis 9:8–17 and Jesus' allusion to Noah at Matthew 5:45.

Only the vindication of Job and the restoration of his fortunes at the end of chapter 42 correspond to the optimism suggested by the exhortation in Proverbs about a suitable reward in this life for those who choose what is just. Some scholars treat this chapter as an epilogue by a hand committed to the optimistic tradition, but it could equally well testify to the author's confidence in divine grace to set things right. Regardless, the bulk of the book of Job is not so much a theoretical answer to the problem of evil as an affirmation that suffering in life must be accepted as part of the mystery of divine providence, often without sufficient explanation, for Job remains unaware of the decisions made in the heavenly council at the beginning of the book, even though the reader knows of them. The task is to preserve one's fidelity to God, even amid great hardship and confusion, trusting that God will sustain and redeem. There is no explanation of the suffering of the innocent, but only strong affirmation of God's creative power and knowledge. There is no talk about recompense in the next life, but only an example of how to speak to God in the midst of this life's tragedies. Considered philosophically, this book presents a kind of objection to the proposal offered in Proverbs and thus begins the debate.

Qoheleth presents a pessimistic, or at least a somewhat skeptical position on the theodicy question. In a strategy that anticipates Descartes's method by holding as "doubtful" whatever can be challenged by even one strong objection, Qoheleth rejects both the traditional confidence in divine reward and retribution as at odds with experience (3:16–18, 7:15, 8:10–9:1) and any trust in human wisdom to chart the course of the "two ways" (8:16–17). If it remains clear to the author that God does direct the universe, he repeatedly insists that we are unable to know anything of God's plans or reasons, and that the right course is simply to enjoy whatever ordinary gifts of prosperity God may send (2:1–11, 5:18, 9:7–10).

Qoheleth seems primarily intent on showing that God's ways simply cannot be known, and it uses the problem of evil only as a dramatic case in point. If anything, the book readily assumes in passing that there is nothing beyond the grave: "one fate comes to all, to the righteous and the wicked. . . . This is an evil in all that is done under the sun, that one fate comes to all" (9:2–3). After men live "they go to the dead." There may be some hope for something better while one is still alive, but there is nothing to recommend the state of the dead: "the dead know nothing, and they have no more reward, but the memory of them is lost. Their love and their hate and their envy have already perished, and they have no more forever any share in all that is done under the sun" (9:5–6). The certain prospect of death and the absence of any hint of heaven leave the reader of Qoheleth with the unexplained discrepancy between the fortunes of the righteous and those of the unrighteous in this life. Experience gives no reason to think that these claims are adjudicated here, and there is no mention of anywhere else. Yet, this does not bring the author to distrust God so much as to distrust human abilities to press the theodicy question.

By contrast, Sirach is filled with respectful allusions to the book of Proverbs and shares its basic confidence that injustice and sin contain the seeds of destruction while virtue, however difficult, is sure to prosper. This book is clearly designed for the education of the young about responsible use of their free choices by stressing the natural links between acts and their consequences as well as the law of divine retribution. But as a justification for thinking that these books contribute to something of an ongoing philosophical debate, we may note that the book is more thematically alert to the problem of evil than is Proverbs, and we find both a melange of citations from earlier wisdom books as well as new material. The author repeats, for instance, the traditional answers about God's control of the universe and history (1:2ff.). Although human beings may not now or ever be able to comprehend this plan, they should rest assured that there is a divine plan by which providence is wisely administering the world (1:6–10). What human beings need is "fear of the LORD" (1:11–20), that is, a firm adherence to true religion, reverence for the one God, trust in His arrangements, and especially observance of divine law (Torah), with which Sirach identifies wisdom (chapter 24). Living out their religion faithfully is the proper and fitting course.

Sirach's contribution to discussion of the problem of evil shows a tremendous sensitivity to the mystery of suffering. Sometimes the LORD must compassionately discipline his children, as a father must do for his son. Suffering can also come as a test of patient endurance (2:1–6). Personal experience of how this works makes the author able to give encouragement that divine providence is operating in everything (33:1), even though full understanding of this operation may remain cloaked in mystery. Unlike Qoheleth, Sirach finds it neither wrong nor impossible to seek to know the meaning God may intend; in fact, this is the point of education in the wisdom tradition. But it would be wrong to presume to understand the divine plan so well as to lose the proper fear of the LORD (33:14–15, 42:24).

The apocalyptic passages about God's redressing of wrongs on the day of judgment and vengeance do imply a judgment of souls after death, with punishment for the wicked and a joyous life with God for the righteous, but there are great textual difficulties here, for these passage are found in late Greek and Latin versions, but not in any of the existing Hebrew manuscripts of the book, which mention immortality only in terms of the memory of one's name by one's descendants (14:11–19). This is the perspective governing the many stories about the courage of the just patriarchs amid their sufferings (chapters 44–50)—the first time that such extensive hagiography is included within the Bible, let alone within Wisdom Literature. Death is usually regarded as final and the proper course is resignation, but there are hints about an afterlife (28:6) and about the retribution which the LORD will bring about on the day of a person's death (11:26–28). What is not clear is whether this means that there will be reward and punishment in the next life, or simply that moral retrospection about how a life was spent cannot be completed until death. On the whole, Sirach seems more concerned with exhortation to virtue and wisdom by the internalization of Torah observance than with the disclosure of a theoretical analysis or the revelation of the solution to the problem.

It is only with the chronologically latest books of the Old Testament that we find a clear and unequivocal teaching on immortality, e.g., in Daniel, 2 Maccabees, and the Wisdom of Solomon. The martyrdom of many Jews faithful to Torah at the hands of Antiochus IV Epiphanes had raised the question anew, and a vision is granted in the apocalypse of Daniel: "Many of those who sleep in the dust of the earth shall awake; some to everlasting life, and some to shame and everlasting contempt" (Daniel 12:2). From this disclosure there comes a more profound sense that the "resurrection" mentioned in the Torah and the prophets refers not merely to the restoration of the nation of Israel but to individuals based on personal merit. This same truth is revealed again in 2 Maccabees by one of the seven brothers facing martyrdom: "But the King of the universe will raise us up to an everlasting renewal of life, because we have died for his laws" (7:9). Their mother is filled with the same inspiration when she says: "The Creator of the world, who shaped the beginning of man and devised the origin of all things, will in his mercy give life and breath back to you again, since you now forget yourselves for the sake of his laws" (7:23).

The Wisdom of Solomon, written just before the Christian era, employs the assumption of immortality of soul throughout and even presents a form of the doctrine of the resurrection, a doctrine that Christ will reveal in its fullness by His teachings. As noted earlier, the opening five chapters present a vision of the judgment in the afterlife to be made by Jews killed for their fidelity to Torah upon their persecutors. The doctrine of immortality thus serves to help resolve the problem of unjust suffering. The other theodicy cases typical of the Bible are also mentioned—the sinless barren woman, the eunuch who has been faithful to the LORD, and the good who die young and without progeny or with name dishonored (chapter 3). The LORD makes them judges of those who scorned their Torah loyalty, and the wicked themselves testify to their surprise at the power of God manifested in this vindication of their victims (chapter 5). Such a revelation offers a strong defense of God as all-just and all-powerful, for the divine plan is here seen to right wrongs and to punish wrong-doers according to the law of retribution suggested in Proverbs.

A second discussion of theodicy issues occurs in the second half of the book by the presentation of a typological interpretation of certain events from the Exodus story. The punishments which the Egyptians receive in the course of the plagues are all shown to have been carefully suited to their crimes, and the implication is that they should have known better. In fact, much of the burden of the address by King Solomon to his fellow kings of the earth in the middle chapters serves to prepare the way for the conclusion that the Egyptians should have recognized the power of God and the signs of Israel's divine protection, but that "the fascinations of evil" blinded them and that devotion to their idols perverted their morality (13:1–15:17).

The Wisdom of Solomon goes beyond the other books of Old Testament Wisdom Literature in its resolution of the problem of evil, by envisioning a post-mortem judgment for souls, which are immortal. Like Job, the book also re-emphasizes the utter sovereignty of God and the divine power at work in the forces of nature to redress sins and injustice against the LORD's people. Two important elements in this teaching deserve special mention.

1. The term "immortality" *(athanasia)*, like the concept it represents, is rare elsewhere in the Scriptures but has long philosophical provenance. It occurs, however, throughout the text of Wisdom to name the gift God will grant the just who persevere in fidelity. Unlike the use of this term in Greek philosophy, where immortality tends to be regarded as an inherent trait of the soul by virtue of its natural structure, immortality is here regarded as a gift that comes from union with Divine Wisdom (8:13, 17) and as a result of God's power. It is clearly more than the immortality of being remembered by later generations that is typical of Sirach, and more than the shadowy existence in Sheol, for after death it is only real life with God that is worthy of the name life. There is real risk of destruction and annihilation (1:12–13, 2:2–3), and yet (ironically) it is the presence of the wicked in the post-mortem vindication scene that allows us to infer that the wicked too have immortality as the condition for the suffering of their punishment.

2. The coming resurrection of the body is suggested by the frequent use of the term "incorruption" *(aphtharsia)*. It occurs in an allusion to Genesis 2:7: "for God created man for incorruption, and made him in the image of his own eternity, but through the devil's envy death entered the world, and those who belong to his party experience it" (2:23–24). This final destiny intended by God for humankind is portrayed as a matter of holy hope, but not as an inevitable outcome of life. In both the vindication scene and in the allusions to the book of Exodus and the rescue from Pharoah, *aphtharsia* does not yet seem to mean "incorruptibility" but "incorrup-

tion," a state that the human being is supposed to share, but a gift that was lost and must be restored again by an act of God. In what the Church has seen as a fascinating anticipation of the connection between the Eucharist and everlasting life, it is the gift of manna, the "food of angels" (16:20), that the Wisdom of Solomon uses to present the utter gratuity of the gift of immortality and incorruption. That with which God fed the people during the Exodus proved "indestructible" by fire (16:22–23, 19:21), a food for immortality; it is no surprise that the Church has taken up the language of Wisdom in the ritual of Benediction to proclaim that the Eucharist, like this manna, "has all sweetness within it" (16:20c). The entire cluster of images around the gift of manna seems to express concretely what abstract terms like *athanasia* and *aphtharsia* express thematically: the LORD alone is the giver of the nourishment that bestows immortality on the just as the reward of their righteousness. God will restore perfect order in justice and mercy in the afterlife, and we are exhorted to live rightly in this life to prepare the way for union with God beyond the grave in eternity.

The near absence of a clear idea of personal immortality in the earlier periods of Israel's history is remarkable, especially in light of the widespread diffusion of this idea in surrounding cultures. But the persistent questions of evil and theodicy provided a context for divine revelation, in God's good time, to disclose partially in the Wisdom Literature, and then fully and completely in the Gospels, an answer consistent with earlier affirmation of God's ultimate justice and providential care for creation, and yet a truth not discussed in the Bible before this time, the immortality of the soul and the resurrection of the body. This is to say that God's plan from the beginning was to share His divine life with His creation and that the education and disciplining of the Chosen People was directed to stimulate their recognition that only life with God is true life. But, as the old adage has it, wisdom comes through suffering. It is precisely by fidelity in suffering that the just are given the gift of life that is incorruptible and eternal, life with God. These Jewish roots of Christian hope anchor our expectations about the last things and the life to come in a profound divine pedagogy. If the fullness of revelation comes about only in Christ, as we are told by the Second Vatican Council's *Declaration on Divine Revelation,* the patience of God in providing the channels to bring about that fullness should fill us with holy awe.

III. The Relation of Faith and Reason in Light of Biblical Wisdom Literature

It would be excessive to claim that biblical Wisdom Literature is philosophical in the generally prevailing sense of the word. But the expansion of the sense of what philosophy is, so as to recover its sapiential dimension, may well be one of John Paul II's most cherished projects in *Fides et ratio*.[17] This review of some of the important themes within biblical Wisdom Literature strongly reinforces the recoverist project envisioned by the pope and exemplies the relation between faith and reason which he articulates in *Fides et ratio.*

Throughout the wisdom books we meet the conviction that both faith in what God has revealed and reasoning about life and its prospects are valid sources of genuine knowledge. The confidence that books like Proverbs and Sirach repose in the Torah as providing

17. Consultation of the definition of "philosophy" in any of the standard dictionaries of philosophy reveals the loss of the sapiential dimension even in definitions which try to be broad and inclusive. By way of example, consider the definition that appears in *The Harper Dictionary of Modern Thought,* ed. Alan Bullock and Oliver Stallybras (New York: Harper and Row, 1977): "Philosophy. A term that cannot be uncontroversially defined in a single formula, used to cover a wide variety of intellectual undertakings, all of which combine a high degree of generality with more or less exclusive reliance on reasoning rather than on observation and experience to justify their claims."

directives for a peaceful and happy life is unbounded. But in the very same books there is no expectation that the specific answers to life's questions are perfectly laid out in advance. One must use one's reason to call to mind the ancestral wisdom of Israel as found in pithy proverbs to think through the issues. What is more, it is not just a matter of thinking one's way through a mental exercise but a matter of developing a character that is constantly disposed to think things through clearly. In doing so, one may expect illumination from the revelation in which one puts one's faith, but one must grow in one's use of reason, as well as in docility to God's Word by a healthy fear of the LORD.

Speculative concerns likewise have a certain prominence in this part of the Bible. Solomon's prayer for understanding of natural processes and the order of the cosmos is clearly deferential: he is, after all, *praying* so that he may understand, but there is no presumption that the understanding he desires will simply come by way of a full direct illumination. Rather, his deferential act of prayer invites the divine illumination of his studies and thus suggests the importance of divine assistance as well as the conviction that what he will be studying is a divinely ordered cosmos. The discovery of its laws and workings will only further his knowledge of God, whose providential care for the universe designed those principles into creation.

Besides these explicit reflections upon speculative wisdom, we have also noticed a tremendous speculative project that runs the entire course of biblical Wisdom Literature. One can trace the give-and-take of positions within these books on questions about evil, suffering, and death. Although these books do not use a methodology that would be recognized as philosophy in the strict sense, they do exhibit an interesting interplay of faith and reason in just the sense that the pope has described in their treatment of the problem. Those books which raise expectations that life will really turn out in a way that rewards the just and punishes the wicked rely on faith in earlier revelation as well as on solid patterns of moral reasoning to make their case. But the discrepancies any reasonable person will readily notice between such expectations and the way life often enough does turn out provokes further reasoning about the limits of human reason as well as more sophisticated understanding of what it is that faith requires. Further reflection drives the question back to its starting point, for reason insists that justice must indeed be done, but further revelation is required in order to supply an answer in terms of immortality and incorruption that is deeply reasonable even if beyond what reasoning seems to have arrived at on its own.

In the final analysis, it is no surprise that God's self-disclosure in that portion of the Scriptures which comes near the close of the old dispensation involves the interplay of human reason and the revelations of faith so fully. For the divine plan of readying a people to receive His Son in the fullness of time meant bringing the Chosen People to ever greater maturity in many respects, including the life of the mind. One crucial aspect of human maturity involves growth in one's powers of thinking in such a way as to be confidently reliant on one's own powers even while humbly receptive to what is, strictly, above and beyond them but accessible under divine assistance. This maturation of human thinking in certain important philosophical dimensions is evident in biblical Wisdom Literature and helps to further illustrate the relation between faith and reason which the pope is anxious to explore in *Fides et ratio*.

THE MEDIEVALISM OF *Fides et ratio*

MICHAEL SWEENEY

The complexity of John Paul II's approach to medieval philosophy and theology in *Fides et ratio* is apparent in the question whether the following statements from that document give rise to a contradiction. We read there that "The Church has no philosophy of her own nor does she canonize any one particular philosophy in preference to others. The underlying reason for this reluctance is that, even when it engages theology, philosophy must remain faithful to its own principles and methods" (§49). Nevertheless, at the same time the encyclical praises the medieval period over all others (§§45, 58, 62), calls Thomas Aquinas a "model for all who seek the truth" (§§43, 78), and follows Pope Leo XIII in commending the philosophy of Aquinas: "More than a century later, many of the insights of his encyclical letter [Leo XIII's *Aeterni Patris*] have lost none of their interest from either a practical or a pedagogical point of view—most particularly, his insistence upon the incomparable value of the philosophy of St. Thomas" (§57).

We can begin to understand the pope's praise of the medievals in general and of Aquinas in particular when we piece together from *Fides et ratio* his account of the history of the relationship between faith and reason. In the Patristic and Medieval periods, he says, there is broad agreement on the unity of faith and reason (§45), though the account of the unity of faith and reason matures in the Middle Ages when the question of their relationship becomes central (§62), and especially when Latin Christendom becomes aware of the accomplishments of Jewish and Islamic philosophers (§43) and becomes more aware of the accomplishments of Greek philosophers (§77). The tendency of late medieval thinkers to separate faith and reason brings the Middle Ages to a close (§45), and the modern period is marked by an increasing separation of faith and reason (ibid.), although there are those who have resisted this severance, many of whom have been neither Thomists nor interested in medieval philosophy (§74).

In this history, *Fides et ratio* expresses more interest in the nature of philosophical inquiry than in particular systems.[1] The principal reason for praise of medieval philosophers is their openness to a philosophical inquiry that transcends human subjectivity and contingent existence (§5). The nature of philosophical inquiry in the Middle Ages coincides with the biblical image of human life as a journey without rest (§18). For most medieval philosophers there is a natural desire—an "eros"—of reason for faith and of philosophy for theology: philosophy makes us aware that our desire to know is a thirst for God without being able to satisfy it.

How the pope's interest in the nature of philosophical inquiry coincides with his praise of the medieval period becomes clearer

---

1. "Yet often enough in history this [the ability to systematize knowledge] has brought with it the temptation to identify one single stream with the whole of philosophy. In such cases, we are clearly dealing with a 'philosophical pride' which seeks to present its own partial and imperfect view as the complete reading of reality. In effect, every philosophical *system*, while it should always be respected in its wholeness, without any instrumentalization, must still recognize the primacy of philosophical *enquiry*, from which it stems and which it ought logically to serve" (§4).

when we take note of the two proofs for the existence of God to which he alludes in *Fides et ratio*. Augustine argues in *De vera religione* XXX and in *De libero arbitrio* II that God is always present in our mind, and every judgment of unity and eternal truth depends upon Him as the standard by which these judgments are made. Returning within our minds, we remember that God has always been present there (§15), although this glimpse makes us more aware of our absence than of God's presence. Anselm's well-known proofs for the existence of God in the *Proslogion* maintain that real and necessary existence are included in the definition of God as that than which nothing greater can be thought, with the result that the non-existence of God becomes unthinkable; and yet, it is not merely that God is that than which nothing greater than can be thought, He is also greater than human thought (§14): proof of God's existence does not make Him any less mysterious.

Aquinas' proofs are not mentioned here, nor does he play a noticeable role in the description of reason's desire that God should reveal Himself, but there is a clear preference for the general medieval view that philosophy can discover God and that something more than philosophy is desirable (Chapter III: "Intelligo ut credam").[2] Likewise commended in *Fides et ratio* is the view widely held in the Middle Ages whereby faith is said to desire reason. Augustine's dictum of faith seeking understanding expresses the eros of faith towards reason (Chapter II: "Credo ut intelligam"). As reason desires to attain what it lacks through faith, so faith desires to complete itself through reason. Since faith is an act of the whole person, it must engage the rational nature of the human being.[3] The submission of intellect in

2. Given the later emphasis on metaphysics and an account of nature within Christian philosophy (see pp. 169–71 below), this focus on Augustine's and Anselm's proofs is striking, and it supports the contention that "nature" and "metaphysics" in *Fides et ratio* are not necessarily tied to a philosophical starting point in the material world.

3. "This is why the Church has always considered the act of entrusting oneself to God

faith is neither a silencing of reason nor separate from reason (§13, n. 15); for, as Augustine notes, although the will leads in faith, the act of belief is an act of both will and intellect.[4]

Anselm is also cited in describing the need of faith for reason. It is not only the case that reason possesses an eros for knowledge of God that surpasses philosophy, says Anselm; faith also possesses a desire to understand that which it loves.[5] There is an incompleteness in faith that leads to a desire for reason, which is able to supply explanations that faith lacks.

The internal necessity of reason towards faith and of faith towards reason is expressed through the examples of Augustine and Anselm.[6] Nevertheless, the desire of reason towards faith and of

---

to be a moment of fundamental decision which engages the whole person. In that act, the intellect and will display their spiritual nature . . ." (§13).

4. "To believe is nothing other than to think with assent. . . . Believers are also thinkers: in believing, they think and in thinking, they believe. . . . If faith does not think, it is nothing" (§78).

5. "For the saintly archbishop of Canterbury the priority of faith is not in competition with the search that is proper to reason. . . . Its [reason's] function is rather to find meaning, to discover explanations which might allow everyone to come to a certain understanding of the contents of faith. St. Anselm underscores the fact that the intellect must seek that which it loves: the more it loves, the more it desires to know" (§42).

6. Such concentration on Augustine and Anselm manifests the importance of their "erotic phenomenology" of faith and reason in *Fides et ratio*. The following passage from Anselm's *Proslogion* exemplifies the erotic element in this perspective:

"'How long, O Lord?' (Psalm 6:3) 'How long, O Lord, will you forget us? How long will you turn your face from us?' (Psalm 13:1). When will you look favorably upon us and hear us? When will you 'enlighten our eyes' (Psalm 13:3) and 'show us your face'? (Psalm 80:3, 7,19) . . . I beseech you. Lord: my heart is made bitter with its desolation; sweeten it with your consolation. I beseech you. Lord: in my hunger I began to seek you; let me not depart from you empty. I have come to you starving; let me not leave unsatisfied. I have come as a beggar to one who is rich, as a pitiful wretch to one who has pity; let me not go back penniless and despised. If indeed 'I sigh before I eat' (Job 3:24), grant that I might eat after I sigh. . . . Teach me how to seek you, and show yourself to me when I seek. For I cannot seek you unless you teach me how, and I cannot find you unless you show yourself to me. Let me seek you in desiring you; let me desire you in seeking you. Let me find you in loving you; let me love you in finding you.

faith towards reason does not necessarily establish that such a union is in fact possible. It is not enough to show that a marriage between reason and faith is desirable, it is also necessary to demonstrate that it is possible. While Augustine and Anselm play important roles in describing reason's desire for faith and faith's desire for reason, Aquinas stands virtually alone in *Fides et ratio* during the discussion of how the desirable is known to be possible.

That the mutual desire of faith and reason *can* lead to their union is demonstrated by the content of revelation (§79) and by the complementarity of faith and reason (§43). With regard to faith's desire to be completed by reason, Aquinas is lauded for the clarity with which he distinguishes the mutual contributions of faith and reason already noted by Anselm (§§42–43). This is best seen through Aquinas' distinction between two types of revealed truths: (1) that which has been revealed and is inherently beyond the capacity of human reason and (2) that which has been revealed but is not inherently beyond the capacity of human reason (§§66–67). Through belief in that which is beyond reason, reason is given an object that it could receive only supernaturally, and from this starting point one can demonstrate truths that follow from it necessarily. Moreover, it is possible to give explanations for those revealed truths, which, although they do not attain the necessity of demonstration, are reasonable—explanations *ex convenientia,* as Aquinas calls them. Anselm in particular did not clearly distinguish in theology between demonstrative arguments and arguments from "fittingness" or *ex convenientia.*[7]

... But I do long to understand your truth in some way, your truth which my heart believes and loves. For I do not seek to understand in order to believe; I believe in order to understand. For I also believe that 'Unless I believe, I shall not understand.'"

Anselm, *Proslogion* 1 in *Monologion and Proslogion,* transl. Thomas Williams (Indianapolis: Hackett, 1995), pp. 98–99.

7. So, for example, with regard to the reason why the second person of the Trinity became incarnate, Anselm says: "If it be necessary [necesse est], therefore, as it appears,

Through the second type of revealed truth, i.e. those truths revealed but accessible to reason, revelation gives to reason a conclusion that it is naturally capable of achieving on its own. Such truths have been revealed, however, not only because few are philosophers and no philosopher is without error; more importantly, truths such as the existence of God and creation are part of the Christian message of salvation (§76). Hence the revelation of truths accessible to philosophy means that not only can faith be united with reason in theology, but that theologians must be philosophers as well, because a portion of what is believed can be understood philosophically.

Now if it is true that Aquinas's distinction between these two types of revealed truth helps to explain why he is being held up as a model in *Fides et ratio,* does this amount to a "canonization" of Aquinas' philosophy? Since his account of philosophy being aided by faith is compatible with widely diverse philosophies, there seems to be no elevation of Aquinas' philosophy to the level of magisterial teaching. It does seem, however, that there is a problem with those philosophies which deny that there are revealed truths attainable by reason. In particular, it is difficult to see how reason can complement the needs of faith if philosophy is unable to achieve metaphysical and objective ethical knowledge (§§83–84, 106). If there is no metaphysical knowledge of God's existence or of creation, and there are

---

that the heavenly kingdom be made up of men, and this cannot be effected unless the aforesaid satisfaction be made, which none but God can make and none but man ought to make, it is necessary [necesse est] for the God-man to make it." *Cur Deus Homo* II.6 in *St. Anselm: Basic Writings,* trans. S. Deane (LaSalle, Ill.: Open Court, 1962), 245.

Compare this to Aquinas' argument in the *Summa theologiae* III.1.1: "[I]t belongs to the essence of the highest good to communicate itself in the highest manner to the creature, and this is brought about chiefly by *His so joining created nature to Himself that one Person is made up of these three-the Word, a soul and flesh,* as Augustine says. Hence it is manifest that it was fitting [conveniens fuit] that God should become incarnate." *The Summa Theologica of St. Thomas Aquinas,* transl. Dominican Fathers (Westminster, Md.: Christian Classics, 1981), vol. 4, p. 2020.

no objective ethical norms, there is no class of revealed truths attainable by philosophy. While Aquinas' model union is compatible with philosophers as diverse as those of Augustine, Boethius, Anselm, Albert the Great, Duns Scotus, Suarez, and perhaps Descartes, its compatibility with analytical or postmodern philosophy, for example, is doubtful.

Aquinas is exemplary, according to *Fides et ratio,* not only because he asserts that a union of reason and faith is achievable in theology but also because such a union is possible in philosophy, inasmuch as philosophy is capable of attaining some revealed truths. This affirmation that philosophy can grasp some revealed truths presupposes that human reason, though weakened by sin, is capable of attaining metaphysical and ethical truths (§43). That such truths are philosophically possible, and thus that this union of faith and reason is possible, is demonstrated by two facts, and here, once again, Aquinas is set apart as a paradigm in *Fides et ratio.* The first fact that accounts for the possibility of human reason achieving metaphysical and ethical truth through philosophy is the achievement of the great pagan philosophers (§75). Ancient Greek philosophy, in particular that of Plato and Aristotle, makes patent the power of unaided human reason to reach metaphysical and ethical truth. Aquinas and medieval philosophers strengthen the union of faith and reason, according to *Fides et ratio,* when they recognize the accomplishments of pagan philosophers (§§43, 76). The second fact supporting the ability of reason to grasp metaphysical and ethical truth is the achievement of Islamic and Jewish philosophers. Aquinas is singled out in *Fides et ratio* as an outstanding example of incorporating Islamic and Jewish philosophy (§43). The fact that philosophy is able to attain metaphysical and ethical truth apart from any faith or apart from a Christian faith supports the position that human reason can grasp some metaphysical and ethical truths that are a part of Christian revelation, and thus it supports the position that a union between faith and reason is not only desirable but possible.

Affirming that some revealed truths are within the grasp of reason presupposes that human reason is capable of attaining metaphysical and ethical truths through its own power, which, in turn, implies that there is such a thing as "nature," and here we find in *Fides et ratio* another reason to consider Aquinas a "model." For Aquinas, the possibility of a unity between faith and reason requires an understanding of nature: faith and reason are complementary only if there is a discernible domain of nature upon which faith builds.[8] The unity of faith and reason through their identical origin in God is balanced by the difference between God and nature. Of course, the question immediately comes to mind whether this understanding of nature must be Aquinas' or whether other versions are possible. There is no indication in *Fides et ratio* that Aquinas' view of nature, derived largely from Aristotle, is the only way to explain "the secularity of the world," as it is called here, but some account of nature whereby there is an internal necessity to created things does appear to be a requirement for explaining how a union between faith and reason is possible.

Fides et ratio is not declaring that Aquinas' philosophy is a condition for the possibility of a union between faith and reason, and yet some concept of nature and some form of metaphysics and objective ethics are presupposed. What is affirmed in *Fides et ratio* is not Aquinas' philosophical system but a general or abstract philosophy

8. The pope summarizes Aquinas' thought on the matter: "Both the light of reason and the light of faith come from God, he argued; hence there can be no contradiction between them.

"More radically, Thomas recognized that nature, philosophy's proper concern, could contribute to the understanding of divine revelation. Faith therefore has no fear of reason, but seeks it out and has trust in it. Just as grace builds on nature and brings it to fulfillment, so faith builds upon and perfects reason" (§43).

with which Aquinas' philosophy is compatible, as are many others, especially among the medievals:

Although times change and knowledge increases, it is possible to discern a core of philosophical insight within the history of thought as a whole. Consider, for example, the principles of non-contradiction, finality and causality, as well as the concept of the person as a free and intelligent subject, with the capacity to know God, truth and goodness. Consider as well certain fundamental norms which are shared by all. These are among the indications that, beyond different schools of thought, there exists a body of knowledge which may be judged a kind of spiritual heritage of humanity. It is as if we had come upon an *implicit philosophy,* as a result of which all feel that they possess these principles, albeit in a general and unreflective way. Precisely because it is shared in some measure by all, this knowledge should serve as a kind of reference point for the different philosophical schools (§4).

There is no contradiction in affirming both that Aquinas is an example of this general philosophy and that other philosophies may reach these conclusions in ways quite different from Aquinas.

Of course, there are many philosophies that are not consistent with the general philosophy described here in *Fides et ratio* because not only do they fail to affirm nature, metaphysics or universal ethical norms, they deny the possibility of such rational knowledge. Thus *Fides et ratio* lays down several conditions under which the Magisterium can and will critique philosophy.[9] The Magisterium's criticism of philosophy occurs only when (1) the error is serious; (2) it is a denial of revelation; and, moreover, (3) the intervention is aimed more at protecting ordinary believers than at correcting philosophical dis-

9. "It is neither the task nor the competence of the Magisterium to intervene in order to make good the lacunas of deficient philosophical discourse. Rather, it is the Magisterium's duty to respond clearly and strongly when controversial philosophical opinions threaten right understanding of what has been revealed, and when false and partial theories which sow the seed of serious error, confusing the pure and simple faith of the People of God, begin to spread more widely" (§50).

course. These limitations on the Magisterium's intervention in philosophy do not come merely from the fact that philosophers who deny the most basic tenets of revelation typically do not have faith and have no interest in the Magisterium's criticism, but from the nature of philosophical inquiry itself, which is autonomous because philosophy possesses the means to arrive at the truth proper to it.[10] If authority is not a constitutive part of the philosophical method, criticisms based on revelation and authority can do little to bring philosophy into harmony with reason. More effective in actually producing a union of faith and reason is to offer examples of philosophy that are persuasive according to philosophical method and yet that are consistent with revelation.

This positive approach of promoting philosophy compatible with revelation was part of Leo XIII's *Aeterni Patris* and its approval of the philosophy of Thomas Aquinas. Nevertheless, *Fides et ratio*, in commending philosophy compatible with revelation, will not focus on any one philosophy, such as that of Aquinas, or even on the medieval period in general. Instead of promoting a single philosophical system, *Fides et ratio* is advocating any number of philosophies compatible with faith because they are consistent with the general philosophy that recognizes metaphysics, nature, and universal ethical truths.[11]

10. "A philosophy which did not proceed in the light of reason according to its own principles and methods would serve little purpose. At the deepest level, the autonomy which philosophy enjoys is rooted in the fact that reason is by its nature orientated to truth and is equipped with the means necessary to arrive at truth" (§49).

"The Church follows the work of philosophers with interest and appreciation, and they should rest assured of her respect for the rightful autonomy of their discipline" (§106).

11. "Yet the Thomistic and neo-Thomistic revival was not the only sign of a resurgence of philosophical thought in culture of Christian inspiration. Earlier still, and parallel to Pope Leo's call, there had emerged a number of Catholic philosophers who, adopting more recent currents of thought and according to a specific method, produced philosophical works of great influence and lasting value. . . . From different quarters, then, modes of

If *Fides et ratio* has the advantage of promoting a philosophical pluralism rather than a single philosophy, it would also seem to have the disadvantage of promoting a vague and ambiguous general philosophy. Because of its abstractness, this philosophy is bound to be less inspiring than a single philosophy that is worked out in detail. Clarity and pluralism seem to be at odds here, and it is difficult to see the effectiveness of this invitation to a nameless and faceless philosophy. *Fides et ratio* does, however, show a recognition of this problem and gives this general philosophy both a name and a face.

The name by which this general and pluralistic philosophy becomes more concrete and inspirational is Christian philosophy:

... Christian Philosophy. In itself, the term is valid, but it should not be misunderstood: it in no way intends to suggest that there is an official philosophy of the Church, since the faith as such is not a philosophy. The term seeks rather to indicate a Christian way of philosophizing, a philosophical speculation conceived in dynamic union with faith. It does not therefore refer simply to a philosophy developed by Christian philosophers who have striven in their research not to contradict the faith. The term Christian philosophy includes those important developments of philosophical thinking which would not have happened without the direct or indirect contribution of Christian faith (§76).

There are several defining characteristics to Christian philosophy thus described. First, neither faith nor authority are part of the philosophical method: all conclusions are explained through reason and through principles that are accessible to natural powers. While a Christian philosopher may be also a theologian, Christian philosophy is distinct from theology because it is not methodologically dependent on revelation, faith, or authority. At the same time, philosophy is assisted accidentally—not essentially—through revelation.

---

philosophical speculation have continued to emerge and have sought to keep alive the great tradition of Christian thought which unifies faith and reason" (§59).

Faith may guide the philosopher to certain conclusions, but philosophy is not achieved until those conclusions are reached through rational means. Three examples of the indirect or accidental impact of Christian revelation on the history of philosophy, especially medieval philosophy, are cited: creation, the problem of evil, and the human being as spiritual (§76).

The term "Christian philosophy" was intensely debated earlier this century, especially by different versions of Thomism, and it has taken on a variety of meanings. The term has a general but definite meaning in *Fides et ratio*, and I think that it expresses much of what this encyclical is trying to promote. To summarize, there are two levels of meaning that go with the name "Christian philosophy," which is not Aquinas' term, although he does give a face to go with that name. The first and most general level has the face of Aquinas insofar as he articulated the relationship of philosophy to faith through the notion of revealed truths accessible to reason: the first level simply asserts that faith can indirectly or externally guide philosophy. The second and less general level consists of those elements that any complete Christian philosophy must include, such as metaphysics, universal ethics, and a concept of nature: it points to *where* revelation and philosophy meet. Aquinas is important here insofar as he exemplifies the necessity to explain these revealed truths accessible to reason through nature, metaphysics, and ethics. No less important to this understanding of Christian philosophy is the refusal of *Fides et ratio* to authorize a third level of Christian philosophy that identifies it with a particular philosophy, e.g., with the philosophy of Thomas Aquinas. The uniqueness of *Fides et ratio* is to posit the second level of meaning for Christian philosophy while leaving the third open. In this way, Aquinas can be used as a model for the union of faith and reason while simultaneously affirming a philosophical pluralism.

If the uniqueness of *Fides et ratio* is in its promotion of this second level of meaning to Christian philosophy, it is there too that the most serious questions arise, including the following: How do we know that truths such as the existence of God, creation *ex nihilo,* and the immortality of the soul are not merely revealed but accessible to reason? Revelation itself says nothing about these truths being accessible to reason. To put the question another way, how do we know *where* revelation and philosophy meet? Why should they meet in metaphysics? Why not merely in ethics, or solely in the area of hermeneutics and language? Perhaps the most forceful expression of the objection is to ask why we do not stop at the first level of meaning to Christian philosophy. In other words, we should assert that there is a point at which faith and reason meet, but it is up to the individual philosophies on the third level to decide the second level—*where* they meet. For some Christian philosophers, the second level will be metaphysics, for others ethics, for yet others both, and some will look to altogether different areas. According to this objection, to determine the second level independently of the third, as *Fides et ratio* does, is to give a non-philosophical answer to a philosophical question, and that is a failure to respect the autonomy of philosophy.

One answer to this question that we can find in *Fides et ratio* is the way that it uses the history of philosophy. The modern failure to look for a union between faith and reason in metaphysics, it is argued, has led not only to the separation of faith and reason, and not only to the diminishment of theology, but to the impoverishment of philosophy:

Abandoning the investigation of being, modern philosophical research has concentrated instead upon human knowing. Rather than make use of the human capacity to know the truth, modern philosophy has preferred to accentuate the ways in which this capacity is limited and conditioned.

This has given rise to different forms of agnosticism and relativism which have led philosophical research to lose its way in the shifting sands of widespread skepticism (§5).

The argument that revelation and philosophy meet in metaphysics is being made through philosophy in the sense that it is based on the history of philosophy, especially the history of modern philosophy. One might claim, however, that this is begging the question because it is imposing a medieval perspective on the post-medieval world, with the result that a rejection of metaphysics appears to be a disaster for philosophy: if the standard of philosophy is medieval, of course modern philosophy will be found deficient. This would be an easy objection to make if the view of modern philosophy in *Fides et ratio* were wholly negative, but it is not. No less complex than the medievalism of *Fides et ratio* is its view of modern philosophy. The account in *Fides et ratio* of reason's decline through its separation from faith during the modern and postmodern periods must be evaluated independently; for, if it is necessary to be alert to the question whether an anachronistic medieval standard is being used to judge modern and postmodern philosophy, it is equally true that there can be no *a priori* exclusion of the possibility that reason has suffered from this separation. The question of the medievalism in *Fides et ratio* is thus inseparable from the type of analysis provided by Timothy Sean Quinn's "Infides et Unratio: Modern Philosophy and the Papal Encyclical."[12]

12. See pp. 177–92 below.

INFIDES ET UNRATIO:
MODERN PHILOSOPHY AND
THE PAPAL ENCYCLICAL

TIMOTHY SEAN QUINN

In his popular novel, *The Name of the Rose,* Umberto Eco entertains the possibility that the reemergence of the fabled second half of Aristotle's *Poetics*—the part concerning comedy and laughter—ignites a spark that eventually consumes a Medieval monastic library and, symbolically, the entire edifice of pagan and Christian learning.[1] Imagine, then, to what deeds of splendid destruction Eco's mad librarian might have been inspired if, by some magic feat of time travel, he had received a rather advance copy of Immanuel Kant's *Religion within the Limits of Reason Alone,* or worse still, of Nietzsche's *The Anti-Christ?* Indeed, the so-called "modern" philosophy was, from its inception, not notorious for its devotion to religious orthodoxies. From the seventeenth through the nineteenth centuries, and even extending into our own, the main lines of philosophy were, in the words of one celebrated scholar of these matters, transfused by an

1. Umberto Eco, *The Name of the Rose,* trans. William Weaver (San Diego: Harcourt Brace Jovanovich, 1983).

"anti-theological ire" which pitted Athens against Jerusalem with a ferocity hitherto unknown. Although the pope's encyclical *Fides et ratio* directly addresses the situation of modern philosophy in relatively few pages, "the drama of the separation of faith and reason" provoked by modernity represents the historical context, and with it, the central motive, for this timely document.

Fides et ratio addresses the state of modern philosophy principally in chapters IV (§§45–49) and VII (§§86–91).[2] According to the document, what began in the work of late Medieval Aristotelians like Albert and St. Thomas as a "legitimate distinction" between philosophy and science, on the one hand, and revelation, on the other, degenerated into a "fateful separation." The "profound unity" of faith and reason was undermined "by systems which espoused the cause of rational knowledge sundered from faith and meant to take the place of faith" (§45). Hence, the verdict concerning modernity at the nerve of *Fides et ratio:* "Deprived of what Revelation offers, reason has taken sidetracks which expose it to the danger of losing sight of its final goal. Deprived of reason, faith has stressed feeling and experience, and so run the risk of no longer being a universal proposition" (§48). The divorce between faith and reason went through as planned, but the children died from lack of support.

This verdict is in the main true of the central protagonists in philosophy from the seventeenth through the nineteenth centuries. But the "fateful separation" of faith from reason did not have to await the rise of the great philosophical systems of the nineteenth century— the Kantian and the Hegelian come to mind. From its inception, the "modern" philosophy understood itself less as a quest for wisdom than as a project of emancipation from any authority, natural or supernatural, to which human reason had allowed itself to become

2. All references are to the Vatican translation published by the Daughters of St. Paul (Boston, 1999).

subject. Kant, writing at the close of the Enlightenment, summarizes the matter nicely. "What is enlightenment?" he asks:

Enlightenment is man's emergence from his self-incurred immaturity. Immaturity is the inability to use one's own understanding without guidance of another. This immaturity is *self-incurred* if its cause is not lack of understanding, but lack of resolution and courage to use it without guidance of another. The motto of enlightenment is therefore: *Sapere aude!* Have the courage to use your own understanding![3]

The "other" whose guidance would no longer be welcome was in particular the Church. Thus, central to this emancipatory aim was the need to replace the "false" rationality of the Middle Ages with a "true" rationality that would sustain the autonomy of reason. Since that false rationality was characterized by its subordination to faith, liberating reason from faith became a primary goal of modern philosophy.

But the founders of Enlightenment found that they could not confront Jerusalem directly, lest their project run afoul of the political authority of the Church. To take one celebrated instance: Descartes, writing in Part VI of his *Discourse on Method,* admits that the trial of Galileo sufficed to restrain him—temporarily, at least—from publishing his own physical treatise, *La Monde,* since "persons to whom I defer, and whose authority over my actions cannot be less than that of my reason over my thoughts," had disapproved of it. A delicious irony, that, since Descartes manages to admit that the Church holds sway *only* over his actions. He'll manage to think what he likes. When, a few sentences later, he reveals that he was forced to move ahead with publication in spite of his fears of the Inquisition, in order to avoid "greatly sinning against the law that teaches us to procure as best we can the common good of humanity," Descartes allows

3. Kant, *Beantwortung der Frage: Was ist Aufklarung?* In *Gesammelte Schriften* (Berlin: Konigliche Preussischen Akademie der Wissenschaften, 1900ff.) volume VIII, 35.

the careful reader to draw the obvious conclusion: the Church has
sinned against the law of humanitarianism by impeding the progress
of the new science.[4] In an earlier acknowledgment of the Church's
moral authority in Part III of his *Discourse*, Descartes recommends
obedience to the Church but consigns such obedience to a "provisional morality," that is, one that will be replaced once modern science is in full swing.[5]

A criticism of Church authority is of course not equal to a criticism of faith, as difficult as it may be to pry them apart. Yet, on the
latter score, Descartes is no less veiled in his criticism. In Part I of his
Discourse, he acknowledges that he wished to go to heaven as much as
the next man; but "having noticed that the road [to salvation] is no
less open to the most ignorant than to the most learned, and that the
revealed truths leading to it are beyond our understanding. . . . I
judged that to succeed in this endeavor one needed extraordinary
assistance from heaven, and to be more than a man."[6] Of course,
Descartes is correct, to an extent: the revealed truths are in some sense
beyond our understanding, else they would not have to be revealed.
But he concludes by implying that theology is not a legitimate human
pursuit: "it is beyond our power." Here we begin to touch the nerve of
the modern "anti-theological ire." It has less to do with annoyance at
apparent excesses of Papal authority than it does with the perception
that Christianity has, in effect, set the bar too high; that by allowing
reason to be held in sway by faith, it has bled humanity of power
over its own destiny; that it is, in effect, dehumanizing.

A harsh judgment, to be sure, but one that could not be made
explicit. Unable to join this argument directly with the Church,

---

4. Descartes, *Discourse on Method,* in *Oeuvres* (Paris: Vrin, 1964ff.), vol. VI: 60–61. Subsequent references to the *Discourse* are to this edition, here cited AT.

5. Descartes, AT 23.

6. Descartes, AT 8.

Descartes, Bacon, Hobbes, Locke, and others took a different tack: they could undermine the Aristotelianism that had, after St. Thomas, come to infuse Christian theology. By thus attacking theology's rational core, theology would perforce collapse: reason would win its divorce from faith. But that meant that the modern philosophy could not simply return to a pre-Christian or "ancient" mode of reason, neutral to faith, which was indeed an option for it. That Aristotle was no proto-Christian was perfectly evident from the polemic surrounding the rise of Averroism—and hence Aristotelianism—in the West during the thirteenth century. On the other hand, Aristotle could still stand accused by the founders of Enlightenment of having achieved a philosophical system that could not militate against takeover by revealed religion. If revelation and theology were to go, or at least be contained, Aristotle would have to go first.

The philosophers of the Enlightenment thus do not simply provoke a conflict between Athens and Jerusalem. They foment civil war within Athens itself. Perhaps the most conspicuous arena of combat was the Aristotelian doctrine of final causality, or teleology: the doctrine that things come to be or occur for the sake of an end or good. This doctrine, in the hands of Medieval philosophers and theologians, had been used to great effect in demonstrating the existence of a providential Deity. St. Thomas, for example, declares in the *Summa Theologica* that the most pervasive evidence of Divine Providence in the world is nature's guidance by final causes.[7] Bacon, by contrast, in his *Advancement of Learning*, accuses Aristotle of having imported metaphysics and theology into the study of nature by means of his doctrine of final causality.[8] In a bolder statement from his *New*

7. See for example *Summa Theologica* I, q. 22, a. 2: "Cum ergo nihil aliud sit Dei providentia quam ratio ordinis rerum in finem, ut dictum est, necesse est omnia, inquantum participant esse, intantum subdi divinae providentiae."

8. Bacon, "Of the Dignity and Advancement of Learning," in *Works*, vol. 3 (Cambridge: Taggard and Thompson, 1863), 508–10: "For the handling of final causes in

Organon, Bacon argues that final causality is in fact neither a natural nor a supernatural but a human sort of cause, a projection of restless minds in search of reasons, and an imputation of order to nature where there is none.[9] The extent to which the new science will do away with final causality as an explanation for the natural order is the extent to which it will remain "metaphysically neutral," if not downright hostile to metaphysical inquiry. And metaphysics, by the seventeenth century, had become in effect code for theology, as Bacon's criticism reveals. Liberation from any supernatural order would henceforth require a tandem liberation from a teleological natural order.

This withdrawal of final causes from the understanding of non-human nature was not, however, met with a corresponding withdrawal on the level of human action and passion. For this conceptual sort of autonomy from guidance of any suprahuman authority was part and parcel of the attempt to secure a genuine autonomy for human beings, and final redemption from the human estate. Thus, the emancipatory project of early modern philosophy culminates, in the words of Bacon and Descartes, in the mastery of nature.[10] The terms

---

physics has driven away and overthrown the diligent inquiry of physical causes, and made men to stay with shadowy causes . . . to the great arrest and prejudice of science. . . . And therefore the natural philosophy of Democritus and others, who removed God and Mind from the structure of things . . . seems to me . . . to have been, as regards physical causes, much more solid and to have penetrated much further into nature than that of Aristotle and Plato; for this single reason, that the former never wasted time on final causes, while the latter were ever inculcating them." Aristotle, Bacon continues, "is more to be blamed than Plato" in this regard.

9. Bacon, *Novum Organum,* §48: "The human understanding is restless; it cannot stop or rest, but presses on, though in vain. . . . Thus it is that in reaching out for things further away, it falls back upon nearer ones, namely final causes, which have relation entirely to human nature rather than to the universe, and have thus corrupted philosophy to an extraordinary degree" (*Works,* I). Compare §45 and §65.

10. Bacon, *The Great Instauration,* "The Plan of the Work," 2; Descartes, *Discourse on Method,* Part VI.

in which Descartes, for one, glosses mastery are instructive: the alleviation of labor, and the indefinite extension of human life—fruits of mastery that evoke the penalties of original sin. The message is clear. Where Christianity has failed, modern science will prevail. Divorcing faith from reason will empower humanity to gain control over its own destiny.

This effort was not, of course, restricted to modern natural science. It came to inform modern political science as well. In fact, the original provocation to the modern scientific project of mastery of nature can be traced, arguably, to the Machiavellian admonition to master *"fortuna"* on behalf of the preservation of political power. Hobbesian and Lockean "state of nature" doctrines that would serve as a basis for modern understandings of natural right and individualism, for example, accepted the modern scientific understanding of nature as a goal-less, indifferent mechanism: the "freedom" and "equality" natural to humanity were premised upon a non-teleological view of nature. To this degree, modern political science was, at the very least, "theologically neutral," if not downright hostile to meddling from theology. Although a vestigal notion of Divine Providence may linger in the Lockean assumption of a "hidden hand" in nature, for example, it is also clear—as Locke himself suggests—that a Biblical foundation for political life would culminate not in civil society but in a state of war.[11] This understanding of political life, non-teleological and non-theological, wedded to the notion of *scientia propter potentiam,* rendered politics instrumental to the project of human emancipation: the liberal regime came to be seen as the sole context in which mastery of nature could flourish. It has been this collusion between science and politics, so potent for good and for ill,

11. See Locke's Second Treatise, *Of Civil Government,* chapter V, §25, where he points out that the biblical notion that God has given the earth to mankind in common is in collision with the very possibility of property necessary for human preservation.

which has made the human future virtually incalculable, as the events of our own century attest.

There was of course a price to be paid for this newfound power. Reason, having come to be restricted to mathematical-scientific uses, neutral to ends or goods, would find itself subordinated to the satisfaction of passions, alone productive of ends for humanity. Reason would, in short, become merely a tool. Or, resisting such reduction, it would resolve to construct systems which could preserve reason's autonomy by serving as surrogates for nature or God, as is revealed by the Enlightenment's subsequent fate in Kant and Hegel. Of course, modern philosophy is not a monolith, no more than was Medieval philosophy, and its story is much richer than what has been outlined here. Nonetheless, the paradoxical effect of modern philosophy has been its liberation of potent currents of irrationalism that have deprived reason of its sovereignty over human life and action. The wages reason paid to ransom itself from faith are the theme of *Fides et ratio*'s discussion of modern philosophy.

Fides et ratio diagnoses a sextet of malaises that by and large emerge in the nineteenth century, in consequence of the Enlightenment: idealism, atheistic humanism, scientific positivism, pragmatism, eclecticism and, finally, nihilism. The first case, idealism, represents an attempt to "transform faith and its contents ... into dialectical structures which could be grasped by reason" (§46). In this instance the pope most likely has in mind Hegel, for whom the phenomena of the Incarnation and Redemption represent Reason's sovereign attempt to comprehend and heal the breach between its "otherworldly" tendency toward self-conscious reflection, and its bondage to the particular and to natural necessities.[12] Christianity so construed

---

12. See the discussion in Emil Fackenheim, *The Religious Dimension in Hegel's Thought* (Bloomington: Indiana University Press, 1967), especially chapter 6, "The Transfiguation of Faith into Philosophy."

comes less to be rejected out of hand than to be absorbed as a moment or stage of reason's own self-disclosure—a view that, at best, places Christianity beyond any confessional differences, and at worst makes nugatory the very notion of faith. The evil twin of idealism, atheistic humanism, turns on the judgment that faith is simply alienating and therewith damaging to reason. This judgment, the pope observes, did not prevent various humanisms from appropriating the mantle of religion for themselves, presenting themselves as humane alternatives to Christianity and calling for a new sort of devotion to the project of human emancipation. The resulting parade of "disastrous totalitarian projects of our own century"—Stalinism comes to mind—has its roots in these emancipatory humanitarian projects.

Scientific positivism represents a third modern philosophical pathology. In this event, the claims of reason come to be narrowed to the sphere of positive science. Aesthetic, moral, and especially metaphysical issues are thus excluded from the charmed circle of rationality— relegated, in a word, to the domain of irrational and subjective "values" over and against the demonstrable articles of "fact." More dire, however, is the service to which these "facts" are put: the technological mastery of nature, now unguided by any knowledge beyond what is necessary to produce these technologies (§§46, 88). "Pragmatism" is the name the pope gives to the political expression of this positivist tendency to the utilitarian (§89). Pragmatism, according to the document, precludes any appeal to theoretical considerations, to ethical principles or "unchanging values," when framing political judgments. Liberalism is the principal but unnamed perpetrator here: unwedded to "unchanging values," liberalism has come to eschew moral decisions for institutional mandates. Pragmatism thus construed shares with scientific positivism a "metaphysical neutrality," the effect of which is to reduce human beings to the level of machines, and human desires to strictly utilitarian or commercial ends.

"Eclecticism" and nihilism are the last two malaises to which *Fides et ratio* draws attention. Eclecticism emerges principally as "an error of method": it is the tendency to treat philosophical ideas out of context, and to patch them together without regard either to their internal coherence or to the conceptual baggage they might carry—the history of philosophy as Chinese menu, if you will (§86). The indiscriminacy with which eclecticism picks and chooses among ideas is not only a threat to rational precision. It suggests as well that the interesting is of greater moment than the true.[13] Eclecticism has its counterpart in historicism, that is, in the conviction that truth is determined by and restricted to "the spirit of an age" and its unique historical situation. Historicism effectively denies "the enduring validity of truth" (§87). In theological reflection, the pope observes, historicism generally appears in the guise of "modernism," or in the unqualified preference for contemporary over traditional concepts and distinctions. In the domain of philosophy, though, its consequences are more dire: historicism sets the stage for nihilism, or "the denial of all foundations and the negation of all objective truth" (§90). This denial has severe human consequences: "a denial of the humanity and of the very identity of the human being." Such a denial culminates either in the apotheosis of "a destructive will to power" or of "a solitude without hope"—alternatives that allude, respectively, to Nietzsche and to Sartre. For "once the truth is denied to human beings, it is pure illusion to try to set them free." Nihilism emerges, in short, when the modern emancipatory projects collapse.

Nihilism in this wise is inseparable from the goals of idealism,

---

13. Consider, for example, the nihilistic aesthete of Kierkegaard's *Either/Or,* Book I; the origin of this conception though can be traced to Kant's doctrine of the aesthetic "state of mind" in his third *Critique.*

atheistic humanism, and scientific and political positivisms. Nihilism emerges, on the one hand, from the failure of modern philosophical attempts to liberate humanity from any overarching natural or supernatural orders that might fetter humanity's control over its own destiny. On the other hand, its immediate provocation is historicism and its implicit denial of the objectivity of truth, or of knowledge that could transcend the immanent human situation. But nihilism's consequences are more far reaching than those of the movements that empowered its rise—a fact evident in the complex of literary and philosophical movements grouped under the name "postmodernism." While "postmodernism," the pope admits, is a difficult phenomenon to comprehend in any summary way, it nonetheless seems to entail, in certain of its manifestations, a conviction that the time for rational certainties has ended; that human beings have therewith been reduced to living "in a horizon of total absence of meaning," wherein "everything is provisional and ephemeral" (§91). The pope admits as well that there is potent attraction to this view of the human situation: "the terrible experience of evil" in our age must tempt even the most reasonable souls to despair. Unfortunately, the solutions to such despair available within modernity are limited. The pope indeed points with approval to certain salutary "discoveries" of modern philosophy—the philosophy of language, logic and epistemology, "the more penetrating analysis of the affective dimensions of knowledge and the existential approach to the analysis of freedom" (§91). However, the principal alternative to nihilistic despair has been sought in scientific positivisms which, while cleaving to notions of truth and objectivity, incline to the view that "man and woman may live as a demiurge, single-handedly and completely taking charge of their destiny" through the agency of modern natural science (§91). In all, *Fides et ratio* pronounces modern philosophic reason "affirmative of the principle of immanence," guilty of liberating profound currents of irrationalism. Reason's failure to satisfy "the baseless demand" that it "be absolutely self-grounded" has led to the abandonment of reason altogether.

Suffice to say that while the foundations are crumbling over at Athens, the news is no less bleak back in Jerusalem. Under the sway of what the pope calls "phenomenalism"—a sort of *esse est percipi,* "to be is to be perceived," cast of mind—faith has become increasingly a matter of personal experience and subjective certainty, less and less a matter of rational assent. We note in passing that the two modern religious thinkers who seem to garner the most universal respect—Pascal and Kierkegaard—were notorious critics of reason. This tendency toward the personal is intensified by the gradual separation of faith and theology from any basis in metaphysics. Given the "metaphysical neutrality," if not hostility, of much of modern philosophy, little light is to be hoped for from that quarter. In fact, how could it be otherwise? The regnant modern philosophical movements, having abandoned any provocation by faith, find no compelling reason to pursue metaphysical inquiries, especially when such inquiries jeopardize the apotheosis of the human latent in modern emancipatory projects. No faith, in short, no metaphysics; and with no metaphysics, faith comes to seek refuge in private experience.

Now, it is useful to note at this juncture something of the logic of the pope's argument. The six named aspects of modern philosophic reason group themselves into three pairs, each pair emphasizing a particular core problem. Idealism and atheistic humanism share a tendency to absorb the idea of religion into the domain of philosophy, and thus in highly secularized forms. They represent a failure of transcendence or of metaphysics. Scientific positivism and pragmatism share a reduction of reason to instrumental uses, and therewith truncate the scope of human moral involvement with the world—a moral or ethical failure. Finally, eclectic historicism and nihilism share a basis in denying the possibility of truth—a failure of knowledge, so to speak, that culminates in the collapse of the entire horizon of human meaning. The pope's diagnosis of the situation of modern rationality thus points to three preeminent areas of concern: metaphysics, ethics, and epistemology. Of course, these three areas intertwine. The scientific-pragmatic tendency to instrumentality, for example, is as much a metaphysical and epistemological problem as it is an ethical one. Similarly, the despair into which nihilism throws humanity is as much a metaphysical and moral dilemma as it is an epistemological one, and nihilism is in fact unintelligible apart from the attempt by the other tendencies of modern thought to secure human autonomy and final redemption from the human estate. To this extent, nihilism represents a culmination, the inevitable consequence of the attempt to establish reason's autonomy from any authority extrinsic to itself. Nihilistic despair, in turn, encourages the tendency to seek solace in utilitarian or commercial modes of satisfaction—it encourages a liberalism without conviction. Perhaps the deepest issue that *Fides et ratio* wishes to expose, though, is the corrosion of any metaphysical basis for human life and thought. Not only does the loss of metaphysics deprive reason of any transcendent foundation. As well, it secures faith's abolition from reason.

This verdict on the fate of reason divorced from faith invites several important questions. One of the most obvious ones is whether the pope's diagnosis of modern philosophy is apt—a question unanswerable within the confines of this paper. To resolve it, one must engage in the sort of careful study of the history of philosophy which *Fides et ratio* recommends as an antidote to eclecticism. To that end, a few preparatory observations are in order.

To begin, it is useful to consider that however dire the progress of modern philosophy may seem, the founding generation of modern philosophers may have had compelling reason to oppose the intrusion of faith into the domain of philosophy. First of all, the much-vaunted synthesis between faith and reason was never as seamless as all that. In the final analysis, one would have to come out on top. It is, after all, Tertullian's rejection of philosophy that led him to coin the phrase "Athens and Jerusalem" at the very outset of the Middle Ages. And it was after St. Thomas that St. Bonaventure condemned philosophy as the very "tree of the knowledge of good and evil."[14] During the Middle Ages, three capital issues came to dominate the intellectual scene: the notion of creation, the existence of a providential God and of divine foreknowledge, and the immortality of the individual soul. It was on these three questions that faith and reason parted company—and not because philosophers doubted the truth of these key doctrines, although some did, but only because they periodically questioned their demonstrability. Yet even delaying assent to these doctrines—to the notion that God is intimately involved with the world in both knowledge and action, and metes out justice in the next—would leave theology in shambles. As a result, and especially in the regnant Scholasticism that confronted the founders of Enlightenment, Medieval theology and philosophy, coming to acquire a rather dogmatic tone which, over time, diminished the role of reason to dialectical or argumentative uses, all but abandoned insight into the fundamental issues that provoked the arguments of the Schools in the first place. The spirit of genuine inquiry—what in Socratic philosophy is the "erotic" character of reason—was, if not lost, then badly hampered by theological dogmatism. It must therefore have seemed to Bacon and others that by attacking the intrusion of faith into the domain of reason, they were doing reason an enormous favor, restoring inquiry to its proper sphere in human life by restoring its skeptical impulse.

14. St. Bonaventure, "Third Sunday of Advent," Sermon 2, in *Opera Omnia* IX.62–3.

That said, it is equally useful to note that early modern philosophy decays rather rapidly into dogmatisms of its own. The radical skepticism of a Descartes, for example, had its counterpart in an equally radical dogmatism, the discovery of unshakable certitudes that could serve as a foundation for both a new natural science and a new science of politics. These certitudes were however achieved only at great price, the price of turning reason away from the speculative quest for first principles and turning it to knowledge "within our power," as Descartes puts it, and therewith to what is "useful for life"—by, in effect, lowering the goal of reason. In this, modern rationality may indeed have been prepared by the subordination of reason to faith within Medieval theology and philosophy. On the other hand, it was precisely because Medieval thought took seriously the natural bent of reason toward consideration of first things, as well as its natural skepticism, that it could insist on reason's subordination to and guidance by faith. In the final analysis, reason enjoyed greater authority to guide human life during the period of its subordination to faith than in that period that strove to assert its autonomy from faith.

In this light, we may say that the problem with modern philosophy was never its unwillingness to accept the various Medieval solutions to the Athens-Jerusalem question. It was, rather, its view of having settled the question once and for all to the exclusion of Jerusalem. During the Middle Ages, the conflict between reason and revelation was never a contest between rival "systems" of thought, Biblical and Aristotelian, say, but between an inevitably dogmatic theology and a particular sort of philosophical skepticism. With the advent of modern philosophy, the contest shifts to one between a theological dogmatism and a new sort of "scientific" dogmatism. In a war of dogmatisms, will, not reason, typically decides the issue. Some of the irrationalism that *Fides et ratio* ascribes to modern philosophy may indeed prescind from the latter's dogmatic opposition even to holding open the question as to the harmony of faith and reason.

We thus return to *Fides et ratio*. Whatever else we may learn from this document, we should be grateful for its ability to awaken a question slumbering within the Western tradition. By inviting us to consider that modern science has not inevitably replaced God and that history has not replaced rational reflection, *Fides et ratio* performs as great a service for theology as it does for philosophy. If we take up this invitation to think once again about this most important question, we may discover, as did our Medieval forebears, that we live in a world transfused with divine and human meaning.

FAITH AND REASON: FROM VATICAN I TO JOHN PAUL II

AVERY CARDINAL DULLES, S.J.

John Paul II's encyclical of September 14, 1998, on "Faith and Reason" takes up a theme that has been a staple of Western theology since at least the time of Augustine in the fourth century. St. Anselm in the twelfth century and St. Thomas Aquinas, in the thirteenth, argued brilliantly for the harmony between faith and reason. The medieval synthesis, already wounded by the inroads of fourteenth-century Nominalism, was sharply contested from two sides in the seventeenth and eighteenth centuries. At one extreme were self-assured rationalists, who belittled the role of faith, and at the other, skeptical fideists, who distrusted the powers of reason. Since some Catholic thinkers of the early nineteenth century were tainted by these two errors, the Roman Magisterium issued condemnations of both rationalism and fideism. The official Catholic position was most authoritatively summarized in 1870 by the First Vatican Council in its Dogmatic Constitution on Catholic Faith, which contained a chapter dedicated to the theme of faith and reason.

Without actually mentioning Thomas Aquinas, Vatican I endorsed his position. A decade later, in 1879, Pope Leo XIII published his encyclical *Aeterni Patris,* proposing St. Thomas as the thinker whose synthesis of faith and reason should be accepted as a solid foundation from which to grapple with more recent questions in philosophy and science.

In the first half of the twentieth century the popes issued a number of further condemnations and admonitions relevant to our question. Early in the century Pius X repudiated the agnostic and historicist theses of Modernism. After World War I, Pius XI censured Marxist Communism for its materialist determinism. Pius XII in 1950 cautioned against the *nouvelle théologie* of the day, in which he detected a tendency toward historicism and dogmatic relativism.

At the Second Vatican Council, in 1962–1965, the problem no longer seemed acute. The Council, displaying a measure of historical consciousness, acknowledged the need to understand the Gospel with all the tools of contemporary scholarship and to proclaim it in ways adapted to existing cultural situations (GS 44, 62). But at the same time it declared that there were unchanging realities and permanent truths (GS 10; DH 3). In the course of its treatment of the autonomy of science and culture, it reaffirmed the teaching of Vatican I on the distinction between the "two orders" of faith and reason (GS 59). Elsewhere Vatican II praised Thomas Aquinas for having given glorious witness to the harmony of faith and reason (GE 10). But these were only passing and disconnected remarks. Vatican II gave no sustained attention to our theme; it was remarkably silent about the role of reason in preparing for the assent of faith—a point that had been of acute concern to the Fathers at Vatican I and to Pius XII.

Since the acrimonious debates of earlier centuries had evidently subsided, Pope John Paul II could easily have left the problem in a state of benign neglect. If he did wish to speak on the subject, he might have been expected simply to enlarge upon the positions of Vatican I, very much as Leo XIII had done in his encyclical on Thomistic philosophy in 1879. But instead, he addressed the problem in a strikingly new way.

The present pope does not, of course, contradict Vatican I. In fact, he quotes or refers to its Constitution on Catholic Faith in favorable terms at least ten times at various points spanning the entire encyclical.[1] He takes over from Vatican I the familiar ideas that reason has the power to establish the existence of God and the preambles of Christian faith (§§53, 67), that faith confirms truths that reason can cannot grasp except with great difficulty (§43), that faith also embraces mysteries that lie entirely beyond the range of unaided reason (§§8, 9), and that reason can render even these revealed mysteries to some degree intelligible (§83). In line with Vatican I, the pope teaches that the Magisterium has the right and duty to condemn philosophical tenets that are opposed to truths of faith (§55, fn. 72), and that there can be no conflict between faith and reason, since both are gifts of the same God, who could never contradict himself (§§8, 53). Also in the footsteps of Vatican I, John Paul II opposes both a rationalism that dismisses the input of faith and a fideism that distrusts the guidance of reason (§§52, 53). He repeats the teaching of Vatican I that faith and reason "mutually support each other" (§100).

Notwithstanding these important continuities, there are striking differences between the approaches of Vatican I and John Paul II. They are speaking to radically diverse situations. At the time of Vatican I, the issues within the Church were rather clearly drawn. At one end of the spectrum were rationalists and semi-rationalists who professed exorbitant confidence in the powers of unaided reason to fath-

---

1. Ten references are listed by Kenneth L. Schmitz in his "Faith and Reason: Then and Now," *Communio* 26 (1999): 595–608, at 598, note 9. He seems to have overlooked the quotation from *Dei Filius* in *Fides et ratio* 9.

om the depths of reality and who regarded faith as unreliable and unnecessary for educated persons. At the other end were fideists and traditionalists who denied the capacity of the intellect to attain truths of a moral or metaphysical nature and who entrusted themselves to faith as a blind movement of emotion or volition or a passive conformity to tradition. Rationalism was more at home in Germany; fideism, in France.

Vatican I, recognizing elements of truth and falsehood in both rationalism and fideism, adopted a mediating position. Against the fideists it affirmed that reason, by its natural powers, could establish the foundations of faith and the credibility of the Christian revelation (DS 3019, 3033). And against the rationalists Vatican I attributed the full assurance of the act of faith to the power of divine grace enlightening the intellect and inspiring the will (DS 3010). The act was therefore reasonable without being a deliverance of pure reason.

By the end of the twentieth century, the proud boasts of autonomous reason, setting itself up against the claims of faith, had been severely muted. The prevailing mood was one of metaphysical agnosticism. Some intellectuals, clinging to a remnant of rationalism, professed a scientism that restricted genuine knowledge to the sphere of measurable physical realities. Logical positivists dismissed all statements not verifiable by experience as "noncognitive" deliverances of emotion, convention, or simple caprice.

In summary, therefore, the rationalist mentality hardly survives today except in the spheres of mathematics, logic, and empirical science. Philosophy, for its part, has practically abandoned the pursuit of transcendent or metaphysical truth. It has narrowed its horizons to the spheres of shifting phenomena, linguistic study, the interpretation of texts, and pragmatic strategies for coping with radical pluralism.

In this situation John Paul II sees no need to restrain the excessive claims of pure reason. Unlike Vatican I he refrains from lamentations and angry condemnations. In the spirit of Vatican II, he prefers to use what Pope John XXIII called "the medicine of mercy."[2] He sees himself as a friend and ally, called to help philosophy to extricate itself from its present state of impoverishment. He exhorts it to recover its original vocation of being a quest for wisdom, as is implied in the very name *philo-sophia,* which means love of wisdom (§§3, 6). This positive stance harmonizes with the tendency of the Second Vatican Council to depict the Church as a partner in the struggles of humanity at large, including its search for truth (§2; cf. GS 16).

Whereas Vatican I spoke in authoritative and judgmental tones, John Paul II, seeking to establish a common ground with all sincere seekers, situates himself by the side of sincere inquirers. The philosophical quest, as he sees it, begins from below, where experience gives rise to questions. All philosophy, he remarks, begins in wonder (§4). The mind ineluctably asks about the meaning of life in the face of suffering and inevitable death (§26). In language reminiscent of Augustine the pope detects in the human heart "a desire to know the truth," (Preface), which he later calls "a seed of desire and nostalgia for God" (§24). Giving scope to this impulse, he interprets the search for wisdom as a pilgrimage or journey of discovery, much along the lines of Bonaventure in his *Itinerary of the Mind to God* (§§33, 105).

The pope's rhetoric is strikingly different from that of the Magisterium in the nineteenth century. Vatican I had called for a submission to the authority of God who reveals; it stressed the obligation of the individual to believe whatever is contained in the word of God and certified by the Magisterium. John Paul II, by contrast, adopts the posture of a physician helping a patient on the road to recovery.

2. John XXIII, "Gaudet Mater Ecclesia," in *The Documents of Vatican II,* ed. Walter M. Abbott and Joseph Gallagher (New York: America Press, 1966), 716.

He portrays the truth of revelation as a fulfillment of the universal human quest for meaning and truth. At the point where reason begins to falter, faith comes to its aid and lights its way.

The pastoral and dialogic tone of John Paul's encyclical has its roots in his own personalist philosophy. In agreement with twentieth-century Jewish philosophers, such as Martin Buber and Emmanuel Lévinas,[3] he is convinced that friendship and dialogue can best sustain reason in its search for truth (§33). Among the merits of contemporary philosophy the pope points out its welcome emphasis on personhood and subjectivity (§48). But subjectivity should not be confused with subjectivism; it is in no way opposed to metaphysics. On the contrary, he says, "the person constitutes a privileged locus for the encounter with being, and hence with metaphysical inquiry" (§83). Metaphysics makes it possible to ground the concept of personal dignity in the spiritual nature of the person.

John Paul II professes a personalist doctrine of faith. Whereas Vatican I had described faith in terms of a faculty psychology as a submission of intellect and will, John Paul II prefers to describe it as a decision engaging the whole person (§13). Knowledge through belief, he asserts, develops in a context of personal trust. The witness of the martyrs inspires confidence and requires no lengthy arguments in order to convince. "The martyrs," he writes, "stir in us a profound trust because they give voice to what we already feel and they declare what we would like to have the strength to express" (§32).

The present pope's emphasis on testimony and dialogue differs markedly from the "scientific" apologetics found in the Scholastic manuals inspired by the First Vatican Council. Whereas they relied heavily on objective evidence, and on miracles as exceptions to the laws of nature, the present pope makes no explicit mention of mira-

---

3. John Paul II discusses the personalism of Buber and Lévinas in *Crossing the Threshold of Hope* (New York: Alfred A. Knopf, 1994), 35–36.

cles and prophecies. He refers instead to "signposts of the Spirit," which invite the mind to explore hidden truths.[4] Where Vatican I spoke of the "evident credibility" of the Christian religion (DS 3013), John Paul II speaks of the need to discern the signs of revelation in the context of interpersonal communication (§13). Here as elsewhere, the pope does not contradict the earlier teaching; he simply adopts a different angle of approach and a new emphasis.

Whereas Vatican I and the popes who followed it relied principally on the medieval Scholastics as sources, John Paul II gives at least equal emphasis to Holy Scripture and the Church Fathers. His second chapter, dealing with revelation, deals at some length with the Wisdom literature of the Old Testament and its echoes in the Pauline letters. He opens his chapter on the relationship between faith and reason (chapter 4) with a discussion of Paul and the Acts of the Apostles, and follows this with a survey of patristic thinking from Justin and Clement to the Cappadocians and Augustine. The Fathers, he concludes, were highly original in welcoming the unlimited dynamism of reason and infusing it with a richness drawn from revelation (§41).

The biblical and patristic predilections of John Paul II affect his categories of thought and language. The vocabulary of Vatican I was Scholastic and abstract. Concerned with universal essences, that Council spoke in an undifferentiated way of "natural reason" (DS 3015), without reference to any historical or cultural context. John Paul II, by contrast, gives close attention to the concrete factors of history and culture. The wisdom tradition of Israel, in his estimation, did not arise through revelation alone; it preserved insights from the ancient cultures of Egypt and Mesopotamia (§16). In referring to

4. For the expression "signposts of the Spirit," see John Paul II, Audience before the Angelus at Castel Gondolfo, September 26, 1999, *L'Osservatore Romano* (English weekly edition), 29 September 1999, p. 1.

philosophical wisdom, the pope does not focus exclusively on the Greco-Roman heritage. Philosophy, he notes, is found in less abstract and technical forms in every great culture, from the ancient Near East to present-day India and Japan (§72).

In view of their different orientations, Vatican I and John Paul II treat tradition in characteristically different ways. Vatican I speaks only briefly of tradition, affirming that it is received from Christ and the apostles and that it belongs to the deposit of faith, of which the Church is the infallible custodian (DS 3006, 3011, 3020). This way of speaking suggests that tradition is something passively received and impervious to change or development.

Vatican II, however, made it clear that apostolic tradition continually develops in the Church with the help of the Holy Spirit (DV 8) and takes different forms in different cultures (UR 14–17). Consistently with this teaching, John Paul II asserts that the content of revelation has been progressively unfolded in the course of the centuries (§65) and that the faith has been differently handed on in different cultural contexts (§71). Tradition, therefore, has always employed the help of concepts and thought-forms drawn from particular philosophical currents (§65). While extolling the merits of the great philosophical tradition that comes down to us from the Greeks, the pope does not see it as a closed chapter. The philosophical tradition, he contends, can be further developed by dialogue with the religious and philosophical traditions of other civilizations, such as those of India, China, and Japan, as well as the traditional cultures of Africa, which are for the most part orally transmitted (§72).

Vatican I adopted a two-stage schematism in which reason, with its natural powers, provided a firm platform upon which faith, as a supernatural gift, could be erected. According to this schema, philosophy, as a work of pure reason, comes first, and theology, as a rational reflection on faith, follows (DS 3015–16). Philosophy, for Vatican I, was a perfectible construct of human ingenuity, but the doctrine of faith was a divine trust that God had committed to the Church to be faithfully preserved and expounded (DS 3020).

John Paul II softens this dualism of reason and faith. In the Wisdom literature of the Old Testament, he points out, we find a harmonious fusion of philosophy and theology. In the biblical Wisdom literature and in the Greek and Latin Fathers, he shows, no sharp distinction was made. The profound unity between the two disciplines, preserved until after the time of St. Thomas, has regrettably been eroded in recent centuries (§48).

John Paul II does not reject the hard-won distinctions between reason and faith, philosophy and theology. He even quotes Vatican I to the effect that "faith is superior to reason" (§53; cf. DS 3017). But when he speaks in his own name he shows a marked preference for circular images. "The relationship between theology and philosophy," he writes, "is best construed as a circle" (§73). God's word comes to meet the human quest for truth, and is itself best understood with the help of philosophy. The revealed word keeps philosophy from going astray and at the same time stirs philosophy to explore new paths that it would not have discovered without revelation. Reason and faith, therefore, are not competitors. Each, according to the pope, contains the other (§17). The simultaneity of faith and reason in the pope's thinking makes him reluctant to speak of either in isolation. As he puts it in the preamble to the encyclical, "Faith and reason are like two wings on which the human spirit rises to the contemplation of truth." The implication would seem to be that truth is unattainable without both together.

Revelation and reason, for John Paul II, are two different paths, neither sufficient unto itself. Revelation perfects the work of reason in its quest for ultimate truth. Faith and reason converge as they turn toward Jesus Christ, the eternal Word of God, who is both Creator and Redeemer. As the Word or Logos, he is the light of reason, and as incarnate Son he reveals the depth of the divinity, making it accessible to faith. The unity of all truth, natural and revealed, is found in a living and personal way in Christ himself (§34). The Christocentricity of *Fides et ratio* stands in marked contrast to what we might call the theocentricity of Vatican I.

Philosophical wisdom and theological wisdom, according to John Paul II, have a deep affinity because both of them aim to explore reality in terms of its ultimate principles. They are two forms of acquired wisdom. But both of them, he notes, can be perfected by the infused gift of wisdom, which enables the human mind to penetrate divine things through a kind of connaturality bestowed by the Holy Spirit (§44). Here again, the pope takes a step beyond Vatican I, which made no reference to this higher synthesis through the gifts of the Holy Spirit.

Another interesting development beyond previous doctrinal teaching, including that of Vatican I, is Pope John Paul II's attitude toward to what we may call philosophical pluralism—if I may here use a term that does not appear in the encyclical. Neither Vatican I nor Leo XIII nor Pius XII had words of praise for modern philosophies outside of the Thomistic, or at least the Scholastic, tradition. Leo XIII, in his encyclical on the study of philosophy, said that the "golden wisdom" of St. Thomas should be used for the defense of the faith, the advance of the sciences, and the refutation of prevalent errors. Pius XII, after calling for the instruction of future priests according to the method, doctrine, and principles of Thomas Aquinas, deplored the current tendency to denigrate the philosophy so long received in the Church as if the erroneous principles of immanentism, idealism, materialism, and existentialism could offset the limitations of classical metaphysics (DS 3878, 3894).

Vatican II gave a slight opening to pluralism. In its Decree on

Priestly Formation it declared that while students should be trained to exercise their speculative intelligence under the tutelage of St. Thomas, they should learn to apply eternal truths to the changing conditions of modern affairs, so as better to communicate the faith to men and women of our own time (OT 16). The Pastoral Constitution on the Church in the Modern World, going a stage further, observed that the findings of science, history, and philosophy raise new questions that demand new theological investigations. The faithful should live in close union with men and women of their time, and be familiar with modern ways of thinking and feeling (GS 62).

John Paul II in *Fides et ratio* shows no lack of esteem for St. Thomas. "The Church has been justified," he declares, "in consistently proposing St. Thomas as a master of thought and a model of the right way to do theology" (§43). He praises Leo XIII for having insisted on the incomparable value of the philosophy of St. Thomas (§57). He is also on guard against eclecticism, which takes over ideas from different philosophical systems without concern for their inner coherence (§86).

Notwithstanding his evident preference for St. Thomas, the present pope is careful to avoid canonizing any one philosophical system (§49). He writes that while the Church has been excellently served by the powerful array of thinkers formed in the school of the Angelic Doctor (§58), philosophers who adopt more recent currents of thought, such as the method of immanence and phenomenology, have helped to keep the tradition of Christian thought alive (§59). In addition to St. Thomas, therefore, philosophers and theologians of other schools receive words of praise in the encyclical. He mentions St. Anselm and St. Bonaventure together with St. Thomas as making up the "great triad" of medieval doctors (§74). Among the baroque philosophers, he pays tribute to Francisco Suárez (§62), and among the moderns he commends John Henry Newman, Antonio Rosmini,

Vladimir Soloviev, and Vladimir Lossky (§74), none of whom could be called a Thomist.

These references to non-Thomistic currents in philosophy call for some explanation. In the first place, it may be noted that the method of immanence, apparently favored by the pope, should not be confused with the philosophy of immanentism that had been previously rejected by the Magisterium. Maurice Blondel proposed the method precisely as a way of demonstrating the aspiration to the transcendent that is inscribed in the human spirit, and therefore as a way of refuting immanentism, which excluded the transcendent. It is surprising that the pope does not mention Blondel by name anywhere in the encyclical.[5]

The reference to phenomenology is by no means surprising. John Paul II encountered it in depth when writing his *Habilitationsschrift* on the ethics of Max Scheler. While he welcomed the personalism and intersubjectivism of Scheler, and some aspects of Scheler's philosophy of values, he was dissatisfied with Scheler's unwillingness to pass from pure phenemenology to ontology. The pope stands closer to Roman Ingarden, who combined Husserlian phenomenology with philosophical realism. Edith Stein, having been a disciple of Edmund Husserl, likewise integrated his phenomenology with the ontology of Thomas Aquinas, thus more closely approaching the positions of the present pope.

Although John Paul II insists that the Magisterium has no mandate

---

5. On this subject see the speculations of Peter Henrici, "The One Who Went Unnamed: Maurice Blondel in the Encyclical *Fides et Ratio,*" *Communio* 26 (1999): 609–21. Henrici is of the opinion that precisely because the pope was following Blondel so closely, he may have feared that an approving reference to Blondel might have suggested that he was imposing Blondel's analysis of immanence. The same explanation might hold for the omission of the name of Henri de Lubac, who set forth positions on faith and reason very similar to those of John Paul II. See my essay "Can Philosophy Be Christian? The New State of the Question" in the present volume.

to teach philosophy, he agrees with earlier popes that it has the right and duty to warn against philosophical errors that can undermine the right understanding of revelation and present obstacles to faith (§§49–50). He recalls with approval the Church's condemnation in the nineteenth century of systems such as fideism, traditionalism, rationalism, and ontologism (§52).

In the list of past condemnations the pope significantly omits any mention of Rosmini, although the Holy Office in 1887 condemned no fewer than forty erroneous propositions drawn from his work (DS 3201–41). Should this omission, taken in combination with the favorable reference I have already mentioned, be understood as a tacit retraction of the earlier magisterial reprobation? Several commentators suggest that the pope is here rehabilitating Rosmini and exercising the kind of ecclesial repentance for past errors that has been an integral part of his program.[6] This interpretation is not indisputable, since John Paul II declares that he is not endorsing all aspects of the thought of the thinkers he praises. Nevertheless, his remarks on Rosmini tend to support a solid scholarly opinion to the effect that Rosmini was misinterpreted and wrongly accused.[7]

Like Vatican I and the popes of the past century, John Paul II enu-

6. Henrici, "Maurice Blondel," 620. Walter Kasper, "Magisterium's Interventions in Philosophical Matters," *L'Osservatore Romano* (weekly English edition), 28 April 1999, 5–6, at 5.

7. Since this paragraph was written, the Congregation for the Doctrine of the Faith has published a "Note Regarding Father Rosmini," confirmed by Pope John Paul II, in which explicit reference is made to *Fides et ratio,* no. 74. The CDF here explains that John Paul II, without endorsing every aspect of Rosmini's thought, pointed to him as "one of the recent thinkers who achieved a fruitful exchange between philosophy and the word of God. According to the Note, the condemnation of 1887 rejected only certain conclusions that could possibly be drawn from the reading of Rosmini's works; it did not state that his work was contrary to Catholic faith and doctrine. The recent Note concedes that Rosmini's system was considered "inadequate to safeguard and explain certain truths of Catholic doctrine" and that his speculations "at times bordered on a risky rashness." For the text of the Note, see *Origins* 31 (August 16, 2001): 201–2.

merates a variety of philosophical systems that he sees as injurious to faith and to authentic wisdom. Instead of impulsive fideism and idealistic rationalism, the prime targets of Vatican I, he names eclecticism, historicism, scientism, pragmatism, and nihilism (§§86–90). All of these tendencies call into question the capacity of the human mind to transcend the factual and the empirical; they implicitly deny the possibility of metaphysics (§83). Some forms of postmodernity, he adds, allege that "the time of certainties is irrevocably past" and contend that we must "learn to live in a horizon of total absence of meaning, where everything is provisional and ephemeral" (§91). In settling for such an absence of meaning, says the pope, philosophy subverts its own project. Abandoning its pursuit of sure and abiding wisdom, it offers a prescription for intellectual despair (§91).

Even when he severely criticizes, John Paul II avoids the harsh language of condemnation. He calls attention to the ingredients of truth in systems that he finds faulty. When discussing historicism, for example, he concedes that to understand a doctrine from the past correctly, it is necessary to set it in its proper historical and cultural context (§87). Later he says that "the currents of thought which claim to be postmodern merit appropriate attention" (§91). He appreciates the difficulty of seeking full and ultimate truth in a world divided into so many specialized fields (§56). Concessions of this kind are not easy to find in Vatican I or in the encyclicals of popes prior to John XXIII.

For John Paul II the negative role of the Magisterium in condemning philosophical errors is secondary and subordinate. The primary purpose of magisterial interventions, he states, is to "prompt, promote, and encourage philosophical inquiry" (§51). No such positive encouragement of philosophy can be found in the decrees of Vatican I. In fact, that Council quoted the words of Paul in the Letter to the Colossians, warning the faithful against philosophy and vain deceit (DS 3018; Col 2:8).

So great is John Paul II's confidence in reason that he is willing to use it critically in the field of theology. Without this rational component, he declares, faith could easily deteriorate into myth and superstition (§48). In an admonition to theologians he voices his dissatisfaction with biblical positivism and with merely narrative styles of theology, which content themselves with retelling the biblical story. For the same reason he is also critical of hermeneutical theology that seriously studies the meaning of ancient texts but tends to dodge the hard questions of truth and falsehood (§94). The very acceptance of God's word, he points out, presupposes the capacity of the human mind for transcendent truth (§103).

A note of positive encouragement resounds through the entire text of *Fides et ratio* like a refrain. In his introduction the pope states his intention "that those who love truth may take the sure path leading to it and so find rest from their labors and joy for their spirit" (§6). Faith, he contends, can stir reason to overcome any false modesty and to run risks with the goal of attaining whatever is beautiful, good, and true, arduous though this may be (§56). A restoration of confidence, he believes, is essential for the renewal of philosophy and for setting all the arts and sciences in their proper context. In his concluding exhortation to philosophers he asks them "to have the courage to recover, in the flow of an enduringly valid philosophical tradition, the range of authentic wisdom and truth—metaphysical truth included—which is proper to philosophical inquiry" (§106).

Throughout this paper I have tried to call attention to the points at which the recent encyclical of John Paul II differs from the statements of Vatican I and some earlier papal teaching. But I would not wish to be understood as dismissing the value of these earlier statements. Vatican I, in particular, is to be esteemed for having established the solid platform on the basis of which further advances could be made. Leo XIII took a positive step forward when he encouraged a revival of Thomistic philosophy. Vatican II made further progress by pointing out the need for Catholics to be men and women of their time, familiar with modern currents of thought.

John Paul II presupposes these earlier documents and in no respect disavows them. But he uses a different method and speaks with new accents. With his keen sense of the variety of human cultures and historical eras, he is able to enter into dialogue with many schools of thought. As a personalist, he brings out hidden resources in the great tradition with which he identifies himself. Standing firmly in that tradition, he issues a ringing challenge to contemporary philosophers and theologians.

For Catholic universities, *Fides et ratio* may provide a beacon light of progress. Taken together with the apostolic constitution *Ex corde Ecclesiae,* it can enable Catholics to overcome the haunting suspicion that their confessional allegiance is an encumbrance for the intellectual life that is the proper business of the university. If John Paul II is right, the light of revelation is no substitute for thought but is the strongest possible ally of reason and science. It can permeate the various disciplines, reenergizing them, and bringing them into an organic unity with one another.

SUMMARY OUTLINE OF *Fides et ratio*

Fides et ratio: INDEX OF TOPICS
AND PROPER NAMES

LIST OF CONTRIBUTORS

SELECTED BIBLIOGRAPHY

INDEXES

SUMMARY OUTLINE OF *Fides et ratio*

The following summary incorporates many phrases from the text of Fides et ratio *in the effort to provide a close summary-outline of the encyclical.*

Introduction

"KNOW YOURSELF"

§§1–2 This maxim from Delphi exemplifies the quest found in all cultures to know the truth about the meaning of life. The Church's *diakonia* (service) of truth involves proclaiming Jesus Christ as the Way, the Truth, and the Life and helping believers to see how every truth they attain is a step toward the fullness of truth.

§§3–4 One of the noblest human tools for seeking truth about life's meaning is philosophy, the love of wisdom. The wonder awakened by contemplating creation can arouse a strong desire for knowledge about the world and about the meaning of human life. However helpful any particular system of thought may be for enhancing knowledge, one must beware the philosophical pride of mistaking any imperfect or partial view of reality for the whole. All sound philosophical inquiry will make use of such principles as non-contradiction, finality, and causality and such concepts as that of "the person" as a free and intelligent subject, with a capacity to know God, truth, and goodness.

§§5–6 Out of the Church's appreciation for philosophy, the present encyclical reflects on its use to attain deeper knowledge of the ultimate truths about God and the meaning of life. What prompts this encyclical is a worry that in some respects philosophy today has lost its way. There have been many advantages gained from philosophy's recent focus on human subjectivity, but this trend has sometimes led to agnosticism, skepticism, relativism, and a general lack of confidence about the human capacity for obtaining truth on some questions. Charged with the mission of being witnesses to truth, bishops should join philosophers and theologians in reflecting on faith and reason as trustworthy sources for gaining knowledge and wisdom.

Chapter 1: The Revelation of God's Wisdom

JESUS, REVEALER OF THE FATHER

§§7–10 The knowledge that comes through faith has its origin not in speculative human thinking but in the Word of God. Against the rationalist claim about the impossibility of any knowledge that is not the product of human rational capacities, the Church affirms that there is also a knowledge proper to faith, a knowledge that in some respects surpasses the knowledge proper to reason. Yet it is not all a matter of faith, for human reason by its own resources can come to recognize God as the creator.

§§11–12 God's self-revelation, culminating in Jesus, occurs in time and this gives time and history a special importance for Christianity. Revealed knowledge not only concerns what God does for humanity in time but also discloses certain truths about Divine Eternity and elucidates the very meaning of human life in a way that is true across all times and cultures.

REASON BEFORE THE MYSTERY

§§13–15 Faith is an obedient response to God, a response that acknowledges God's divinity, transcendence, and supreme freedom. Freely entrusting oneself to God in the obedience of faith engages the whole person, including intellect and will. The knowledge that comes through faith in no way diminishes the importance of reason's autonomous exploration or reality. But faith is needed for knowledge about mysteries such as the inner life of God and the extent of the Father's love for creation that are communicated by the sacramental dimension of revelation. It is Christ who fully reveals man to himself as the sort of creature who is fulfilled only when open and freely responsive to the transcendent. The truths offered by revelation are not the products of human reason but the free gift of God, designed to stir up our thinking and to evoke our loving acceptance.

Chapter 2: *Credo ut intelligam*—I Believe So That I May Understand
"WISDOM KNOWS ALL AND UNDERSTANDS ALL" (WIS. 9:11)

§§16–18 The Bible's wisdom books show the deep-seated relation between the knowledge conferred by faith and that conferred by reason, including certain basic rules about how reason can be fully true to itself, namely: (1) human knowledge is a journey that allows no rest; (2) such a path is not for the proud who think that everything worth knowing is the fruit of personal conquest; and (3) with due fear of the Lord reason must recognize the transcendent sovereignty and providential love of God in governing the world. To abandon these rules is to risk failure and to end up in folly.

§§19–20 Texts like the Book of Wisdom affirm that in reasoning about nature the human being can rise to knowledge of the Creator. This is to value reason without overvaluing it, for the truths accessible to reason have their full meaning only within the larger horizon of faith.

"ACQUIRE WISDOM, ACQUIRE UNDERSTANDING" (PROV. 4:5)

§§21–23 Mindful of the strains that the mind feels when reaching its limits, revelation shows that the reliance of our human mind on God can lead to an understanding of some things otherwise beyond hope of attainment. The Genesis story about the Garden of Eden explains the impairment of reasoning that flows from aversion to God, the source of truth. Christ's death on the Cross shows that the divine plan for human salvation employs a generosity that human logic could never have suspected and can scarcely comprehend but must gratefully accept.

Chapter 3: *Intellego ut Credam*—I Understand So That I May Believe
JOURNEYING IN SEARCH OF TRUTH

§§24–27 Paul's Areopagus sermon relies on the desire for God that is deep in every human heart. Truth is the proper object of the human desire to know, a desire constantly manifested in daily life as well as in learned disciplines, and found not just in theoretical questions but also in such practical matters as the quest for happiness. The experience of suffering and the inescapability of death make people ask whether life has a meaning. Through the ages philosophy has pursued the question of what happens after death as well as the proper orientation for our choices during life.

THE DIFFERENT FACES OF HUMAN TRUTH

§§28–29 Mindful of the many ways in which the search for truth can be frustrated, we may nevertheless define the human being as "one who seeks truth." It is unthinkable that a search so deeply rooted in human nature would be completely vain and useless. Only the expectation that one can reach an answer leads one to take the first step.

§§30–32 Truth has various modes, for the type of evidence, experiment, and argumentation proper, say, to scientific research differs from that found in philosophy or religion. The truths of philosophy should not be understood as limited to the teachings of professional philosophers, for the reflections by which all men and women seek to direct their lives are philosophical precisely they involve the quest for wisdom. In all philosophizing the need for belief of some sort is inescapable. It is impossible to acquire everything that one needs to know by personal verification. For this reason there are many areas of life in which we need to entrust ourselves to knowledge acquired by other people; in fact, human development depends on learning how to entrust oneself to others and to give what one knows to others. In this way warranted belief is often part of the normal process of gaining knowledge and certitude. The lives of the martyrs exemplify how much certitude about the ultimate meaning of life can come from encounter with Christ.

§§33–35 It is characteristic of human nature to seek the truth, and especially the ultimate truth about the meaning of life toward which the religious impulse impels us. The truths needed for life are attained not only through reason but also through relations of trust in others who can guarantee the authenticity and certainty of these truths. Not just the sort of reasoning that is involved in faith but all kinds of reasoning need to be sustained by trusting dialogue and sincere friendship. The human journey of discovery is a search for truth and for another person to whom one can entrust oneself. Christian faith offers a concrete answer, a truth about Christ that is not opposed but complementary to those truths that rigorous philosophical thinking can provide and thus a way to truth in all its fullness. It is the same God who established the intelligibility of the natural order and who reveals Himself as the Father of Jesus.

Chapter 4: The Relationship Between Faith and Reason

IMPORTANT MOMENTS IN THE ENCOUNTER OF
FAITH AND REASON

§§36–40 Paul's use of the natural knowledge of God and the voice of conscience in order to reach the pagans shows a respect for classical philosophy's concern to purify human notions of God from mythological elements and to provide a rational foundation for belief in divinity. Church Fathers such as Justin Martyr, Clement of Alexandria, Origen, the Cappadocians, Dionysius the Areopagite, and especially Augustine showed both prudence and creativity in bringing to light certain links between reason and religion. Avoiding gnosticism, they found much that was useful in Stoicism and Platonism, even while remaining convinced that salvation comes only through Christ. Often the work of these Church Fathers disclosed truths that had remained implicit or only partial in the great pagan philosophers. The Gospel offered such a satisfying answer to the hitherto unresolved question of life's meaning that delving into the philosophers seemed to early Church Fathers something remote and in some ways outmoded. Figures more skeptical of philosophy (such as Tertullian) accentuated the limits of any attempt to state the truths of the faith in philosophical categories.

§§41–42 As time went on, there was increasing recognition of certain points of convergence between reason and revelation as well as a sense of various points of divergence. By careful adaptation of the philosophical frameworks they received, Christian thinkers were able to elaborate sophisticated forms of theology and to make major advances on such questions as the immortality of the soul and the origin of evil. Of special importance is Anselm's sense of the role of philosophical reasoning in the *intellectus fidei* (the understanding of faith). For him, the priority of faith is not in competition with the search that is proper to reason. Reason is not asked to pass judgment on faith, but to seek its meaning.

THE ENDURING ORIGINALITY OF THE THOUGHT
OF SAINT THOMAS AQUINAS.

§§43–44 Aquinas stresses the harmony between faith and reason. Both the light of reason and the light of faith come from God; hence, there can be no contradiction between them. Nature can contribute to the understanding of divine revelation, and so faith need have no fear of reason. Illumined by faith, reason is set free from the fragility and limitations that derive from the disobedience of sin and receives the strength needed to rise to knowledge of the Triune God. Aquinas stresses both the supernatural character of faith and its reasonableness. In taking note of the Holy Spirit's role in the process by which knowledge matures into wisdom, Aquinas distinguishes between the wisdom named among the gifts of the Holy Spirit and the wisdom found among the intellectual virtues acquired through discipline and study.

DRAMA OF THE SEPARATION OF FAITH AND REASON

§§45–48 A need to accord philosophy and the various sciences their proper autonomy accompanied the rise of the universities and the progressive separation of disciplines. In some quarters there came to be a deep mistrust of reason; some preferred to focus on faith alone and others to deny the rationality of faith altogether. As modern philosophy progressively distanced itself from Christian revelation, the separation of disciplines sometimes turned into outright hostility, and theology often became marginalized. An atheistic humanism arose that regarded faith as damaging to rationality. The rejection of metaphysics by positivism included a denial of absolute values that some used to justify using a purely market-driven logic. In some quarters the crisis of rationality provoked a kind of nihilism, and in general there was a profound change in the perception of the role that philosophy should play within culture. From being respected as universal wisdom, philosophy became just one of the many fields of human learning, and a peripheral one at that. The loss of metaphysics leaves culture open to the utilitarian reduction of the human being to just one more item in the world, one whose use-value is to be calculated by instrumental reason. When tied to weak reason, faith runs the risk of withering into myth or superstition.

Chapter 5: The Magisterium's Interventions in Philosophical Matters

THE MAGISTERIUM'S DISCERNMENT AS
DIAKONIA OF THE TRUTH

§§49–51 The Church has not declared any one philosophy her own in preference to others. While it is not the Magisterium's task to make up what is lacking in any particular brand of philosophy, it does belong to the Magisterium to intervene when controversial philosophical views threaten right understanding of what has been revealed and thus threaten the faith of the People of God. Within the Magisterium's competence is the identification of widespread presuppositions that are incompatible with revealed truth, such as about God or the human person. The Magisterium's interventions need not be negative; they are intended to prompt further philosophical inquiry. The vast pluralism of systems, methods, and philosophical approaches makes this a daunting, yet urgent, task.

§§52–56 There is a long history of such ecclesiastical discernments, including the censures of fideism and excessive rationalism. It was in this light that Vatican Council I spoke about the relationship between faith and reason, treating them as distinct but inseparable. Likewise, there have been warnings against mistaken interpretations of evolution, existentialism, liberation theology, and Marxism. In the present day there is need to address the declarations of postmodernism about the alleged end of metaphysics as well as certain rationalist tendencies in theology and in biblical interpretation. Biblical exegetes are reminded that every form of hermeneutics has philosophical assumptions that need careful evaluation before being applied to the sacred texts. Philosophers are exhorted to trust again in the genuine powers of reason and not to set for themselves goals that are too modest.

THE CHURCH'S INTEREST IN PHILOSOPHY

§§57–63 Developing the teachings of Vatican Council I, Pope Leo XIII's encyclical *Aeterni Patris* showed certain ways in which philosophy contributes to faith and to theological learning. In recommending a renewed study of Aquinas, this encyclical prompted much thinking and research that proved important for the Second Vatican Council and its renewal of the Church. During the same period various Catholic philosophers adopted approaches other than Thomism and produced much of value, especially in the areas of epistemology and anthropology. Complementarily, the biblical anthropology of *Gaudium et spes* offers many insights that deserve philosophical reflection, especially on the dignity and freedom of the human person and on the inadequacies of atheism. The Council also affirmed the importance of philosophy in seminary education. Regrettably, Vatican II's encouragement of the continued study of scholastic philosophy as well as of philosophy in general have not always been heeded, perhaps because of the distrust in reason typical of much contemporary philosophy but also because of exaggerated trust in the ability of the social science to replace philosophical inquiry. The present encyclical would thus like to reemphasize the Church's interest in philosophy by stressing the bond between the work of theology and the philosophical search for truth.

Chapter 6: The Interaction Between Philosophy and Theology
THE KNOWLEDGE OF FAITH AND THE DEMANDS
OF PHILOSOPHICAL REASON

§§64–65 The Magisterium does not claim the competence to decide on the particular methods that theology should use, but it does insist on reminding theologians of the importance of philosophical distinctions for certain tasks of theology. The methodological principles of sound theology are two: (1) *auditus fidei*—attentively receiving the content of revelation as gradually expounded in Tradition, Scripture, and the Magisterium, and (2) *intellectus fidei*—carefully developing an understanding of what has been received through disciplined, speculative thought. Philosophy can assist the *auditus fidei* by its study of the structures of knowledge, language, and communication. For the development of the *intellectus fidei*, philosophy can contribute by its analysis of the logical and conceptual structures in which the Church's teachings are articulated.

§§66–71 In order to discuss many issues in *dogmatic theology* (such as the use of human language to speak of God, or the union of divine and human natures in the one person of Christ), it is crucial to have sound philosophical distinctions at hand. The discipline of *fundamental theology* is specifically concerned with articulating the relation between faith and philosophical thinking and thus deals with such topics as the natural knowledge of God, the credibility of revelation, and the reasonableness of the free assent of faith. In even greater need of philosophy is *moral theology*, for the responsible use of human freedom requires a sound vision of human nature and society as well as of the general principles of ethical decision-making and the proper formation of conscience. Helpful as an awareness of other fields of learning and of diverse cultural traditions is, the focus on the universal that is typical of philosophical reasoning is indispensable. For two millennia the Church has tried to reach out to all cultures with its universal message of salvation for all in Christ. Evangelization should respect what is best in each culture, and yet it may also involve transforming a culture, thereby giving people access to the unchanging truth of God through Jesus Christ. No one culture can ever become the criterion of judgment. The Gospel brings to all cultures both a genuine liberation from the various disorders caused by sin and a call to the fullness of truth.

§72 It was not chance but divine providence that brought Christianity so early on to encounter Greek philosophy. There are new tasks of inculturation today, and Christians in lands such as India need to draw from that land's rich spiritual heritage the elements that are compatible with their faith. But in this work certain criteria must be kept firmly in mind: (1) The universality of the human spirit, whose basic needs are the same in the most disparate cultures. (2) In engaging great cultures, the Church cannot abandon what has been gained from inculturation in the world of Greco-Latin thought, to which divine providence led the Church early in its history. (3) Care must be taken lest (contrary to the very nature of the human spirit) the legitimate defense of the uniqueness and originality of a culture's thought be taken as a reason for refusing to be open to being transformed by the Gospel.

§§73–74 Philosophy and theology need one another. Theology's source must always remain the Word of God revealed in history, while its goal will be an understanding of faith that needs to increase with each new generation. But the human search for truth (especially when pursued by philosophy operating with its proper autonomy) can only help to understand God's Word better, for God's Word is Truth. The believer needs to use all the powers of reason in search of ever better understanding of God's word and can be stirred by these revealed truth to paths that reason of itself might never have suspected. Given this mutually beneficial relation, it is no surprise that the history of theological discovery has so often involved great philosophical discoveries.

DIFFERENT STANCES OF PHILOSOPHY

§§75–79 This historical review has highlighted three distinct stances of philosophy toward faith and theology: (1) Philosophy as completely independent of the Gospel's revelation (modeled on the philosophy practiced by the ancient Greeks in their search for truth within the natural order). (2) "Christian Philosophy," properly understood not as an official philosophy of the Church but as a way of philosophizing in which speculation is dynamically united with faith so as to purify reason from presumption (the typical temptation for a philosopher) and to promote a humble readiness to appreciate rather than to ignore the data of revelation on such questions as the problem of evil and suffering or the personal nature of God. (3) Philosophy as ready to supply assistance to theology (conceived as a work of critical reason in light of faith) by confirming the intelligibility and universality of theology's truth-claims. This third stance affirms philosophy's autonomy, and in this regard the thought of Thomas Aquinas remains an important model. Philosophy must always remain faithful to its own principles, but the unity of truth implies that reason must be as ready to be questioned as to ask questions. A philosophy consonant with the revealed Word of God will provide a privileged place of encounter between Christian faith and human cultures.

Chapter 7: Current Requirements and Tasks

THE THREE INDISPENSABLE REQUIREMENTS
OF THE WORD OF GOD

§§80–81 The scriptural vision of the human being and the world manifest great profundity. To regard the world as created and non-absolute is to begin to appreciate that God alone is the Absolute. To understand the human being as an *imago Dei* is to begin to appreciate the intrinsic value of human life, freedom, and immortality, even while affirming the essential dependence of every creature on God. Revelation's full answer to the problem of evil and to the challenge of properly exercising human freedom is found in Jesus Christ, the Incarnate Word of God. Now, one of the great tasks of the present moment is to address the crisis of meaning brought on by the fragmentation of knowledge and the maelstrom of data. These easily lead to skepticism, indifference, and nihilism. If human life were confined to its own immanence without reference to the transcendent, it would be immeasurably poorer. Hence, the first requirement is that philosophy must recover its *sapiential* dimension as a search for the ultimate and overarching meaning of life. This recovery is especially crucial today, given the vast expansion of technological thinking and technical capacity, for technology that is not ordered to something greater than merely utilitarian ends can easily prove inhuman and even destructive. The Word of God reveals the dignity of men and women and offers a way to unify all that they do in the world. Hence faith invites philosophy to engage in the search for the natural foundations of the meaning of life, which corresponds to the religious impulse innate in every person.

§§82–84 The second requirement is that philosophy must verify the human capacity to know objective truth about the intrinsic goal of human life. A radically phenomenalist or relativist philosophy would be ill-suited for the project. The third requirement is for philosophy to have genuinely metaphysical range by going beyond empirical data so as to attain absolute, ultimate, and foundational truth. This is not to champion any particular school of metaphysics, but simply to note the importance of verifying the capacity to know such truths and thus to ground the dignity of the human person in the spiritual nature of the human person. What has been revealed by the Word of God could not be rendered theologically intelligible if human knowledge were strictly limited to the world of sense experience. For this project metaphysics plays an essential role of mediation in theological research. Metaphysics is likewise important for making the best use of recent scholarly developments in hermeneutics and the analysis of language.

§§85–91 However daunting these challenges may seem, a sapiential philosophy can assist people to come to an interior unity precisely by addressing the splintered approach to truth in academe and the consequent fragmentation of meaning. A unified and organic vision of knowledge can be helpful spiritually, even while respecting philosophy's proper autonomy. Strategic in this effort is the cultivation of a close relationship between contemporary thought and the philosophy and theology as developed in the Christian tradition. Among the more risky and error-prone trends are eclecticism, historicism, scientism, pragmatism, and nihilism.

CURRENT TASKS FOR THEOLOGY

§§92–99 Theology today needs to renew its specific methods in order to serve evangelization more effectively and needs to keep its focus on the ultimate truth that revelation has entrusted to it. These dual tasks of theology require appropriate assistance from philosophy. The chief purpose of theology remains to provide an understanding of revelation and the content of faith, and for this project there must be a careful analysis of the texts of the Scriptures and the texts that express the Church's living Tradition. Among the specific problems that will require the help of philosophy are these: (1) the relationship in a text between meaning and truth, (2) the reconciliation of the absoluteness and universality of truth with the inescapably historical and cultural condition of the formulas that express that truth; (3) the problem of the enduring validity of the conceptual language used in conciliar definitions, (4) the understanding of revealed truth by the articulation of the *intellectus fidei*, both for dogmatic theology and for moral theology. The development of genuine reciprocity between philosophy and theology can greatly help to clarify the relationships between truth and life, between historical event and dogmatic teaching, and between transcendent truth and humanly comprehensible language.

Conclusion

§§100–102 The significance of philosophy for the development of culture and its influence on patterns of personal and social behavior is evident. But philosophy also has an importance for the understanding of the faith, and so the Church remains convinced of the need for faith and reason mutually to support each other. Both philosophy and theology can benefit from being related to one another, even while respecting their own proper methods and appropriate autonomy. The Church's interest in these questions flows from its duty to defend human dignity and to proclaim the Gospel message. Through the mediation of a sapiential philosophy people can come to appreciate that their humanity is all the more affirmed the more they entrust themselves to the Gospel and open themselves to Christ.

§§103–108 As a mirror that reflects the culture of a people, philosophy can serve the new evangelization, the evangelization of cultures. Often philosophical thought is the only available ground for understanding and dialogue with those who do not share the same faith. Theologians and those responsible for priestly formation will do well to give great attention to the work of sound philosophy. Philosophers should have the courage to recover the full range of authentic wisdom and truth that is proper to philosophy and to be open to the compelling questions that arise from the Word of God. Scientists too are encouraged to embrace a sapiential perspective in their scientific and technological endeavors. But for everyone whatsoever, the most important thing is to contemplate Christ and the way in which he has saved humanity and provided the ultimate answers to the unceasing human search for truth and meaning. Like the Virgin Mary, whose vocation it was to offer herself entirely so that God's word might take flesh and dwell among us, so too philosophy is called to offer its rational and critical resources so that theology, as the understanding of faith, may be fruitful and creative. In giving her assent to the divine initiative, Mary lost nothing of her freedom or her true humanity, and neither will philosophy lose its proper autonomy in heeding the summons of the Gospel's truth.

Fides et ratio

INDEX OF TOPICS AND PROPER NAMES

Numbers refer to section numbers of the encyclical (1–108).

CONTRIBUTORS

AVERY CARDINAL DULLES, S.J., an internationally known author and lecturer, is currently the Laurence J. McGinley Professor of Religion and Society at Fordham University, a position he has held since 1988. Cardinal Dulles received the doctorate in Sacred Theology from the Gregorian University in Rome in 1960. Before coming to Fordham, he served on the faculty of Woodstock College from 1960 to 1974 and that of The Catholic University of America from 1974 to 1988. He has been a visiting professor at colleges and universities in the United States and abroad. The author of 700 articles on theological topics, Cardinal Dulles has published twenty-one books including *Models of the Church* (1974), *Models of Revelation* (1983), *The Assurance of Things Hoped For: A Theology of Christian Faith* (1994), and his latest book, *The New World of Faith* (2000). Past President of both the Catholic Theological Society of America and the American Theological Society, Cardinal Dulles has served on the International Theological Commission and as a member of the United States Lutheran/Roman Catholic Dialogue. He is presently an advisor to the Committee on Doctrine of the National Conference of Catholic Bishops. He is the first American theologian who is not a bishop to be named to the College of Cardinals.

PRUDENCE ALLEN, R.S.M., is Chair of Philosophy at St. John Vianney Theological Seminary, Denver, Colorado and Distinguished Professor Emeritus, Concordia University, Montreal. She received her Ph.D. from Claremont Graduate University in 1967. She is the author of a two-volume work, *The Concept of Woman: The Aristotelian Revolution (750BC–1250 AD)* and *The Concept of Woman: The Early Humanist Reformation (1250–1500)* published by Eerdmans. She has published in such journals as *The American Catholic Philosophical Quarterly, Maritain Studies, Dialogue, Lonergan Workshop, International Philosophical Quarterly, Thought,* and *Communio.*

JOSEPH W. KOTERSKI, S.J., is Chair of Philosophy at Fordham University (Bronx, New York), where he has taught since 1992. He received his undergraduate degree from Xavier University and his Ph.D. in philosophy from St. Louis University, where he studied under the late Prof. James Collins. He has also taught at the University of St. Thomas (Houston, Texas) and Loyola College (Baltimore, Maryland). At Fordham he also serves as the editor-in-chief of *International Philosophical Quarterly* and as chaplain and tutor at Queen's Court Residential College for Freshmen. His academic interests include natural law ethics, Thomistic metaphysics, and the history of medieval philosophy. Besides authoring articles in ethics and the history of philosophy, he has recently recorded two series of lectures for The Teaching Company, "Aristotle's Ethics" and "Natural Law Ethics."

DAVID FOSTER has taught philosophy to seminarians at Seton Hall University since 1987. He earned his doctorate from The Catholic University of America and his baccalaureate from Notre Dame University. He also earned an S.T.B. from the Dominican House of Studies in Washington, D.C., in 1980. His doctoral dissertation studied St. Thomas' arguments for the immateriality of the intellect. In a dozen articles and reviews, he has focused on the problems of metaphysical structure and the philosophy of person. As chairman of the American Catholic Philosophical Association Committee on Priestly Formation, David Foster has hosted regular meetings on how to improve the philosophy curriculum in seminaries. To this end he has published articles on how theology uses philosophy and the recent history of philosophy in seminaries.

DAVID VINCENT MECONI, S.J., a Jesuit scholastic, was visiting instructor for philosophy and classics at Xavier University in Cincinnati and is currently in theology studies at the University of Innsbruck. He holds Masters degrees in theology and philosophy from Marquette University. He has published numerous articles on the early Church, especially on the thought of St. Augustine and Pseudo-Dionysius. Many of his current projects focus on pneumatology and Christian deification.

ALLEN H. VIGNERON is an Auxiliary Bishop of the Archdiocese of Detroit and Rector of Sacred Heart Major Seminary, where he has served on the faculty since 1986. He received his S.T.L. in fundamental theology from the Pontifical Gregorian University, Rome, in 1977, and his Ph.D. in philosophy from The Catholic University of America in 1987. His work in phenomenology and the history of philosophy has provided him with resources for exploring the stance of the Second Vatican Council toward modernity and the implications of the conciliar and post-conciliar Magisterium for some of the more controversial elements of Catholic life today, for example, seminary education, particularly formation in celibate chastity.

TIMOTHY SEAN QUINN, associate professor of philosophy at Xavier University, joined the faculty in 1987. He received his Ph.D. from The Catholic University of America in 1985, and taught for two years at Albertus Magnus College in New Haven, Connecticut, before moving to Xavier University. While at Xavier, he directed the Honors Bachelor of Arts Program (1992–1998). He has written on Aristotle, Boethius, and Kant, and is currently preparing an essay concerning philosophy and mythology for inclusion in a collection of essays on mythology.

MICHAEL J. SWEENEY, associate professor of philosophy, has been at Xavier University in Cincinnati since 1995. He received a Ph.D. in philosophy from The Catholic University of America in 1994, an S.T.B. from the Gregorian University in Rome in 1989, and an M.A. in medieval studies from the University of Toronto in 1985. During the 1998–99 academic year, he was a Fulbright teaching fellow at the Greco-Latin Kabinet and Institute of Philosophy (Russian Academy of Science) in Moscow, Russia. The Greco-Latin Press published his Srednevekovaya Khristyanskaya Filosofiya *(Medieval Christian Philosophy)* in 2001, and Politicheskaya Filosofiya Srednikh Vekov *(Political Philosophy of the Middle Ages)* is forthcoming. His publications in English have focused on Thomas Aquinas and medieval philosophy.

SELECTED BIBLIOGRAPHY

I. Works of Pope John Paul II / Karol Wojtyła

Redemptor hominis. English, *The Redeemer of Man*. Washington, D.C.: United States Catholic Conference. Vatican translation from Vatican Polyglot Press. 1979

"The Task of Christian Philosophy Today," in *The Human Person,* ed. G. F. McLean. Proceedings of the American Catholic Philosophical Association 53 (1979).

The Acting Person. Trans. Anna Teresa Tymeniecka. Dordrecht and Boston: D. Reidel, 1979.

"Catholic Higher Education." *Origins* (1 October 1987): 269.

Mulieris dignitatem. English, *On the dignity and vocation of women*. Boston: Daughters of St. Paul, 1988.

Centesimus annus. English, *On the hundredth anniversary of Rerum novarum*. Washington, D.C.: United States Catholic Conference, 1991.

Pastores dabo vobis. English, *I will give you shepherds*. Vatican City: Libreria Editrice Vaticana, 1992.

Veritatis splendor. English, *The splendor of truth*. Washington, D.C.: United States Catholic Conference, 1993.

Crossing the Threshold of Hope. New York: Alfred A. Knopf, 1994.

Evangelium vitae. English, *The Gospel of Life*. Washington, D.C.: United States Catholic Conference, 1995. Text and format from Libreria editrice vaticana, Vatican City."

The Theology of the Body: Human Love in the Divine Plan. Foreword by John S. Grabowski. Boston: Pauline Books & Media, 1997. Reprinted with permission from *L'Osservatore Romano*.

Fides et ratio. English, *Faith and Reason.* Washington, D.C.: United States Catholic Conference, 1998. Text and format from Libreria Editrice Vaticana, Vatican City."

Audience before the Angelus at Castel Gondolfo, September 26, 1999. *L'Osservatore Romano* (English weekly edition), (29 September 1999), 1.

"Faith involves the whole person," in *L'Osservatore Romano* (20 October 1999), 1.

II. Other Church Documents

Vatican I. Constitution on Catholic Faith, *Dei Filius.* 1870. DS 3016.

John XXIII. "Gaudet Mater Ecclesia." October 1962. In *The Documents of Vatican II,* edited by Walter M. Abbott and Joseph Gallagher. New York: America Press, 1966.

Gaudium et spes (Constitution on the Church in the Modern World). December 1965. In *Documents of Vatican II,* Austin P. Flannery, ed. Grand Rapids, Mich.: Eerdmans, 1984.

Optatam Totius (Decree on Religious Formation). October 1965. In *Documents of Vatican II,* Austin P. Flannery, ed. Grand Rapids MI: Eerdmans, 1984.

The Letter of the Congregation For Education, *The Study of Philosophy in Seminaries* (20 January 1972).

Catechism of the Catholic Church. Libreria Editrice Vaticana, 1994. English translation of the Catechism of the Catholic Church: Modifications from the Editio Typica copyright 1997, United States Catholic Conference, Inc.

Pontifical Council for Culture, *Toward a Pastoral Approach to Culture.* Boston: Pauline Books and Media, 1999

III. Other Authors

Anselm. *Proslogion in Monologion and Proslogion.* Translated by Thomas Williams. Indianapolis: Hackett, 1995.

Arendt, Hannah. *The Life of the Mind.* New York: Harvest Books, 1971.

Balthasar, Hans Urs von. *Theo-Drama III: Dramatis Personae: Persons in Christ.* San Francisco: Ignatius Press, [1978] 1992.

Blenkinsopp, Joseph. *Wisdom and Law in the Old Testament: The Ordering of Life in Israel and Early Judaism.* Oxford University Press, 1995.

Blondel, Maurice. "La philosophie chrétienne existe-t-elle comme philosophie?" *Bulletin de la Société française de philosophie* 31 (1931): 86–92.

———. *Le problème de la philosophie catholique.* Paris: Bloud & Gay, 1932.

Bloom, Allan. *The Closing of the American Mind*. New York: Simon and Schuster, 1987.

Bréhier, Émile. "Y a-t-il une philosophie chrétienne?" *Revue de métaphysique et de morale* 38 (1931): 133–62.

———. *Historie de la philosophie,* vol. I: *L'Antiquité et le moyen âge*. Paris: Alcan, 1927.

———. *La philosophie du moyen âge*. Paris: Albin Michel, 1949.

Cere, Daniel. "Newman, God, and the Academy." *Theological Studies* 55 (1994): 3–23.

Cessario, Romanus. "Thomas Aquinas: A Doctor for the Ages," *First Things* 91 (March 1999): 27–32.

Clarke, W. Norris, S.J. "The Complementarity of Faith and Philosophy." *Communio* 26 (1999): 562–63.

Collins, James. *A History of Modern Philosophy*. Milwaukee: Bruce Publishers, 1954.

———. *God in Modern Philosophy*. Chicago: Regnery Press, 1959.

Congar, Yves M.-J. *A History of Theology*. Garden City, N.Y.: Doubleday, 1968.

Covolo, Enrico da. "The Encounter of Faith and Reason in the Fathers of the Church," *L'Osservatore Romano* (weekly English edition) (17 March 1999), 9.

Day, John, Robert P. Gordon, and H. G. M. Williamson, eds. *Wisdom in Ancient Israel*. Cambridge University Press, 1995.

Del Noce, Augusto. "Thomism and the Critique of Rationalism: Gilson and Shestov." *Communio* 25 (1998): 732–45.

Duggan, Michael. *The Consuming Fire: A Christian Introduction to the Old Testament*. San Francisco: Ignatius Press, 1991.

Dych, William V. "Philosophy and Philosophizing in Theology." In *Continuity and Plurality in Catholic Theology: Essays in Honor of Gerald A. McCool, S.J.,* ed. Anthony J. Cernera, pp. 13–34. Fairfield, Conn.: Sacred Heart University Press, 1998.

Ellis, John Tracy. "The Catholic Church and Her Universities." The 1986 Archbishop Gerety Lecture at Seton Hall University. Printed by Immaculate Conception Seminary, Seton Hall University, South Orange, N.J.

Fisichella, Rino. "Reason finds in Revelation the possibility of being truly itself." *L'Osservatore Romano* (13 January 1999), 14.

George, Robert P. "The Renaissance of Faith and Reason." *Crisis* (January 2000): 19–22.

Gilson, Étienne. *The Spirit of Mediaeval Philosophy.* New York: Charles Scribner's Sons, 1936.

————. *The Philosopher and Theology.* New York: Random House, 1962.

————. "La notion de philosophie chrétienne." *Bulletin de la Société française de philosophie* 31 (1931): 37–93.

Henrici, Peter. "The One Who Went Unnamed: Maurice Blondel in the Encyclical *Fides et Ratio.*" *Communio* 26 (1999): 609–21.

Hook, Sidney. *Academic Freedom and Academic Anarchy.* New York: Cowles, 1970.

Kasper, Walter. *Jesus the Christ.* Trans. V. Green. London: Burns and Oates, 1976.

————. *The God of Jesus Christ.* Trans. Matthew J. O'Connell. New York: Crossroad, 1984.

————. "Magisterium's Interventions in Philosophical Matters." *L'Osservatore Romano* (weekly English edition), (28 April 1999), 5–6.

Leclerq, J. "Maria Christianorum Philosophia." *Melanges de science religieuse* 13 (1956): 103–6.

Leff, Gordon. *Paris and Oxford Universities in the Thirteenth and Fourteenth Centuries: An Institutional and Intellectual History.* New York: John Wiley and Sons Inc., 1968.

Levinas, Emmanuel. *Totality and Infinity: An Essay on Exteriority.* Trans. Alphonso Lingis. Pittsburgh: Duquesne University Press, 1969.

Lienhard, Joseph T. *The Bible, The Church, and Authority: The Canon of the Christian Bible in History and Theology.* Collegeville: The Liturgical Press, 1995.

Lubac, Henri de. "On Christian Philosophy." *Communio* 19 (1992): 478–506.

Maritain, Jacques. *An Essay on Christian Philosophy.* New York: Philosophical Library, 1955.

————. *The Person and the Common Good.* Translated by John Fitzgerald. New York: Charles Scribner's Sons, 1947.

Marsden, George M. *The Soul of the American University: From Protestant Establishment to Established Nonbelief.* New York: Oxford University Press, 1994.

McCool, Gerald A. "How Can There Be Such a Thing as a Christian Philosophy?" In *Philosophical Knowledge.* Edited by J. B. Brough et al. Proceedings of the American Catholic Philosophical Association 54 (1980): 126–34.

————. *From Unity to Pluralism: The Internal Evolution of Thomism.* Bronx, N.Y.: Fordham University Press, 1989.

McDermott, John M. "Dogmatic theology needs philosophy." *L'Osservatore Romano* (5 May 1999), 9.

Melina, Livio. "The 'Truth about the Good: Practical Reason, Philosophical Ethics, and Moral Theology'" *Communio* 26 (1999): 640–61.

Nédoncelle, Maurice. *Is There a Christian Philosophy?* Trans. Illtyd Trethowan. New York: Hawthorn Books, 1960.

Neuhaus, Richard John. "The Public Square." *First Things* 90 (February 1999): 68–80.

Newman, John Henry Cardinal. *Fifteen Sermons Preached Before the University of Oxford Between A.D. 1826 and 1843.* Edited by Mary Katherine Tillman. Notre Dame, Ind.: University of Notre Dame Press, 1997.

———. *The Scope and Nature of University Education.* New York: E. P. Dutton, 1958.

———. *The Idea of a University.* Notre Dame, Ind.: University of Notre Dame Press, 1982.

O'Connell, M. *Theotokos: A Theological Encyclopedia of the Blessed Virgin Mary.* Wilmington, Del.: M. Glazier Press, 1982.

Peters, F. E. *Greek Philosophical Terms: A Historical Lexicon.* New York: New York University Press, 1967.

Pieper, Josef. *Leisure the Basis of Culture.* South Bend, Ind.: St. Augustine Press, [1948] 1998.

Prades, Javier. "The Search for the Meaning of Life and Faith." *Communio* 29 (1999): 622–39.

Putnam, Hilary. *Many Faces of Realism.* Lasalle, Ill.: Open Court, 1987.

———. *Realism with a Human Face.* Cambridge: Harvard University Press, 1990.

Rahner, Karl. *Foundations of Christian Faith.* New York: Crossroad, 1982.

Rashdall, Hastings. *The University of Europe in the Middle Ages.* 3 vols. London: Oxford University Press, 1958.

Ratzinger, Joseph Cardinal. "Culture and Truth: Reflections on the Encyclical." *Origins* (25 February 1999): 630.

Sala, Giovanni B. "The Drama of the separation of faith and reason." *L'Osservatore Romano* (31 March 1999), 9–10.

Schindler, David. "God and the End of Intelligence: Knowledge as Relationship." *Communio* 23 (1996): 510–40.

Schmitz, Kenneth L. "Faith and Reason: Then and Now." *Communio* 26 (Fall 1999): 595–608.

———. "Community, the Elusive Unity." *Review of Metaphysics* 37 (1983): 243–64.

Scola, Angelo. "Human Freedom and Truth." *Communio* 26 (Fall 1999): 492.

Sokolowski, Robert. *The God of Faith and Reason: Foundations of Christian Theology.* Notre Dame, Ind.: Notre Dame University Press, 1982.

Spalding, John Lancaster. *Religion, Agnosticism and Education.* Chicago: A. G. McClure Company, 1902.

Sweeney, Leo. *Christian Philosophy.* New York: Peter Lang, 1997.

Thomas Aquinas. *Summa theologica.* Westminster, Md.: Christian Classics, 1981. 5 vols.

———. *Summa contra Gentiles.* Trans. Anton Pegis. Notre Dame, Indiana and London: University of Notre Dame Press, 1975.

Van Steenberghen, Fernand. *Aristotle in the West: The Origins of Latin Aristotelianism.* Trans. Leonard Johnston. Louvain: Louvain University Press, 1970.

———. *Thomas Aquinas and Radical Aristotelianism.* Trans. D. J. O'Meara, J. F. Wippel, and S. F. Brown. Washington, D.C.: The Catholic University of America Press, 1980.

———. "Philosophie et christianisme." In his *Études philosophiques,* pp. 11–57. Quebec: Éditions du Préambule, 1985.

Viola, Francesco. "The human person as seeker of truth." *L'Osservatore Romano* 37 (15 September 1999), 9–10.

Weigel, George. *Witness to Hope: The Biography of John Paul II.* New York: Harper Collins, 1999.

Wildberger, Hans. *Isaiah 1–12: A Commentary.* Minneapolis: Fortress, 1991.

Wippel, John F. "The Condemnations of 1270 and 1277 at Paris." *Journal of Medieval and Renaissance Studies* 7 (1977): 169–201.

———. "The Possibility of a Christian Philosophy: A Thomistic Perspective." *Faith and Philosophy* 1 (1984): 272–90.

INDEX OF PROPER NAMES

INDEX OF TOPICS

INDEX OF REFERENCES TO *Fides et ratio*

THE TWO WINGS OF CATHOLIC
THOUGHT: ESSAYS ON *Fides et ratio*
was designed and composed in Columbus
by Kachergis Book Design of Pittsboro,
North Carolina. It was printed on sixty-
pound Glatfelter Writers Offset B21
Natural and bound by Thomson-Shore,
Inc., Dexter, Michigan.